Environment, employment and development

ENVIRONMENT, EMPLOYMENT AND DEVELOPMENT

Edited by A.S. Bhalla

A WEP study

International Labour Office   Geneva

Bhalla, A. S.
Environment, employment and development
Geneva, International Labour Office, 1992

/Environmental policy/, /Environmental protection/, /Ecodevelopment/, /Employment/, /Employment policy/, /Developed country/s, /Developing country/s. 16.03.1
ISBN 92-2-108250-4

ILO Cataloguing in Publication Data

Printed in Switzerland

PCL

PREFACE

It is now widely accepted that economic development in both industrialised and developing countries, especially during the past half century, is not environmentally sustainable. This is evident from the current debate on alternative approaches to sustainable development, which has been intensifying with the approaching United Nations Conference on Environment and Development to be held in Rio de Janeiro in June 1992. It is also generally recognised that the question of sustainable development is a *global* problem, emphasising the increasingly interdependent nature of relationships among nations. Solutions to the problem are as much political as they are economic and technological. The current debate, besides raising difficult questions, challenges the very concept of development. More than measuring incomes per capita is involved when such matters as the quality of life, as well as its sustainability over time, are included.

Notwithstanding the deepening and widening of the debate on sustainable development, its implications for employment — a major concern of the ILO under its World Employment Programme — have remained largely unexplored. This volume is intended to shed light on this issue. It does not provide quantitative estimates of employment gains and losses that would result from the adoption of development strategies that are environmentally sustainable. The reasons are obvious. With so many unsettled questions regarding the elements of a sustainable development strategy, it would be premature to attempt to measure the employment impact. Even more serious is the question of data availability. Methodologies to measure the employment impact pose a serious constraint too. This volume therefore has a very modest objective, namely to place the employment question on the policy agenda in the context of the current debate on environment and development.

The design of environmental policies, it is argued, should allow for the differences that exist between countries with a high level of development and technological dynamism and those with a low level of development and low technological capability. Sustainable development is a delicate concept and should be interpreted carefully, with due emphasis being placed on poverty, particularly in the Third World. Similarly, one must distinguish between short-term and long-term consequences of promoting sustainable development. One must also recognise the costs imposed by adjustment and the consequent distributional impact.

In the long term, technology choice plays a crucial role in promoting sustainable development in both industrialised and developing countries. It is not only environment-friendly technologies that need to be developed and diffused; in the case of the least developed countries, technological transformation needs to be accelerated in order to minimise their dependence on natural resources for economic growth. Such a strategy would contribute not only to sustainable development but also to higher growth, employment and productivity, especially in the poor countries. For the latter group of countries other areas such as population, poverty reduction and urbanisation also deserve policy attention. In the short and medium term, one would no doubt have to rely upon various direct and indirect economic instruments, including command and control approaches and state involvement. The combination of these instruments doubtless varies between industrialised and developing countries, depending on the extent to which markets are developed. These and other related issues are the subjects dealt with in this volume.

The volume has greatly benefited from the comments on earlier drafts of Rolph van der Hoeven and Larry Kohler of the ILO and Anil Markandya of the International Institute of Environment and Development, University of London. Thanks are due to Peter Haag and Rohit Mohindra, who provided valuable research assistance, and to Ronald Kirkman for his very vital editorial contribution under severe time constraints. Finally, special thanks are due to Mary Hamouda and Micheline Batailley for their unfailing support in the preparation of this manuscript for publication.

CONTENTS

LIST OF TABLES

LIST OF BOXES

LIST OF FIGURES

INTRODUCTION

1

S. V. Sethuraman *

Economic performance, especially in the industrialised countries and parts of the developing world since the Second World War, has been claimed as a success by any standard. The rate of economic growth witnessed during the short span of a few decades far surpassed what had been achieved earlier over centuries. That the key to this success is technological advancement has been proved beyond doubt. The application of technologies based on modern science has contributed to an unprecedented growth in productivity. Much of this growth has often been considered as a windfall. Productivity gains have yielded benefits well above the cost of developing improved technologies. (See for example the literature on growth accounting.)

ENVIRONMENT VERSUS DEVELOPMENT

However, the emergence of environmental concerns, especially during the past two decades, has led people to question whether in fact this spectacular economic growth, particularly in the industrialised countries, has been "costless" and whether there has been any windfall at all. There is a growing consensus that this growth is, at least in part, attributable to the "cost" imposed on the environment through the depletion of non-renewable natural resources and damage to the physical environment. For example, according to a recent study by the World Resources Institute, "although the GNP of Indonesia increased at 7 per cent a year between 1970 and 1984, the true growth rate would fall to 4 per cent a year" if one allowed for the depreciation of natural capital resulting from environmental degradation (Warford and Partow, 1989). It is now widely recognised that the global warming caused by the "greenhouse gases" is in a large measure related to growth in industry and agriculture, especially in

---

* ILO, Geneva.

the developed countries. Perhaps half of this damage is attributable to carbon dioxide produced mostly by the burning of fossil fuels — coal, oil and natural gas — and deforestation. Natural capital, consisting of both natural resources and the biosphere, has long been considered as almost a free good; and natural resources, finite in quantity, were underpriced. Negative externalities of the growth process on the environment were rarely taken into account. One can therefore understand why technological change that led to rapid economic growth failed to respect the environment. There is a growing consensus that such growth cannot be sustained for long except at the risk of our very survival.

What has aggravated this concern for environmental degradation is the rapid rate at which natural resources are being depleted in the Third World. Though such depletion is in part motivated by growth considerations, such as the easing of resource constraints for development, it is also the result of growing population pressures and poverty in developing countries. Economic growth, based on modern technologies borrowed from the developed countries has no doubt also played an important role.

This global concern for the environment comes at a time when Third World countries are just beginning to hope that they too could follow the path trodden by the industrialised countries and rely on improved technologies for their economic growth. The timing is critical, for the issue of sustainable development is being raised precisely when these developing countries have an urgent need to increase their rate of economic growth more than at any time in the past, owing to increasing population pressure. From around 2 billion in 1960, the population in developing countries is projected to reach 5 billion by the year 2000 (UNDP, 1991, table 42, p. 190). Without rapid economic growth there is little chance that these countries will be able to absorb the millions of new entrants to the labour force or raise the living standards of the masses.

If the developing countries cannot follow the path of the developed countries because it leads to development which cannot be supported from the environmental point of view, what options do they have? What are the implications of these options for employment generation and poverty alleviation? For example, is it possible that environmentally sustainable development could also lead to a greater alleviation of poverty? Would it result in a lower rate of economic growth and employment than is otherwise possible? It should be noted in this context that the rate of growth, under a strategy of sustainable development, could be even higher if the relevant magnitudes are measured properly. The environment debate, though largely originating from the developed countries of the world, is therefore highly relevant to the Third World. It raises difficult questions, such as whether developing countries should compromise their growth objectives in order to accommodate the environmental objectives if there is a trade-off between the two.

2

The current debate on the environment unfortunately does not discuss the consequences for employment. Though some micro-level studies have examined the employment consequences of environmental protection measures, the macro-level issues, particularly as they concern the developing countries, have hardly received any attention. Perhaps the major reason for this lacuna is the absence of relevant data. This study takes a first look at the employment implications, especially for the developing countries, of the current environment debate; it does not provide any quantitative indications. The focus is limited to an assessment of the direction of the impact wherever possible. Another objective is to review the instruments and approaches that are currently being utilised to reduce, if not arrest, environmental degradation. It is not evident that the instruments and approaches deployed by the developed countries can be applied in the developing world without modification. Besides the level of development and the magnitude of poverty, deficiencies in institutional capacity would also seem to be an important factor which limits their application in the Third World.

Two key concepts need to be clarified before elaborating on the relationship between the two objectives of environment and growth, i.e. "environment" and "sustainable development". In the relevant literature one finds that "environment" can be defined as broadly or as narrowly as one wishes. Since this study is concerned with environment versus employment, a more pragmatic approach is taken here, and "environment" is defined as the sum of all natural resources, including the biosphere, which sustain life on earth. Defined in terms of resources, one can talk about the degradation of environmental resources or about measures on how to arrest it. The issue of what constitutes "sustainable development" is, however, more complicated (see Chapter 2).

To ensure sustainable development, does one have to abandon certain technological advances that have already been made, including improved processes, products and techniques? Would that imply fewer technological options for developing countries? Alternatively, can sustainable development in these countries be achieved by incurring additional costs on "appropriate" activities to compensate for environmental degradation, which would then imply fewer resources for development? Is there a trade-off between "protecting the environment" and "economic growth"? Is the trade-off the same for both developing and developed countries? For example, can the developing countries use more labour than capital in preserving their environment intact and thereby generate more growth as well as more employment (e.g. labour-intensive soil conservation measures)? Are there conflicts between policies to promote growth and preserve the environment? For example, it is clear that the developing countries will experience a rapid increase in the demand for energy as they grow. The extent to which such growth depends on energy derived from fossil fuels will determine the extent of damage to the environment.

Policies to promote growth can therefore conflict with policies to contain environmental pollution.

If indeed alternative, environment-friendly technologies exist, it would imply that one need not be confronted with a reduced set of technological options; one could maintain the desired rate of economic growth while at the same time fully respecting the environmental objectives. But this depends on the following two questions. First, are the environment-friendly technologies more or less costly than the ones they replace? Second, can they be made accessible to developing countries at no extra cost? If indeed such a substitution between technologies that are detrimental to the environment and those that are friendly is possible at no extra cost, it would imply that there really is no trade-off between environmental protection and economic growth. All this of course assumes that such environment-friendly technologies exist. In reality, it is generally recognised that they do not exist in many domains and that they imply a need for massive investment in R & D. While such a substitution may prove costly for developed countries because they have to incur additional expenses (i.e. abandon investment already made and make new investments in skills, equipment, infrastructure, etc.), the developing countries that are about to choose the technologies would be in a more advantageous situation. This of course assumes that the environment-friendly technologies developed mostly in the North would be made available freely to the South. A related issue, important from the employment point of view, is whether such a substitution between technologies results in more or less aggregate employment, taking into account both direct and indirect effects.

Besides the two possibilities discussed above (i.e. the adoption of environment-friendly technologies and labour-using techniques to prevent environmental degradation), there is a third possibility to promote sustainable development, namely to follow a pattern of development different from that followed by the developed countries. Here one must consider the role of population growth and its implications for alternative patterns of development.

There are indeed other factors internal and external to the Third World countries which also influence the choice. Growing global competition and interdependence among countries would seem to suggest that the developing countries, to benefit from competition from world trade, cannot adopt patterns of development totally divorced from those of the developed countries. And yet it is clear that the Third World, with a large proportion of its population below the poverty line, cannot blindly follow the development patterns pursued elsewhere. In this context, one would like to know if development strategies emphasising poverty alleviation cause less harm to the environment. Similarly, would development strategies placing greater emphasis on small enterprises cause less damage to the environment?

In the context of the Third World there is yet another complicating factor. Even in the absence of economic growth environmental degradation could occur, and indeed has been occurring, owing to the interaction between demographic growth and urbanisation, on the one hand, and the environment, on the other (Chapter 6). In the rural areas (of developing countries) too, one can observe a similar relationship (Chapter 5). Population growth combined with increasing poverty could result in the consumption of natural capital (deforestation, for example) and a polluted environment resulting from increased population density on a limited infrastructure. If population growth has an independent negative impact on the environment, say due to greater poverty, can it be corrected through a higher rate of economic growth? The answer naturally depends on whether such growth is accompanied by a reduction in poverty or not. If indeed poverty is reduced, one could reduce the environmental degradation. For example, the poor, with increased incomes, would opt to replace wood by other forms of energy for cooking and thereby reduce the rate of deforestation. Another critical factor is, of course, whether such growth was generated through the use of environment-friendly technologies or not. For example, the use of certain chemicals in agriculture may lead to higher output and employment (and hence be favourable to the poor) but cause environmental degradation (Chapter 5). Such conflicts may not always arise. The substitution of synthetic fibres (which are not environment-friendly) by natural ones may be both employment-generating and an environment-friendly solution.

Perhaps a more complicated case of potential conflict arises when the direct impact of an activity is detrimental to the environment but when its output may have substantial indirect social benefits through multiplier or linkage effects (e.g. energy based on nuclear power). These illustrations suggest that the choice of strategies and policies for development can be difficult if environmental objectives are also to be taken into account, besides employment generation and poverty alleviation. They also raise issues of the intergenerational transfer of welfare in so far as they involve trade-offs such as "less poverty now" and a "better environment later".

UNDERSTANDING THE EMPLOYMENT-ENVIRONMENT NEXUS: INDUSTRIALISED VERSUS DEVELOPING COUNTRIES

Environmental degradation, it is generally recognised, has been taking place in both developed and developing countries, although for different reasons, as noted earlier. As the *Human Development Report 1991* pointed out, "It is ironic that significant environmental degradation is usually caused by poverty in the South — and by affluence in the North" (UNDP, 1991, p. 28). A clear understanding of the environment-employment nexus is important not only for the developing countries but for many industrialised countries too. For these countries, facing recession and serious unemployment problems, it provides a basis for designing appropriate policies and interventions (see Chapters 4 to 6).

There is growing recognition that the industrialised countries in the North are using up the earth's natural resources, which are finite, in such proportions that the process cannot continue for too long. In the developed countries technological change including new products and processes has been identified as the major factor contributing to environmental degradation, i.e. the depletion of limited natural resources and the damage caused to the biosphere through atmospheric pollution. Both rapid growth and the level of development, measured in terms of income per capita in the developed regions, would seem to explain why the pace and extent of environmental degradation has been so marked in recent years. For example, the developed countries are estimated to account for about half the 6 billion metric tons of greenhouse gases emitted each year — even though they have only a fifth of the world's population (see Chapter 7). These countries have no doubt introduced measures to remedy the situation. But one should recognise the limited possibilities of such measures to bring about any appreciable change in the near future. Besides raising complex technological challenges, these measures also impinge on such fundamental factors as lifestyle and social organisation. Preventing environmental degradation in developed countries may include curbing the growth of activities or sectors which contribute to heavy pollution; the employment implications of this are not obvious. Clearly it raises serious questions about distributional costs — who gains and who loses. Also, there may be trade-offs between short- and long-run effects. One should not therefore underestimate the immense task involved in bringing about a new international "environmental" order (see South Centre, 1991, for a fuller discussion of the problems of adjustment). Besides finding appropriate technological solutions, one must find ways to minimise the costs of adjustment.

The problems confronting the developing world are somewhat different. First, even in the absence of growth, they must act in order to prevent environmental degradation resulting from population growth. This implies additional resource costs as well as enhanced institutional and technological capacity. Such action would seem necessary if these countries are not to jeopardise the well-being of future generations. Second, income distribution and the changes affecting it can have a significant impact on environment. As in the case of the poor who, of necessity, are driven to exploit natural resources, one may argue that the rich also contribute to environmental degradation through the consumption of products that cause greater pollution and through greater waste generation (e.g. non-recyclable products leading to a negative effect on the environment.) The former may be described as the "substitution effect", since the poor draw on natural resources in the absence of adequate purchasing power. The second may be called the "income effect", since with a rise in incomes the demand for polluting products also rises.

If indeed these hypotheses are borne out by empirical evidence (as seems to be the case), this would suggest certain options in terms of the patterns of development to be followed by developing countries. For example, it would strengthen the case for poverty alleviation and restrain wasteful consumption (or expenditures that are not environment friendly) by the rich. One could of course attempt to prevent environmental degradation by the poor through "administrative controls". Another course would be to use fiscal incentives encouraging consumers to move towards environmentally sustainable alternatives (see Chapter 4). With this approach, much depends on how elastic the demand is with respect to price and income. These and other mechanisms to arrest environmental degradation are discussed in the following chapters. But these problems also suggest why the State should play a more active role in the Third World in bringing about environmentally sustainable development. Another area where the problem differs from that of the developed countries is in the field of urbanisation and the location of industrial activities (see Chapter 6). Rapid urbanisation in many developing countries portends environmental degradation, not only because of an increase in energy consumption but also because of overcrowding and the consequent worsening of the balance between population and infrastructure. Perhaps the fundamental reason for environmental degradation in the poor countries is, as will be argued in Chapter 2, that economic growth in them is heavily dependent on natural resources; improved technologies play a relatively insignificant role in generating growth. It follows that economic growth in these countries, accompanied by poverty alleviation and based on technological transformation, holds the key to sustainable development in the long term.

PROMOTING ENVIRONMENTALLY SUSTAINABLE DEVELOPMENT: THE INSTRUMENTS

Much of the discussion above has focused on what the State can do to cope with the problem of environment and employment. For example, the State can undertake direct investments to compensate for the loss of natural capital and thus arrest, and possibly reverse, the negative trends. In the developing countries the State can adapt development strategies to take particular account of the environmental objective. The State can likewise influence the choice of products and technologies through appropriate mechanisms. For example, it can encourage (or discourage) investments in specific sectors or subsectors of the economy; it can also influence consumers in their choice of products and services. There are a number of ways in which the State can play this role. The most obvious is, of course, to depend on policy instruments which operate through markets. These might include taxes and subsidies aimed at curbing the consumption of natural capital and the degree of pollution; such instruments are generally designed to internalise the external costs imposed on society so that the factors causing damage to the environment are forced to behave in such a way as to take environmental objectives into account. But one should also recognise the existence of "missing markets" (see Chapter 2) in using the market-based instruments; consequently the State has to resort frequently to what is known as the "command and control" approach, which defines the environmental norms to be respected in the production of goods and services in the economy (Chapter 4). As a corollary one might add that, in certain vital areas, the State itself might choose to take responsibility for the production of certain services, such as ensuring a cleaner urban environment through improved waste disposal systems, water purification, etc. The State can also encourage the development of environment-friendly technologies through funding and other support mechanisms, besides creating the appropriate market environment that would lead to development of environment-friendly technologies.

ORGANISATION OF THE VOLUME

The chapters in this volume are organised as follows: Chapter 2 discusses the crucial role played by technology in the environment-employment debate. In particular, it deals with the question of whether environmental policy necessarily involves a trade-off between employment and output. The chapter argues that in the long run environmental protection and economic growth are indeed complementary, although in the short run there might be some trade-off. The extent to which industrialised and developing countries depend on natural resources for their growth is identified as a key factor in determining the environment-development interrelationship. Finally, it emphasises the role of structural constraints in dealing with the environmental problems of the Third World and introduces a new definition of the term "sustainable development" based on the notion of "desired rate of natural resource depletion". The chapter concludes with an empirical analysis of data on agriculture in sub-Saharan Africa and underlines the need to distinguish between "growth and technological dynamism" and "underdevelopment and technological stagnation" in designing environmental policies.

A review of the employment-environment relationship in the developed countries is presented in Chapter 3. Quantitative evidence of the employment implications of environmental policy measures in specific sectors is presented and discussed. The chapter also deals with the compatibility of environmental and employment policies and identifies areas of potential conflict and suggests measures to resolve them.

Chapter 4 deals with the instruments of environmental policy as they have been applied in industrialised countries. It also examines the relevance and limitations of these policies for the developing countries at their present stage of development. Besides economic instruments, it also deals with the role of environmental standards and other measures to control environmental damage. It concludes with a discussion of the *scope* for applying such market-based instruments as well as of their limitations for developing countries.

Chapter 5 briefly discusses the meaning and significance of the current environment debate for the Third World and identifies some of the major environmental concerns, especially in the rural areas of the developing countries. The chapter traces the trends in environmental degradation, giving concrete examples, and analyses the causes underlying them as well as their consequences, especially for the rural poor in these countries. It provides an assessment of the current efforts to deal with the environment issue and identifies their shortcomings with a view to drawing policy conclusions. In particular, it emphasises the role of policies directed towards population growth, energy consumption and poverty alleviation in dealing with environmental problems in developing countries.

Given the projected increases in urban population in developing countries (half their total population is expected to be urban in two decades) and given the rapid deterioration in the urban environment, there is growing concern that future growth in urban employment in these countries is almost certain to cause further environmental degradation. Chapter 6 analyses the problem of urbanisation, especially the growth of employment in the urban informal sector in developing countries. Issues relating to urban employment, poverty and environment are discussed. The chapter concludes with a discussion of the options before policymakers if they wish to pursue the employment objective on an environmentally sustainable basis.

The forthcoming United Nations Conference on Environment and Development in 1992 in Brazil clearly underscores the importance of "global" solutions to deal with the "global" dimension of the environmental problem. Chapter 7 briefly reviews the issues and approaches currently in vogue to deal with the "global commons". It also discusses the employment implications in the developing countries of environmental standards and measures introduced in the developed countries.

Finally, Chapter 8 synthesises the findings from the previous chapters in respect of concepts, employment implications and policy issues. It also identifies the areas where further research needs to be carried out.

References

South Centre. 1991. *Environment and development: Towards a common strategy of the South in the UNCED negotiations and beyond.* Geneva.

United Nations Development Programme (UNDP). 1991. *Human Development Report 1991.* New York.

Warford, J.; Partow, Z. 1989. "Evolution of the World Bank's environmental policy", in *Finance and Development* (Washington, DC, International Monetary Fund), Dec.

ENVIRONMENT, DEVELOPMENT AND EMPLOYMENT: SOME CONCEPTUAL ISSUES *

2

M. Karshenas **

In this chapter we discuss the analytical aspects of environmental, developmental and employment interrelationships. The literature on environmental and economic development has grown apace in recent years. The role of employment in environment-development interrelationships, however, has not been adequately analysed in this literature. Here we argue that, in fact, employment plays a key role in the environmental degradation processes, particularly in the least developed countries. We emphasise the central role of employment creation in the environmental processes by introducing a new operational concept of sustainable development. The chapter is organised in four sections. In the first section we elaborate the interrelationship between employment, technology and the environment. This section highlights the role of employment as a key variable in the process of environmental degradation and economic development. The second section reviews environmental and growth relationships, including possible trade-offs. The third section discusses the key issues relating to environmental degradation and introduces a new, more general concept of sustainable development. It also examines the process of "forced environmental degradation" in the context of sub-Saharan Africa. The last section deals with policy issues.

EMPLOYMENT, TECHNOLOGY AND ENVIRONMENT

The relationship between employment and environment, the main theme of the book, is a complex one. In economic models, while full employment is assumed to be continuously maintained, environment-growth trade-offs and complementarities are translated into

---

* This chapter is an abridged version of a larger study prepared for the ILO World Employment Programme.

** Department of Economics, School of Oriental and African Studies, University of London.

labour productivity, income per head, and working conditions as well as quality of life in general. For example, environmental protection policies which in the short run may lead to a slower growth of income per head (the trade-off aspect) would be necessary to ensure the long-term sustainability of income growth and improvements in the quality of life (the complementarity aspect). The level of employment is not affected as such.

The real world, however, is far from the full employment models. Even in the case of industrialised countries which may happen to be working near full employment, conventional theory is unlikely to apply, because the painless and instantaneous adjustments assumed certainly do not hold. Long time-lags and high adjustment costs often lead to outcomes which are very different from the frictionless world of the theory. Pollution taxes, for example, can render some factories uneconomical and lead to factory closures and unemployment. Even if the net benefits of pollution abatement turn out to be positive in the short run, and if in addition the economy is assumed to be endowed with forces which drive it towards the reinstatement of full employment, the adjustment may still take a long time, with high costs for those affected (see Chapter 3). Under these circumstances, retraining schemes and other policies which may facilitate the mobility of labour will contribute to a more smooth adjustment. It would nevertheless not be surprising to find a certain resistance to the introduction of such preventive-type policies because of the short-term economic dislocations to which they may give rise. A gradual approach to the introduction of such policies may therefore be necessary.

Of course, in none of the industrial economies at present could the economic conditions be described as anything near full employment. Some economists have even put forward the opinion that this may be a part of a secular trend towards growing unemployment resulting from the fast rates of factory automation. Under these circumstances there may be trade-offs and complementary relations between employment and environment.

There are cases where one can mistakenly be led to believe that environmental policy becomes a matter of trade-off between employment and output. The problem of the fisheries is a case in point (see box 1). Here free access to fishing which leads to a suboptimal stock and hence suboptimal output of fish seems to create maximum employment. Environmental protection policy which leads to optimal stock and hence optimal output of fish at the same time seems to reduce employment. However, considering that greater output now can lead to greater investment and hence greater employment in the future, the trade-off really becomes one between increased employment now and much greater employment in the future.

The problem is similar to the familiar question of choice of the labour intensity of production techniques where a similar trade-off exists. Output- or growth-enhancing environmental protection policy would in the long run have a corresponding complementary relation with employment as well (see Chapter 3 for empirical evidence).

Box 1. Fisheries in developing countries: Output and employment with environmental deterioration

The main proposition in the economic analysis of fisheries is that overfishing can lead to reduced output. If access to the fishery is open, fishing units will be attracted to fish there for as long as revenues are above costs and if costs are low enough, overfishing will result.

If the fishery serves only a local market, which is often the case in developing countries where transport and preservation facilities are poor and tropical climates cause fish to spoil within hours of being caught, prices can be driven up as fish supply falls, continuing to attract new fishing units despite yields falling from the depletion of the fish stocks. Indeed, in an unregulated fishery, as population and incomes rise, demand steadily increases, making a market with high prices, low output and overfishing eventually inevitable.

With overfishing, the output of fish is below the maximum that it is possible to sustain, and more fishing resources are engaged to make catches from the depleted fish stock than would be the case if access to the fishery could be regulated to allow either the maximum output of fish, or the maximum income per fishing unit.

However, open access will lead to maximum fishery employment. There is thus a potential trade-off between output and incomes, on the one hand, and employment, on the other. In a labour market with no unemployment, the objective should be to maximise economic surplus and hence revenue per fisherman. However, when there is unemployed or underemployed labour, distributional considerations might make it desirable to maximise employment by allowing open access, even though this may lead to lower output and incomes.

Regulatory policy seeks to reduce the number of fishing units by such methods as licensing boats, imposing catch quotas, taxing output or controlling fish prices, with the addition of restrictions on minimum net mesh sizes. Quotas will work only in maintaining the fishery at its desired optimum — to attain this optimum, fishing activity has to be reduced. Various regulation methods have different side-effects on efficiency and income distribution which need to be taken into consideration. For example, restricting fishing effort requires that the fishing techniques for each boat be specified, as well as the number of boats; and this can preclude the introduction of more efficient methods. Controlling prices passes all the benefits of regulation to the fish consumers rather than to the fishermen.

Fisheries are extremely sensitive to changes in the environment. The building of a dam can reduce downstream fish stocks by reducing the flow of nutrients. Dams themselves typically have high catches soon after completion, but then they often fall dramatically over just a few years. Forestry projects can cause run-off to waterways which destroys fisheries. A demand for water for irrigation or industrial usage can lower water levels, reducing the ability to sustain fish stocks. Industrial water pollution can destroy fisheries. Harmful fishing methods such as dynamite fishing, bottom trawling and splash-fishing can reduce stocks and destroy breeding grounds. When there is environmental degradation, each of the possible alternative objectives, be it employment, output or revenue per fisherman, is lower.

Projects and practices which affect the environment to reduce fishing stocks impose considerable costs on fishing communities through lower employment or lower incomes. Society bears the cost of lower fish output and the associated higher price of fish. These costs need to be considered in the appraisal of projects and in designing a regulatory framework for fisheries.

Similarly, as with the case of employment adjustment costs discussed above, environmental protection policy, particularly of the preventive type, can also lead to resistance on the side of the affected parties because of its extra costs and the reduction of competitiveness which it may bring about. Such considerations may also lead governments to postpone environmental protection policy, particularly if the benefits happen to be spread well into the future. Under such circumstances, international coordination in introducing environmental protection measures, similar to those initiated with regard to global environmental problems, could facilitate the enactment of such policies by individual national States.

With a similar logic, clearly the more technologically dynamic economies and those with a competitive edge over the other countries may find it more convenient to implement environmental protection policies. A neglect of environmental protection policies in countries with lower technological dynamism and with regard to non-competitive industries could in fact be interpreted as a short-term subsidy to the producers. In the long run and from the point of view of the development of the economy as a whole, however, this would be highly counterproductive. The role of technological progress in environmental protection, therefore, goes far beyond the development of "clean" technologies or technologies that are less intensive in environmental resource use. Technological progress also leads to increasing productivity of labour and incomes and improvements in competitiveness, which increases the capability to cope with environmental problems and makes the necessary adjustments, so to speak, more affordable. This explains the empirical observation that the more advanced a country and the higher its technological level and standards of living, the cleaner its environment becomes. At the lower end of the spectrum we observe countries where technological retrogression and declining productivity of labour are combined with fast environmental degradation — the process may be referred to as "forced environmental degradation". The relation between employment, technology and environment in these countries is radically opposite to that of the advanced countries.

Empirical evidence on the extensive occurrence of the forced environmental degradation process in developing countries, particularly in the least developed countries and in relation to the agricultural sector, is now overwhelming (see Chapter 5). The crucial constituent elements of this process are said to be population growth and growing poverty associated with the marginalisation of labour. As is demonstrated in Chapter 5, employment generation, particularly in the non-farm sector, constitutes a key element in alleviating the environmental degradation in the least developed countries. This is a clear example where economic growth is not only complementary to environmental protection, but in fact is a necessary precondition for the latter.

The above point is often too easily missed in the recent literature on environment and economic development, where environmental protection policy is seen as a direct augmentation of the natural capital stock and where even underdevelopment is sometimes explained in terms of the inadequacy of the natural resource base. For example, it is not uncommon in the literature to attribute the causes of poor economic performance and environmental degradation in sub-Saharan Africa to the low natural capital stock/population ratio. For example, Pearce and Turner (1990, p. 47) maintain that "in the Sahel . . ., it is difficult to envisage development without natural resource augmentation". However, the causes of both underdevelopment and environmental degradation processes seem to be the technological backwardness, meagre stock of man-made capital and lack of adequate employment generation in non-farm activities, rather than low relative natural capital stock (see below). The consequences of such misconceptions in terms of development policy prescription can be grave. This brings us to the question of the environment-development relationship.

ENVIRONMENT AND ECONOMIC DEVELOPMENT

In an analysis of the different dimensions of the interaction between the environment and economic development, it is important to distinguish between the conditions prevailing in industrialised countries and those in developing countries.

In the case of industrialised countries we are dealing with post-industrial economies, characterised by the growing share of services both in the national income and in exports. Growth in such economies is embodied in the production of goods and services with high and increasing technological sophistication and skill intensity, and declining natural resource intensity. Unemployment in these economies is either a cyclical phenomenon or one that is related to the high rate of automation in the economy rather than to a shortage of capital and other complementary resources. Their environmental concerns at the local level are more to do with improving the quality of life than with warding off the threats to their subsistence posed by environmental degradation. Despite the relatively low and declining natural resource/value added ratio in their final output, they are nevertheless the major consumers of natural resources at a global level and are the main sources of global environmental problems such as global warming, ozone layer depletion, acid rain, etc. (see Chapter 7).

The developing countries, on the other hand, are still in the process of changing from primary-sector-based economies into industrial economies. The natural resource/value added ratio in these economies is much higher than in industrialised countries, and in addition they still have a higher output elasticity of natural resource use than the latter. The majority of the population in these economies are immediately dependent for their livelihood on the natural resource base. Their man-made capital stock is meagre, and technologically they are well behind the industrialised countries. They also suffer from massive unemployment and underemployment of labour, which is more the result of a shortage of man-made capital and complementary resources than a cyclical phenomenon or one related to high rates of automation. Environmental degradation in many instances is related to economic backwardness and slow economic growth rather than being a matter of a growing economy pressing against the limits of the natural resource base.

The distinct features of the advanced and developing countries do not, of course, imply that the environmental problems facing the two groups of countries are totally independent of each other or have nothing in common. Global environmental problems constitute important examples of the interdependence of environmental processes in the two country types. For example, global warming, though being to a larger extent caused by industrial pollution in the advanced countries of the North, is likely to have more deleterious effects for the developing economies of the South (see Chapter 7).

In addition to such interdependences, there are also various examples of environmental degradation which are common to both the developing and the advanced countries. Pollution caused by modern industry, environmental issues related to the consumption habits of the high-income groups in the developing countries, e.g. exhaust fumes from motor cars, environmental effects of the modern agricultural inputs such as fertilisers and pesticides, can be counted as such examples. Therefore, it may be more useful to classify the environmental problems into two groups: in the first group are those related to the application of modern technology, to economic growth, to advances in technology and to high income and consumption levels; and in the second are the problems related to economic backwardness, poverty, unemployment, stagnant technology and slow growth in general. The first group of problems is shared between the advanced countries and the modern sectors of the developing countries, and the second is largely specific to the marginal subsector of the developing economies. In analysing both types of the environmental issues, however, it is important that we keep in mind the kind of economy in which they originate. The institutional set-up and the technological capabilities which condition the policy context in the two cases are very different.

Trade-offs between the environment and economic growth

What is the relationship between economic growth and environmental degradation? Is the relationship one of complementarity or is there an inevitable trade-off between the two processes? The issue has raised a great deal of controversy in the literature, and there seems to be some confusion as to the meaning of complementarities and trade-offs in this context. This seems to have been caused partly by the contradictory nature of the factual evidence, and partly by the analytical context in which the problem is posed.

Empirical evidence appears to support both the complementarity and the trade-off points of view. For example, urban pollution seems to be much worse in most of the megacities in developing countries as compared with their industrialised country counterparts (see Chapter 6). Land degradation and loss of forest cover also seem to be taking place more extensively in the developing countries than in the advanced countries. Time-series evidence from the past experience of the industrialised countries also suggests that there has been an improvement over time in many aspects of environmental management. Per unit of GDP, surely, the rate of environmental resource depletion in the industrialised economies has been declining throughout the past century. Even in absolute terms, however, there have been improvements in certain environmental areas, e.g. urban pollution following the switch from coal-based heating to other, cleaner types of energy over the past four decades, improvements in the working environment in factories, etc.

All this evidence seems to suggest a negative correlation between economic development and environmental degradation, or in other words a complementarity relationship between economic development and the environment.

Evidence to the contrary, however, also seems to be available. For example, global environmental problems such as the emission of greenhouse gases seem to have been increasing with the level of economic development. Policies aimed at environmental protection without exception involve costs in terms of real resources (see Chapter 4), and the opportunity cost of environmental protection therefore appears to be reduced consumption or investment. In this case there seems to be a trade-off between the environment and economic development.

How does one reconcile this apparent contradiction? The issue of complementarity and trade-off between economic development and the environment crucially depends on the following set of factors: (a) the structure of the economy in question; (b) the time span of the analysis; and (c) the level of analysis, i.e. a micro or localised as against a macro or holistic level of analysis. The first factor, namely economic structure, determines institutional and technological capabilities as well as the possible existence of a slack in the economy (idle resources) which can be mobilised to protect the environment as well as to promote economic growth. The second factor, i.e. the time scale of the analysis, poses the problem in an intertemporal context — what in the short term appears as a trade-off may turn out to be a complementary relation when viewed from a long-term perspective. The third set of issues, i.e. the micro-macro distinction, poses the question in an economy-wide perspective — what may seem as a cost- or growth-inhibiting factor when looked at from a localised or micro point of view could turn out to be a growth-inducing factor when viewed from the point of view of the economy as a whole. Much of the confusion in the literature on the trade-off between environment and development seems to be caused by lack of due attention to these factors.

Let us consider the case of an economy in full employment equilibrium and growing along a steady state growth path at a rate equal to the rate of population growth. The technology is given and the economy is in full employment. Steady state growth in the present context, of course, means that the rate of environmental resource depletion is at or below the natural regeneration rate, and therefore the environmental constraints are ignored. This was the paradigm within which most of the conventional economic growth theory was discussed in the literature. Now let us assume that at a certain point in time it is realised that, given the environmental constraints, the prevailing growth path is no longer sustainable. Measures have to be introduced to protect the environment in order to avert the collapse of economic growth in the long term.

The possible environmental protection policies can be one of three types. The first type are *preventive* policies aimed at reducing the rate of environmental resource depletion at source. The polluter-pays-principle and various other policy instruments discussed in more detail in Chapter 4 are examples of such measures, which are in principle aimed at influencing the behaviour of economic agents (polluters). In the context of global warming, for example, this group of policies is aimed at reducing the emission of greenhouse gases. The second type of policies are *corrective* policies. These normally take the form of investments aimed at cleaning up the pollution or compensating the environmental resource depletion after the event. Taking the example of greenhouse gases again, this type of policy is exemplified by the recent suggestions for, for instance, fertilising the oceans with trace iron and shooting particulate matter into the stratosphere. The third type of policies are *adaptive* policies. They normally take the form of investments to adapt the economy to be able to cope with the undesirable side-effects of environmental degradation. Fish farms to compensate the loss of fish resulting from polluted rivers, the building of dykes to prevent ocean invasion in the event of global warming, etc., are examples of this type of measure. Of course, under certain circumstances it may be optimal to consider a combination of all three types of measure.

What is common to all three types of policy discussed above is that in all the cases the economy incurs a cost in terms of the real resources (i.e. labour, capital and raw materials) which have to be devoted to environmental protection. Given that the economy is assumed to be in full employment equilibrium, these resources have to be diverted from other activities, and therefore environmental protection appears to be taking place at the expense of economic growth. It is also intuitively clear that the addition of an extra binding constraint (the environmental resource constraint) would lead to a reduction in the rate of growth of the economy. Under the above assumptions (i.e. full employment equilibrium and given technology), therefore, there seems to be a trade-off between environmental protection and growth.

The trade-off, however, is only a short-term one. This becomes clear as soon as we recognise the fact that the environmental protection measures had to be introduced in the first place because the economy was not on a sustainable growth path. Failure to introduce such measures would in the long term have implied a loss of income as a result of the depletion of the natural resource base. This need not necessarily take a catastrophic form such as the eventual collapse of the economy. Environmental degradation could take its toll through a gradual decline in the production potential — for example, increasing pollution leading to growing health problems and loss of working days of the workforce. Given this information, optimal environmental policies by definition would lead to a higher overall output or well-being in the long run than could be procured in their absence. Environment and economic growth, therefore, would have a complementary relation in the long run even in an economy in full employment equilibrium and with given technology.

Even in the short run there need not necessarily be a trade-off between the environment and economic growth in such an economy. This depends on the balance between the localised costs and the economy-wide benefits of environment-improving policies. For example, pollution control may lead to an increase in the supply of fish in the rivers and hence an improvement in the productivity of fishermen. The gains in productivity may outweigh the cost of pollution control even in the short run. In this case the relation between environment and economic growth becomes a complementary one, even in the short run and in an economy with full employment and with fixed technology. This need not always be the case, however, as environmental policies may be introduced with a view to the long-term sustainability of the economy rather than their short-term benefits.

So far we have assumed that the economy is in full employment equilibrium. If the economy happens to be in a state where there is a slack of resources, e.g. where there exists a large pool of unemployed and underemployed labour, these resources could be mobilised to protect the environment without necessarily being at the expense of economic growth. The analogy with Keynesian policies of demand management in an economy suffering from cyclical unemployment is all too clear. In the case of developing countries where one is faced with long-term structural unemployment and underemployment of labour, the relations become more complicated. In such a case the final outcome depends on the kind of constraints which happen to hinder the growth of the economy in the first place, and the way in which environmental policy impinges on this constraining factor.

For example, if the shortage of capital is the main cause of unemployment, environmental protection policies which take the form of labour-intensive public works could be introduced, and these will be growth-inducing and employment-generating, both in the short run and in the long run (see Chapter 3 for more details on this point). In an economy constrained by balance of payments problems, on the other hand, it is often difficult to reconcile the twin aims of growth and environmental protection in the short run. This is obvious in cases where environmental protection requires the import of more technologically sophisticated and environmentally clean machinery. However, even in the case of environmental protection activities with minimal immediate foreign exchange requirements, e.g. labour-intensive hand and shovel public works, the foreign exchange constraint may not be accommodating — as the indirect foreign exchange requirements resulting from the multiplier effect of such activities have to be taken into consideration.

So far we have assumed a given technology of production. This is a very restrictive and unrealistic assumption, particularly in relation to the environmental issues. The most significant changes in the economy-environment interrelationships in the past have arisen as a result of technological change. The enormous power of technological progress to bypass many of the constraints which in earlier times were feared to put an end to economic growth (e.g. shortages of labour, land and raw materials) lead to an optimistic assessment of the possibilities for dealing with possible future environmental resource shortages as well. In the absence of such technological changes, environmental protection has to take the form of factor and product substitutions or a slower growth of output. "Technological fixes" therefore allow *ceteris paribus* for a higher rate of growth to be achieved, while keeping the economy on the sustainable path in the long run.

The above discussion has been conducted in the context of a growing economy, the implication being that we have so far been considering the first type of environmental problems, namely those that arise in the context of a growing and technologically progressive economy. The second type of environmental problems, namely those associated with underdevelopment, technological backwardness and slow growth, introduce a new set of considerations. In the former type, discussed above, environment is primarily seen as a constraint to economic growth. With the second type of environmental problems, the causal relationships take a different turn. Here it is the slow growth and the lack of technological capabilities associated with it that cause environmental degradation.

ENVIRONMENTAL DEGRADATION AND SUSTAINABLE DEVELOPMENT

Two fundamental problems are addressed by the new literature on environmental degradation: the valuation of environmental resources (i.e. optimum depletion of the resources), and the question of implementation (i.e. policy intervention in the face of missing markets). The first problem, valuation, is closely connected with the concept of sustainable development discussed below.

On the implementation side, various policy tools ranging from command and control methods to economic incentive programmes such as taxes and subsidies, marketable permits, fines, etc., have been suggested and some have been tried in relation to environmental regulation in a number of advanced countries (see Chapter 4).

The basic idea behind the economic incentive programmes is to give the correct price signals to resource users by charging them with the cost of environmental resources depletion inflicted by them. The economic incentive approach, mainly advocated in the form of the "polluter-pays-principle", is therefore put forward as the general policy tool for dealing with environmental degradation. An important factor in the effectiveness of the economic incentive approach is the market power enjoyed by the polluter. Maximum effectiveness is of course attained under perfect competition where the polluter is a price taker in the product and factor markets. With growing market power on the side of the polluter, however, the market incentive schemes become increasingly blunt instruments, as the polluter can pass on a large part of the pollution charges to other parties.

The applicability and effectiveness of this seemingly general principle depends on some very important basic assumptions. First, it presupposes a developed market economy and the generalisation of exchange relationships in both the commodity and the factor markets. Missing markets, however, seem to be more pervasive in Third World agriculture than is presupposed by the new environmental paradigm (see Chapter 5). Second, the economic agents are assumed to have the technological capability to respond to price incentives. This is basically a question of the existence of alternatives for the economic agents. The close connection between extreme poverty and environmental degradation that is revealed in the development literature suggests that the range of such alternatives may be extremely narrow. Third, the economy is assumed not to suffer from major and persistent disequilibria and structural imbalances, as for example is evident in the sizeable and persistent unemployment and underemployment of labour in many Third World countries. Such imbalances may be the result of more pervasive price distortions or they may result from some fundamental "structural" causes rooted in the underdevelopment of these economies. What is important in the present context is that the existence of such imbalances may have important implications for the environment, and in fact their alleviation may be a prerequisite for the effectiveness of policies specifically designed for environmental regulation.

Any examination of the empirical evidence on environmental problems in the Third World, particularly in agriculture, will quickly reveal that in fact some of the most important instances of environmental degradation are closely related to the above factors (see Chapter 5). These environmental problems usually have deep-seated structural reasons related to the underdevelopment of the economies concerned, which may not be remedied by the simple application of a general policy rule such as the polluter-pays-principle. To deal with these questions, however, it is first necessary to investigate under what set of conditions it is possible to equate natural resource depletion with environmental degradation. In other words, we need a working definition of what is meant by environmental degradation and when it should be a cause of concern. This is the familiar question of the desired rate of depletion of resources, which is intricately connected to the concept of sustainable development discussed below.

The concept of sustainable development

Many definitions of the concept of sustainable development have been put forward in the literature. The proliferation of the literature on sustainable development followed its popularisation by the report of the World Commission on Environment and Development (1987) — also known as the Brundtland Report — where it played a central role in defining the environmental aspects of economic development. The report defines sustainable development as:

Development that meets the needs of the present without compromising the ability of future generations to meet their own needs ... A process of change in which exploitation of resources, the direction of investments, the orientation of technology development, and institutional change are all in harmony and enhance both current and future potential to meet human needs and aspirations (WCED, 1987, pp. 43 and 46).

This definition, by rightly making the long-term realisation of human needs and aspirations central to the concept of sustainable development, distances itself from the ecocentrist definition of sustainable development in the so-called "deep ecology" approach (see, for example, Naess, 1973, and Devall and Sessions, 1985). Deep ecologists define sustainable development in terms of the imperatives of the preservation of the ecosystem rather than the satisfaction of "human needs and aspirations". They believe that technological fixes would be likely to lead to more intractable and costly environmental problems and by implication, given their prognosis that the world economy has for many years been on an unsustainable path, they adopt an anti-growth stance. At the extreme, some of the advocates of deep ecology "expect the whole world to return to pre-industrial, rural lifestyles and standards of living" (Colby, 1990). Nevertheless, their anti-growth stance does not withstand the test of rigorous examination. As we shall argue below, many instances of environmental degradation arise from lack of development and growth rather than excessive growth.

Pearce et al. (1988), starting from the same general definition of sustainability as the Brundtland Report and shunning the technological pessimism and anti-growth stance of the deep ecologists, still define the condition of sustainability in terms of the constancy of the natural capital stock. These authors offer the following definition of sustainable development:

We can summarise the necessary conditions for sustainable development as constancy of the natural capital stock; more strictly, the requirement for non-negative changes in the stock of natural resources, such as soil and soil quality, ground and surface water and their quality, land biomass, water biomass, and the waste-assimilation capacity of the receiving environments (Pearce et al., 1988, p. 6).

Under this definition all instances of soil erosion and environmental resource depletion documented in the literature cause immediate concern and automatically call for policies for their reversal. It is fair to say that in almost all the empirical literature on environment, where quantitative evidence of environmental resource depletion is presented with expressions of alarm, this definition of sustainable development is implicitly assumed.

A new definition

A more illuminating and operationally useful concept of sustainable development, or the long-term viability of environmental resource depletion, is to define it in terms of feasible growth paths. Sustainable development may be defined in terms of the pattern of structural change in natural and man-made capital stock (including human capital and technological capabilities), which ensures the feasibility of at least a *minimum socially desired rate of growth* in the long run. A minimum socially desired rate of growth could be defined in different ways depending on the level of development and the specific socio-historical characteristics of the country in question. For the majority of Third World countries a useful definition may be the rate of growth which is necessary to cater for the basic needs of the population.

The specification of the minimum socially desired rate of growth in terms of the basic needs of the population is significant here because of the often-discussed relation between poverty and environmental degradation in the literature. Below this minimum rate of growth, options open to the economy in terms of environmental resource depletion rates become increasingly limited, and a process of *forced environmental degradation* will take place (more on the relation between environment and poverty follows below). Of course, forced environmental degradation can also take place in an economy which is witnessing rapid growth, because of lack of adequate employment generation, maldistribution of income and pervasive poverty in the increasingly marginalised sections of the labour force.

To the extent that this pattern of lopsided or uneven growth leads to environmental degradation at a scale which endangers the long-term viability of the growth process (that is, the minimal growth process defined above), it falls outside our definition of sustainable development. However, even in cases where such a lopsided or uneven development path can be shown to fulfil the conditions of environmental sustainability, one may still find unsustainable subeconomies consisting of the marginalised sectors within such economies. The definition of sustainability with regard to subeconomies, however, carries the danger of losing sight of the interlinkages between the overall pattern of development and the prevailing economic conditions in the marginalised subeconomies. In fact, it is precisely through the existence of such interlinkages that significant interactions between technology, employment and environment can be detected. It is important to keep in mind, therefore, that although empirical case studies which locate instances of unsustainable development in subeconomies are by their very nature localised, in an analysis of the evidence one should not lose sight of the broader dimensions of the problem.

As we noted above, not all instances of environmental resource depletion are necessarily equivalent to environmental degradation which endangers the sustainability of the development path. In some cases it may be necessary to deplete the environmental resource base at an early stage of development in transition from a natural-resource-based economy to an industrially diversified and technologically mature economy. It is important therefore to be able to single out at the outset those instances of environmental resource depletion which endanger the sustainability of the development path in the long run.

The above definition of sustainable development in terms of minimal feasible growth paths immediately brings to the fore the case of the least developed countries or subsectors within countries which are perilously close to the forced environmental degradation frontier, as important cases for concern. It also warns us against treating every case of environmental resource depletion as environmental degradation and a cause for policy action. The central question is whether such resource depletion is accompanied by a simultaneous accumulation of man-made capital stock, the acquisition of technological know-how, and an appropriate pattern of structural change and growth, such that the sustainability of the development process is ensured. This in turn points to the important fact that environmental resources should not be treated as exogenous constraints to the growth of the economy. Rather, they are endogenous to the development process in the sense that the same rate of growth may be achieved at different rates of resource depletion, depending on the pattern of growth and the required technological capabilities of the economy. This of course relates to the more general question of complementarity and trade-offs between environment and economic growth, which we discussed earlier. What has to be emphasised here, however, is that in the case of the least developed countries undergoing a process of forced environmental degradation there is an unambiguous complementarity between economic underdevelopment and environmental degradation.

Of course, the relation between basic needs and the environment, highlighted in our definition of sustainable development, has already been discussed in the literature even as far back as the 1970s. This relation was, for example, central in the Bariloche report (see Herrera et al., 1976) and in the paper by Matthews (1976), as clearly suggested by its title *Outer limits and human needs*. In these earlier studies, however, it was the trade-offs between the environment and human needs and the possible ways of restructuring the world economy to deal with the dual objectives of ensuring the provision of human needs and safeguarding the environment, that was the central question. What is new, and indeed essential to the new definition of sustainable development discussed above, is the unambiguous complementarity between economic underdevelopment and environmental degradation witnessed in some of the least developed countries undergoing a process of forced environmental degradation. The reason for non-sustainability in this set of countries appears to be the low stock and rate of increase in man-made capital stock, technological backwardness and stagnation, combined with population growth which forces the economy to eat into its natural capital stock — a clear case of forced environmental degradation. This situation is not uncommon in the developing world; there is strong reason to suggest that, for example, in many sub-Saharan African countries non-sustainability arises from the general backwardness of the economy rather than from poor per capita natural resource endowment.

Sustainability in sub-Saharan agriculture

As the sub-Saharan economies are largely agrarian, the unsustainability of their agricultural sectors is most likely also to imply the unsustainability of their overall development path. Although this is the impression conveyed by a large number of either specific country or regional case studies, no systematic attempt has been made to establish the unsustainability of the economies in question, and to relate the differences in country performances to their technological and employment policies and their overall development strategies (FAO, 1986). We present a comparative statistical analysis of agricultural performance both within the region and with some of the more successful Asian and North African economies. The main purpose is to examine the popular idea that what is hindering the growth of African agriculture is its relatively low natural capital base and the high population/natural capital stock ratio.

Although in the recent literature there has been a tendency to discuss the problems of African agriculture in a regional setting, it is important to note the substantial differences amongst African countries in terms of their natural resource base, climate, vegetation and agricultural systems and overall economic structures. To take account of the effect of ecosystem variations in agricultural performance, we have selected 22 countries from four subregions in Africa, i.e., the arid and Mediterranean North Africa, arid and semi-arid Sudano-Sahelian Africa (including Ethiopia and Kenya from East Africa), humid and sub-humid Central and West Africa, and sub-humid and semi-arid South-East Africa (for a list of countries see tables 1 to 9 in the statistical appendix to this chapter). The overall African performance is further compared with that of other broad regions such as the Far East, Latin America and developing countries in general, as well as a selected number of Asian countries (China, India, Indonesia, Malaysia and Thailand).

The growth of per capita production of total agricultural crops and food crops for the countries and regions in the sample between 1961 and 1990 is depicted in table 1, which brings into clear relief the sharp contrast between the performance of Africa and that of other developing regions and countries. The contrast is particularly glaring in comparison with the Far East. While both per capita food and crop production in Africa declined by about 14 per cent between 1961 and 1990, the Far East as a whole registered 50 and 40 per cent increases in per capita food and crop production respectively during the same period. The figures for developing countries as a whole were 30 per cent and 23 per cent respectively. With regard to individual country comparisons, with the exception of North

African countries, the same glaring contrast emerges in the performance of almost all sub-Saharan countries compared with the selected Asian countries in our sample. With the exception of Mali and Côte d'Ivoire, all the sub-Saharan economies registered a decrease in per capita food and crop production, some by as much as 40 per cent.

A number of important observations may be made about the pattern of growth in African agriculture. First, with the exception of North Africa, the adverse growth performance seems to be shared amongst all agro-ecological regions in Africa. As the agro-ecological conditions in the agricultural regions of North Africa are shared by the semi-arid and sub-humid regions of sub-Saharan Africa, the better performance of the countries in the former region are more likely to be due to socio-economic rather than to natural causes. Furthermore, though the growth performance in sub-Saharan Africa seems to have somewhat deteriorated successively over the past three decades, their lagging behind the Asian and other developing countries dates back to the 1960s (see table 2). The overall decline in the average precipitation rate in Africa during the 1970s and the 1980s, therefore, can be only partially responsible for the bad performance of African agriculture. This is further reinforced by the absence of any systematic relation between the growth performance and agro-climatic location of the countries in the sample.

Second, although population growth rates in most African countries are amongst the highest in the world, the decline in per capita agricultural production is not solely due to the high population growth factor.[1] A comparison of growth rates in total crop and food production levels between sub-Saharan Africa and other countries in the sample shows that the African countries, with one or two exceptions, systematically lag behind the latter countries throughout the past three decades (see tables 3 and 4). A comparison of growth rates between different African countries, presented in tables 3 and 4, also reinforces the observation made above that there seems to be no systematic relation between growth performance and the agro-ecological location of countries in the sample. An examination of the growth performance of different countries over the three decades shown in tables 3 and 4 also further supports the conclusion made above about the absence of any clear correlation between average rainfall and output growth. For example, some of the countries in the Sudano-Sahelian region, e.g. Chad, Mali and Senegal, showed their fastest growth rates in the 1980s, which witnessed the lowest average rainfall in the postwar period.[2] Of course, notwithstanding these and a few other

---

[1] In fact, Côte d'Ivoire, with one of the highest population growth rates in Africa (see table 8), was one of the few sub-Saharan African economies with a positive per capita agricultural production.

[2] Of course, average annual rainfall as an indicator of the favourability of climatic conditions for agriculture is very deceptive. The monthly, or even daily, variation of rainfall is the more crucial variable for performance in rain-fed agriculture. Nevertheless, a long and

exceptions, the general trend in the growth of agricultural output in Africa over the successive three decades shown in the tables was downward.[3]

The above conclusions are further supported by a comparison of the level and growth of cereal yields between the sub-Saharan countries and the other countries in the sample. As table 5 shows, cereal yields in sub-Saharan Africa were amongst the lowest in the Third World both in 1961 and in 1990, and the gap between them and other countries was growing all the time. With the exception of the Sudano-Sahelian region, which seems to have the worst performance both in levels and in growth terms, again no systematic correlation could be established between the level and growth of yields and the agro-ecological location of the countries in Africa.

The question is: To what extent is the poor agricultural performance in sub-Saharan Africa related to environmental degradation? FAO (1986) refers to environmental resource depletion as one of the causes of poor agricultural performance in Africa. Others have, in the same vein, referred to poor agricultural performance as a symptom of environmental degradation (see, for example, Perrings, 1991). Although unsustainable agricultural practices would no doubt in the long run lead to a decline in agricultural productivity, it would still be a mistake to regard the long-term growth performance of the agricultural sector as an indicator of the intensity of environmental degradation. The main reason is that poor agricultural growth performance may be related to various other causes. FAO (1986), for example, enumerates six main causes for the crisis in African agriculture, one of which is environmental degradation (namely, government policy, population growth, poor land development, lack of technological change, environmental degradation, and the conditions of the world economy).

A third important observation to be made is that, although per capita agricultural output in most of sub-Saharan Africa declined rapidly between 1961 and 1990, the picture of the output per head of agricultural population is totally different. The overall trend in agricultural production per head of agricultural population for Africa as a whole was positive between 1961 and 1990, and with the exception of Chad, Congo, Mozambique, Niger and Senegal, the rest of the countries in sub-Saharan Africa showed an increasing output per head of agricultural population. This was due to the relatively high rates of growth of the non-agricultural

(Note 2 continued)
sustained period of below average rainfall, as in Africa during the 1970s and 1980s, is surely to be considered a negative factor for agricultural productivity. We shall return to this issue shortly.

[3] It would be a mistake to attribute this downward trend entirely to increasingly adverse climatic conditions. Amongst other important economic factors one can mention the debt crisis of the 1980s and the resulting restructuring measures which undercut government investment and support services for agriculture, the difficulty of importing essential agricultural inputs owing to mounting foreign exchange shortages, and the downward movement in agricultural terms of trade in the international market during the 1980s.

population in sub-Saharan Africa (see table 8). Sub-Saharan economies nevertheless exhibited higher rates of growth in agricultural population compared with North Africa and the rest of the countries and areas represented in the sample, as shown in table 8. It is the manner and nature of absorption of this increase in agricultural population into the agrarian system which is said to be in part responsible for soil degradation and the depletion of agricultural environmental resources in sub-Saharan Africa. A comparison between the experience of sub-Saharan Africa and other countries in the sample in this regard helps to make this point clear.

As table 9 shows, despite the faster rates of growth of the agricultural population in Africa, in 1990 population pressure on land as measured by the agricultural population/land ratio was still below the figure for the Far East as it stood in 1961. However, the glaring gap between Africa and the rest of the world, as emerges from a first glance at tables 6 and 7, is in its extremely low and stagnating man-made capital stock — as indicated, for example, by fertiliser and tractor use and irrigation, and their rate of change over time.

POLICY IMPLICATIONS

The new definition of sustainable development discussed above introduces important new dimensions to the environmental policy debate in developing countries, particularly in relation to the least developed countries. First and foremost, it implies that policies which may be appropriate in the context of environmental problems related to growth and technological dynamism may not be appropriate for environmental problems resulting from underdevelopment and technological stagnation. It also highlights the fact that environmental problems, which in the first instance appear in the form of environmental resource depletion of one kind or another, may have their ultimate causes in developmental processes which are far removed from the immediate environmental issues. In such cases, the objective of environmental policy should be the removal of these ultimate causes rather than the adaptive or corrective type of policy aimed at repairing the environmental damage or at alleviating its effects.

This can be clearly demonstrated if we take the example of a country which is undergoing a process of forced environmental degradation. Inadequate man-made capital, stagnant technology, lack of employment opportunities, inability to cater for basic human needs, combined with a growing population, has forced the economy into a state where survival necessitates eating into the natural or environmental capital stock. Project aid which is directed solely towards repairing the environment or replenishing the natural capital stock, to the disregard of the broader developmental issues, may turn out to be ineffective under such

29

circumstances. Rebuilding the stock of man-made capital and employment generation, even in areas or sectors far removed from the immediate environment, may be a more effective means of environmental preservation. In certain circumstances it may even be necessary to run down the natural resource stock in the short term in order to achieve these broader developmental goals. This is not of course to underestimate the significance of environmental policy as such, but to emphasise the broader developmental aspects of environmental policy, which could be easily neglected if one takes a purely ecological perspective.

References

Colby, M. E. 1990. *Environmental management in development: The evolution of paradigms.* World Bank Discussion Paper No. 80. Washington, DC.

Devall, B.; Sessions, G. 1985. *Deep ecology: Living as if nature mattered.* Salt Lake City, Utah, Peregrine Smith Books.

Eckholm, E. P. 1976. *Losing ground: Environmental stress and world food prospects.* New York, Norton.

Food and Agriculture Organization (FAO). 1986. *African agriculture: The next 25 years.* Rome.

Herrera, A., et al. 1976. *Catastrophe or new society? A Latin American world model.* Ottawa, International Development Research Centre.

Matthews, W. H. (ed.). 1976. *Outer limits and human needs: Resources and environmental issues of development strategies.* Uppsala (Sweden), Dag Hammarskjöld Foundation.

Naess, A. 1976. "The shallow and the deep, long-range ecology movements: A summary", in *Inquiry* (Oslo), Vol. 16, pp. 95-100.

Pearce, D. W. et al. 1988. *Sustainable development and cost-benefit analysis.* Paper presented at the Canadian Environment Assessment Workshop on Integrating Economic and Environmental Assessment. Vancouver, Canadian Environmental Assessment Research Council.

———; Turner, R. K. 1990. *The economics of natural resources and the environment.* Hemel Hempstead (United Kingdom), Harvester-Wheatsheaf.

Perrings, C. 1991. *Incentives for the ecologically sustainable use of human and natural resources in the drylands of sub-Saharan Africa: A review.* Mimeographed WEP working paper (WEP 2-22/WP.219). Geneva, ILO.

World Commission on Environment and Development (WCED). 1987. *Our common future.* Oxford, Oxford University Press (also known as the Brundtland Report).

Table 1. Per capita crop and food production indices, 1961-90

Continent and country	Crops [1] (1979-81 = 100)		Percentage increase	Food (1979-81 = 100)		Percentage increase
	1961/62	1989/90	1961-90	1961-62	1989-90	1961-90
Africa	**111.43**	**95.24**	**-14.53**	**109.95**	**95.26**	**-13.37**
Morocco	97.41	145.89	49.76	98.54	31.62	33.57
Tunisia	81.66	92.98	13.86	91.03	99.19	8.96
Egypt	97.41	101.99	4.70	97.95	122.67	25.24
Sudan	110.63	64.51	-41.69	94.73	67.41	-28.84
Niger	110.84	74.89	-32.44	114.66	75.54	-34.12
Chad	108.73	105.42	-3.04	111.98	94.13	-15.94
Mali	114.37	125.13	9.40	96.69	97.01	0.33
Senegal	165.73	97.44	-41.21	148.53	105.26	-29.13
Ethiopia	99.64	82.69	-17.01	113.30	85.04	-24.94
Kenya	102.89	93.05	-9.56	121.43	106.77	-12.07
Côte d'Ivoire	79.41	91.76	15.55	79.01	94.87	20.07
Ghana	123.52	108.20	-12.40	115.43	106.79	-7.49
Nigeria	127.37	119.51	-6.17	122.07	114.11	-6.52
Cameroon	2.83	84.92	-8.52	94.28	88.46	-6.17
Zaire	112.14	97.01	-13.49	116.11	95.80	-17.49
Congo	118.24	89.42	-24.37	116.11	90.26	-22.26
Tanzania, United Rep. of	96.72	83.83	-13.33	93.64	88.09	-5.93
Mozambique	128.30	82.46	-35.73	115.25	85.47	-25.84
Malawi	88.95	84.80	-4.67	89.28	81.81	-8.37
Madagascar	106.62	89.95	-15.63	102.94	90.14	-12.43
Far East	**81.98**	**114.38**	**39.52**	**80.01**	**121.71**	**52.12**
India	102.89	115.80	12.55	98.59	119.77	21.48
China	69.15	120.16	73.76	66.32	133.91	101.92
Indonesia	80.78	125.13	54.90	79.38	129.72	63.41
Thailand	77.50	109.92	41.83	78.35	104.19	32.99
Latin America	**93.93**	**99.84**	**6.29**	**89.17**	**102.16**	**14.57**
Developing countries	**88.00**	**108.39**	**23.17**	**86.21**	**112.36**	**30.33**

[1] Indices refer to two-year averages for 1961/62 and 1989/90 respectively.
Source: AGROSTAT, FAO, 1991.

Table 2. Average annual growth rates in per capita food and crop production, 1961-90

Continent and country	Total crops			Food		
	1961-70	1971-80	1981-90	1961-70	1971-80	1981-90
Africa	**0.45**	**−1.88**	**−0.45**	**0.12**	**−1.50**	**−0.53**
Morocco	4.46	−0.77	2.20	2.48	−0.42	1.49
Tunisia	−0.37	3.22	−0.66	−0.89	2.48	−0.41
Egypt	1.63	−0.09	0.18	1.27	−0.48	2.24
Sudan	1.02	−1.91	−4.18	0.14	0.25	−3.90
Niger	−1.99	1.52	−3.58	−1.31	0.25	−3.22
Chad	0.06	−0.27	0.10	−0.60	−0.30	−0.84
Mali	−1.47	−0.35	2.31	0.81	−0.63	−0.07
Senegal	−5.73	−2.68	1.36	−4.07	−2.40	1.84
Ethiopia	0.20	−0.26	−1.77	−0.36	−1.00	−1.54
Kenya	1.42	−1.08	−0.97	−0.07	−2.12	0.90
Côte d'Ivoire	1.59	0.48	−0.89	1.45	1.58	−0.72
Ghana	1.24	−3.39	0.22	1.28	−2.74	0.25
Nigeria	0.39	−2.57	1.52	0.36	−2.14	1.08
Cameroon	2.29	−1.37	−1.56	1.81	−1.19	−1.13
Zaire	−0.45	−0.67	−0.53	−0.67	−0.84	−0.63
Congo	−1.02	−0.81	−0.92	−1.09	−0.58	−0.85
Tanzania, United Rep. of	0.32	−0.06	−2.22	0.16	0.31	−1.52
Mozambique	0.67	−3.00	−2.11	0.89	−2.20	−1.69
Malawi	0.02	1.19	−1.73	0.29	0.96	−2.13
Madagascar	1.03	−1.34	−1.34	0.92	−1.00	−1.30
Far East	**1.62**	**0.56**	**1.46**	**1.63**	**0.88**	**2.07**
India	−0.02	−0.72	1.54	−0.09	−0.15	1.85
China	3.41	0.87	2.18	3.61	1.29	3.21
Indonesia	0.68	1.72	2.33	0.84	1.86	2.64
Thailand	1.51	1.50	0.59	1.34	1.49	0.05
Latin America	**0.00**	**0.44**	**0.06**	**0.82**	**0.38**	**0.19**
Developing countries	**1.14**	**0.30**	**0.88**	**1.18**	**0.52**	**1.22**

Source: AGROSTAT, FAO, 1991.

Table 3.   Growth and variability in crop production, 1961-90

Continent and country	Average annual growth rates			Standard deviation [1]		
	1961-70	1971-80	1981-90	1961-70	1971-80	1981-90
Africa	**3.08**	**0.98**	**2.61**	**2.65**	**3.62**	**3.91**
Morocco	7.24	1.59	4.77	25.24	19.92	23.99
Tunisia	1.58	5.42	1.82	13.86	10.19	20.18
Egypt	4.04	2.03	2.66	8.36	3.10	2.35
Sudan	3.20	1.08	−1.18	14.18	9.04	22.66
Niger	1.00	4.46	−0.33	13.93	19.91	21.97
Chad	1.83	1.77	2.48	5.89	5.02	10.22
Mali	0.79	1.90	5.26	5.66	8.91	12.53
Senegal	−3.05	0.18	4.16	17.53	41.09	30.52
Ethiopia	2.56	2.09	0.63	3.54	7.36	8.47
Kenya	4.64	2.61	2.71	6.42	5.08	7.87
Côte d'Ivoire	5.38	4.44	2.93	9.42	7.08	5.85
Ghana	3.57	−1.19	3.58	4.67	7.69	27.13
Nigeria	3.31	0.69	4.77	3.86	5.83	4.77
Cameroon	4.53	1.32	1.57	4.28	3.69	4.75
Zaire	2.12	2.15	2.52	1.20	2.25	1.35
Congo	1.46	1.98	2.16	2.13	1.62	3.24
Tanzania, United Rep. of	3.33	3.28	1.48	4.98	4.15	3.55
Mozambique	2.97	−0.47	0.47	3.11	6.00	3.24
Malawi	2.50	4.33	1.74	7.35	7.69	4.17
Madagascar	3.37	1.31	1.78	2.47	5.57	2.64
Far East	**4.05**	**2.63**	**3.32**	**1.83**	**3.78**	**2.19**
India	2.27	1.44	3.67	4.37	6.80	6.55
China	5.85	2.69	3.52	4.40	4.21	3.92
Indonesia	2.95	3.99	4.32	5.26	2.51	3.18
Thailand	4.56	4.18	2.35	8.23	7.86	5.27
Latin America	**2.69**	**2.83**	**2.18**	**3.82**	**3.24**	**4.02**
Developing countries	**3.63**	**2.53**	**2.98**	**1.37**	**2.19**	**1.46**

[1] Refers to standard deviation of annual growth rates for each subperiod.
Source: AGROSTAT, FAO, 1991.

Table 4.   Growth and variability in food production, 1961-90

Continent and country	Average annual growth rates			Standard deviation [1]		
	1961-70	1971-80	1981-90	1961-70	1971-80	1981-90
Africa	**2.75**	**1.36**	**2.53**	**2.04**	**2.81**	**3.12**
Morocco	5.26	1.93	4.06	16.54	13.35	15.78
Tunisia	1.06	4.67	2.07	8.78	8.89	17.09
Egypt	3.68	1.65	4.73	5.44	2.01	2.23
Sudan	2.32	3.24	-0.90	8.72	4.88	18.42
Niger	1.69	3.19	0.03	7.38	13.31	13.08
Chad	1.17	1.74	1.54	2.87	3.94	8.16
Mali	3.07	1.61	2.87	2.85	7.69	6.89
Senegal	-1.39	0.47	4.64	14.12	30.83	22.50
Ethiopia	2.00	1.35	0.86	1.87	5.30	6.12
Kenya	3.15	1.57	4.59	2.57	3.17	10.68
Côte d'Ivoire	5.25	5.54	3.10	5.19	6.26	6.77
Ghana	3.61	-0.54	3.61	3.90	6.44	21.91
Nigeria	3.28	1.12	4.33	3.32	5.18	4.09
Cameroon	4.05	1.51	2.00	3.73	3.64	1.64
Zaire	1.90	1.99	2.41	1.08	2.22	1.12
Congo	1.39	2.21	2.23	1.87	1.67	2.86
Tanzania, United Rep. of	3.17	3.65	2.18	3.78	4.12	2.78
Mozambique	3.19	0.33	0.89	1.75	3.38	1.81
Malawi	2.77	4.10	1.35	7.71	7.92	2.86
Madagascar	3.26	1.65	1.82	2.09	4.46	1.41
Far East	**4.05**	**2.95**	**3.93**	**1.76**	**2.94**	**1.63**
India	2.19	2.01	3.99	4.02	5.81	5.42
China	6.06	3.11	4.55	4.60	3.43	2.11
Indonesia	3.11	4.13	4.64	5.86	2.95	3.09
Thailand	4.40	4.17	1.81	6.21	8.26	5.60
Latin America	**3.51**	**2.77**	**2.30**	**1.28**	**1.92**	**2.18**
Developing countries	**3.66**	**2.75**	**3.31**	**1.10**	**1.63**	**1.06**

[1] Refers to standard deviation of annual growth rates for each subperiod.
Source: AGROSTAT, FAO, 1991.

Table 5.   Increase and variability in cereal yields, 1961-90

Continent and country	Yields [1]			Standard deviation [2]		
	1961/62	1989/90	Growth	1962-70	1971-80	1981-90
Africa	**0.75**	**1.03**	**0.48**	**6.69**	**7.01**	**8.03**
Morocco	0.74	1.24	1.86	62.80	36.77	55.66
Tunisia	0.61	0.84	1.13	18.67	23.45	45.50
Egypt	3.08	5.35	1.97	5.64	2.75	3.3
Sudan	0.86	0.41	−2.65	21.79	15.28	43.72
Niger	0.53	0.38	−1.13	17.62	13.80	29.03
Chad	0.57	0.59	0.16	16.65	13.27	24.37
Mali	0.72	0.96	1.03	8.75	27.96	19.45
Senegal	0.55	0.81	1.40	23.50	34.61	25.94
Ethiopia	0.72	1.22	1.87	3.39	11.47	12.51
Kenya	1.35	1.71	0.84	7.46	5.70	16.96
Côte d'Ivoire	0.70	0.89	0.82	8.73	12.36	10.64
Ghana	0.81	1.00	0.74	13.07	7.01	42.91
Nigeria	0.76	1.07	1.20	9.67	17.72	14.33
Cameroon	0.81	1.22	1.46	6.41	10.02	11.13
Zaire	0.72	0.76	0.18	5.90	3.11	4.24
Congo	0.71	0.78	0.30	15.85	19.71	15.72
Tanzania, United Rep. of	0.82	1.47	2.08	10.53	18.27	15.75
Mozambique	0.87	0.55	−1.62	5.17	16.41	6.86
Malawi	1.01	1.09	0.27	23.14	10.95	8.11
Madagascar	1.77	1.97	0.37	4.40	4.06	3.46
Far East	**1.20**	**2.86**	**1.34**	**2.89**	**2.88**	**2.49**
India	0.94	1.90	1.10	7.32	8.41	6.17
China	1.28	4.11	1.81	4.88	4.82	4.16
Indonesia	1.55	3.79	1.39	5.72	3.47	3.45
Thailand	1.71	2.03	0.27	4.52	10.61	5.00
Latin America	**1.30**	**2.09**	**0.73**	**4.40**	**4.11**	**4.16**
Developing countries	**1.14**	**2.39**	**1.14**	**2.50**	**2.39**	**1.82**

[1] Tons per hectare.   [2] Refers to standard deviation of annual growth rates for each subperiod.
Source: AGROSTAT, FAO, 1991.

Environment, employment and development

Table 6.   Agricultural land use, 1961 and 1989 (thousand hectares)

Continent and country	1989			Increase 1961-89		
	Total crops	Irrigated	% share of irrigated	Total crops	Irrigated	% share of irrigated
Africa	**186 995**	**11 186**	**6**	**31 330**	**3 391**	**11**
Morocco	9 241	1 265	14	2 271	390	17
Tunisia	4 700	275	6	450	210	47
Egypt	2 585	2 585	100	17	17	100
Sudan	12 510	1 890	15	1 710	410	24
Niger	3 605	32	1	1 425	16	1
Chad	3 205	10	0	305	5	2
Mali	2 093	205	10	425	145	34
Senegal	5 226	180	3	926	110	12
Ethiopia	13 930	162	1	2 444	12	0
Kenya	2 428	52	2	638	38	6
Côte d'Ivoire	3 660	62	2	1 030	58	6
Ghana	2 720	8	0	250	8	3
Nigeria	31 335	865	3	2 535	65	3
Cameroon	7 008	28	0	1 498	26	2
Zaire	7 850	10	0	900	10	1
Congo	168	4	2	34	4	12
Tanzania, United Rep. of	5 250	153	3	2 170	133	6
Mozambique	3 100	115	4	451	107	24
Malawi	2 409	20	1	450	19	4
Madagascar	3 092	900	29	947	600	63
Far East	**382 227**	**128 518**	**34**	**23 865**	**51 978**	**218**
India	168 990	43 039	25	8 004	18 354	229
China	96 115	45 349	47	−9 119	14 947	−164
Indonesia	21 260	7 550	36	4 160	3 500	84
Thailand	22 126	4 230	19	10 733	2 609	24
Latin America	**180 090**	**169 522**	**94**	**48 970**	**66 945**	**137**
Developing countries	**804 135**	**19 849**	**2**	**107 588**	**4 819**	**4**

Source: AGROSTAT, FAO, 1991

36

Table 7. Manufactured fertiliser and tractor use, 1961-89

Continent and country	Fertiliser use[1]		Kg/ha	Tractors per 1,000 ha
	1961/62	1988/89	1988/89	1989
Africa	**748**	**3 773**	**20**	**1.5**
Morocco	37	316	34	3.8
Tunisia	18	105	22	5.5
Egypt	241	1 040	402	20.4
Sudan	22	48	4	1.8
Niger	0	3	1	0.1
Chad	0	5	2	0.1
Mali	0	12	6	0.4
Senegal	8	28	5	0.1
Ethiopia	1	88	6	0.3
Kenya	12	121	50	4.0
Côte d'Ivoire	7	41	11	1.0
Ghana	2	11	4	1.5
Nigeria	2	345	11	0.4
Cameroon	3	34	5	0.1
Zaire	1	6	1	0.3
Congo	1	1	6	4.2
Tanzania, United Rep. of	3	45	9	3.5
Mozambique	4	2	1	1.9
Malawi	4	53	22	0.6
Madagascar	2	11	4	0.9
Far East	**2 273**	**46 562**	**122**	**6.2**
India	395	11 342	67	5.5
China	859	25 375	264	9.0
Indonesia	143	2 481	117	0.8
Thailand	20	794	36	6.8
Latin America	**1 039**	**8 582**	**48**	**7.7**
Developing countries	**3 970**	**62 128**	**77**	**6.3**

[1]Refers to averages for the periods 1961-62 and 1988-89, in 1,000 tons.
Source: AGROSTAT, FAO, 1991

Table 8.   Population growth rates by sector, 1961-90

Continent and country	Population 1990			Growth rates 1961-90		
	Agri-cultural	Non-agri-cultural	Total ('00s)	Agri-cultural	Non-agri-cultural	Total
Africa	**389 141**	**252 971**	**642 112**	**2.02**	**4.44**	**2.78**
Morocco	9 105	15 955	25 060	0.59	4.57	2.56
Tunisia	1 986	6 194	8 180	–0.60	4.01	2.22
Egypt	21 230	31 196	52 426	1.13	3.50	2.34
Sudan	15 183	10 020	25 203	1.54	6.13	2.74
Niger	6 748	983	7 731	2.74	7.06	3.06
Chad	4 237	1 442	5 679	1.28	6.92	2.07
Mali	7 447	1 766	9 213	2.07	5.24	2.49
Senegal	5 749	1 578	7 327	2.56	3.75	2.79
Ethiopia	36 732	12 508	49 240	1.84	4.71	2.37
Kenya	18 496	5 536	24 032	3.12	5.51	3.54
Côte d'Ivoire	6 682	5 316	11 998	2.42	7.49	3.86
Ghana	7 544	7 484	15 028	1.84	3.70	2.64
Nigeria	70 323	38 219	108 542	2.74	4.06	3.15
Cameroon	7 228	4 605	11 833	1.43	6.90	2.71
Zaire	23 387	12 181	35 568	1.97	5.50	2.82
Congo	1 349	922	2 271	2.39	3.48	2.79
Tanzania, United Rep. of	21 673	5 645	27 318	2.86	6.48	3.36
Mozambique	12 780	2 876	15 656	2.21	3.98	2.47
Malawi	6 574	2 181	8 755	2.31	7.46	3.05
Madagascar	9 189	2 815	12 004	2.30	4.59	2.72
Far East	**1 713 167**	**1 073 151**	**2 786 318**	**1.37**	**3.74**	**2.10**
India	535 601	317 493	853 094	1.78	3.01	2.19
China	768 396	370 664	1 139 060	1.14	4.04	1.85
Indonesia	81 845	102 439	184 284	0.57	4.38	2.18
Thailand	33 675	22 026	55 701	1.48	4.97	2.48
Latin America	**118 350**	**329 729**	**448 079**	**0.37**	**3.54**	**2.39**
Developing countries	**2 287 463**	**1 758 424**	**4 045 887**	**1.40**	**3.87**	**2.26**

Source: AGROSTAT, FAO, 1991

Table 9. Sectoral share of population and population/land ratio, 1961-90

Continent and country	Share of agricultural population in total		Population / land ratio[1]			
			Agricultural		Total population	
	1961	1990	1961	1990	1961	1990
Africa	**75.64**	**60.60**	**170.03**	**248.53**	**224.81**	**410.10**
Morocco	64.41	36.33	110.10	98.53	170.95	271.18
Tunisia	54.95	24.28	55.62	42.26	101.22	174.04
Egypt	57.48	40.50	595.79	821.28	1 036.45	2 028.09
Sudan	85.15	60.24	89.85	121.37	105.52	201.46
Niger	96.01	87.28	140.00	187.18	145.83	214.45
Chad	93.77	74.61	100.69	132.20	107.38	177.19
Mali	91.38	80.83	245.20	355.81	268.35	440.18
Senegal	83.72	78.46	63.60	110.01	75.98	140.20
Ethiopia	87.11	74.60	187.81	263.69	215.59	353.48
Kenya	86.98	76.96	418.04	761.78	480.61	989.79
Côte d'Ivoire	84.54	55.69	125.97	182.57	149.01	327.81
Ghana	63.38	50.20	179.19	277.35	282.71	552.50
Nigeria	72.94	64.79	110.18	224.42	151.07	346.39
Cameroon	88.46	61.08	86.70	103.14	98.00	168.85
Zaire	84.25	65.75	190.13	297.92	225.68	453.10
Congo	66.77	59.40	503.73	802.98	754.48	1 351.79
Tanzania, United Rep. of	91.63	79.34	306.62	412.82	334.64	520.34
Mozambique	88.13	81.63	254.13	412.26	288.37	505.03
Malawi	93.06	75.09	171.77	272.89	184.58	363.43
Madagascar	86.38	76.55	219.91	297.19	254.59	388.23
Far East	**76.00**	**61.48**	**320.97**	**448.21**	**422.33**	**728.97**
India	70.63	62.78	198.27	316.94	280.73	504.82
China	82.78	67.46	524.28	799.45	633.33	1 185.10
Indonesia	70.68	44.41	405.38	384.97	573.53	866.81
Thailand	80.79	60.46	192.47	152.20	238.24	251.74
Latin America	**47.38**	**26.41**	**81.06**	**65.72**	**171.10**	**248.81**
Developing countries	**72.71**	**56.54**	**219.00**	**284.46**	**301.20**	**503.14**

[1] Persons per 1,000 hectares.
Source: AGROSTAT, FAO, 1991

EMPLOYMENT CONCERNS AND
ENVIRONMENTAL POLICY

3

J. A. Doeleman *

Environmental policy, as we saw in the previous chapter, comes in different guises. At a macro level, policy may concern itself with demographic growth, the health of the population, the overall size and composition of the economy in relation to the natural resource base, the regime of work-hours, or other wider aspects of the environment-economy relationship. At a micro level, on the other hand, policies aim at specific environmental problems. Specific policy, for instance, addresses a category or source of pollution, a form of urban congestion, a type of recycling, or the loss of a feature of the natural heritage. Specific environmental measures revolve around two main approaches, i.e. "command and control" regulation and the use of "economic instruments". Both approaches to environmental policy will be discussed in detail in the next chapter. In the present chapter we are interested in the employment effects of such policies for the economy as a whole and at sectoral level.

Environmental policy, like any new policy, is a source of anxiety. By definition, new policies bring change. The possibility of change, however, invites resistance because what is implied is a critique of established values and practices. Moreover, the changing of values and practices brings to the status quo a redistribution of interests with which the losers — be the losses absolute or relative — can be expected to take issue. In the case of environmental policy, anxiety is centred on a concern that employment, profitability and competitiveness in a number of economic sectors might be placed in the balance. As one British author puts it: "An environmentally friendly Britain may be good for our health but how will it affect our wealth? Are we now heading for a scenario of new job losses or is a greener Britain actually a major opportunity for employment?" (McGavin, 1991).

The question can be given an answer at the outset. Our main finding is that, whilst environmental policy will bring both job losses and job gains,

* ILO, Geneva; and University of Newcastle (Australia). With research assistance by R. Mohindra.

the evidence suggests a net gain in employment. This result is not entirely surprising. In the end, the aim of environmental policy is to bring more care to the environment than would otherwise be the case, and additional care is likely to mean additional work. Theoretically, however, it seems ill-advised to be categorical on this point. Environmental policy alters consumer and producer choices directly and intentionally. However, it also carries indirect effects by impacting on the price structure, on incomes and on technology. Repercussions will feed into the labour and capital market in ways that are different for each sector and difficult to anticipate on an *a priori* basis.[1] None the less, as a first approach, we find that the economic sectors likely to be adversely affected by environmental policy are relatively capital intensive. Examples include energy, chemicals, mining and transport. By contrast, economic activities that are likely to benefit from environmental policy are relatively labour intensive, e.g. sewerage schemes, rural rehabilitation, energy conservation, recycling.

The expected favourable employment implications of environmental policy are phrased particularly boldly by the Kreisky Commission. The Commission writes: "Environmental protection is not a jobkiller, but a jobmaker. The positive net employment effects of environmental protection will be the higher, the more active environmental policies are" (Kreisky Commission, 1989, p. 163). Such a positive overall assessment is, of course, welcome to the environmentalist's cause. However, it is insufficient to settle anxiety over the employment issue. The gain of jobs by others is small consolation for those who stand to lose their own. For this reason, environmental policymakers need to be mindful of the dislocations that their measures may bring during the transition stage and, accordingly, pay attention to the minimisation of transition costs as well as to the need for compensation. The case for compensation rests on the assumption that the costs of economic adjustments resulting from environmental policy are outweighed by the gains to society of that policy. Given these societal gains, it can be argued that persons employed in an adversely affected economic sector ought not to bear the brunt of a change which benefits the whole of society and that, instead, the burden might better be shared by all who benefit. Accordingly, it seems equitable and constructive to offset the burden of policy by paying those who bear the cost of adjustment, with the aim of leaving no group worse off. In other words, environmental policy must be considered in terms of the soundness of its political design as well as of the economic features that will be raised in the following chapter.

This chapter is divided into two parts, the first part concentrating on gains in employment and the second part concentrating on losses and

---

[1] An input-output model is required to predict sectoral responses. However, the structure of this model (the input-output coefficients) itself would be affected, as environmental policy is meant to improve technological choices. Besides, the model would need to be augmented with sectoral price-response functions.

remedial actions. The first part commences with a review of the evidence, focusing on the macroeconomic effects of environmental policy, particularly in respect of employment. This is followed by a sectoral account of the economic activities that may be expected to gain from environmental policy initiatives and thus indicating where new employment and investment opportunities could arise and how planning and training might be directed. Separate attention is paid to the role of government in its public works programme.

The second part of this chapter begins by focusing on losses in employment resulting from environmental policy, and recommending features of environmental policy that will facilitate the adjustment process. Next, consideration is given to those economic sectors most likely to be adversely affected by environmental reforms. The chapter continues by referring briefly to the environmental debate in respect of population growth and of working hours, in view of the significance of each for the labour market. A final section looks at the costs that might arise in the absence of environmental policy. The costs of not undertaking environmental policy include the prospect of loss of livelihood and, in severe cases, of displacement and starvation.

EMPLOYMENT PROSPECTS AND ENVIRONMENTAL POLICY

A review of macro-economic evidence

During recent years a number of studies have been conducted to measure or simulate the economic impacts of environmental policies for the economy as a whole. Some of the studies are qualitative assessments but most are based on macro-econometric models of national economies. In this section the findings of these studies have been summarised and compiled.[2] In considering these findings, one must remember that differences in the methodologies used to derive the results inevitably detract from the comparability of the studies.

The OECD, and its members, have been especially active in carrying out the research. Nevertheless, the evidence to date remains sketchy. Moreover, it concentrates on macroeconomic consequences, leaving sectoral implications as a matter in which there is much scope for speculation. Whilst the weakness of the current state of knowledge is a cause for concern for environmental policymakers in more developed economies, the lack of information is particularly worrisome for developing economies. Not only have we found that the operation of environmental policy is hampered by low levels of development (see

---

[2] In compiling this summary of environmental policy effects, we wish to acknowledge particular reliance on three sources, i.e. OECD (1985), Pearce (1991) and Renner (1991).

Chapter 2), but a range of environmental problems poses a greater threat to livelihood in conditions of poverty.

Part of the problem of registering the employment implications of environmental policy (or lack of it) is that a formal concept of unemployment is often unapplicable or inappropriate in developing countries. In the absence of unemployment benefits, many of the "unemployed" must somehow employ themselves to survive. They may find work in the so-called informal sector, thereby disguising the shortage of productive work opportunities. Therefore, the loss of livelihood due to environment-related causes may be observed only partially and indirectly: in the growth of the informal sector, the level of poverty prevailing, and in out-migration within and between countries.

Findings on the impact of environmental policy have been summarised in box 2 and are arranged according to the country or countries of study; the period under consideration; the type of environmental policy; and its expected effects, especially in respect of employment. Studies have been ordered in reverse chronological order.[3]

Box 2. A review of macro-economic studies regarding the effects of environmental policy

A. *Region*
   United Kingdom;
   Period
   1995-2010;
   Policy
   fourfold increase in pollution abatement expenditure by 2000 and intensified water protection measures;
   Findings
   compared to base levels, GDP first increases but falls by the year 2010, albeit by less than 1 per cent; employment gains 682,000 jobs by the year 2005 while unemployment falls by 365,000 jobs (at that point, the model reaches full employment) (Barker and Lewney, 1991, using the Cambridge Multisectoral Dynamic Model, cited in Pearce, 1991).

B. *Region*
   United Kingdom;
   Period
   1995-2010;
   Policy
   a tax of £30 per ton of carbon emission;

---

[3] Depending on the date of commencement of each study period.

Findings

slight reduction in baseline GDP; unemployment reduced by 70,000 (Sondheimer, 1991, cited in Pearce, 1991).

C. *Region*

United States;

Period

next 75 years;

Policy

slowing global warming (prevention) versus adapting by sea walls, flood mitigation works, relocation, etc. (repression);

Findings

adapting is cheaper in commercial terms as no more than 13 per cent of American production is sensitive to climatic change; employment implications are uncertain. (Note: (a) environmental losses of a repressive policy are considered only in respect of the impact on human exploitation of such resources; (b) not considered are the advantages of carbon-cutting measures, e.g. in terms of reducing air pollution and its damaging effects on ecosystems, urban centres and human health as well as in terms of reducing the external costs ensuing from a less heavy reliance on private motor cars (Nordhaus, 1991, cited in Cairncross, 1991, and Pearce, 1991. Related work by Nordhaus was reported in *The Economist* (London), 7 July 1990.)

D. *Region*

Norway;

Period

1990-2010;

Policy

carbon tax designed to keep emissions at the level of the year 2000;

Findings

GDP annual growth rate falls from 2.7 to 2.3 per cent; imports and exports decline by 4.7 per cent; investment falls by about 1 per cent; net employment effects appear negligible (Glomsrod et al., 1990, cited in Pearce, 1991).

E. *Region*

United Kingdom;

Period

1990-2005;

Policy

carbon tax which achieves a 20 per cent reduction on the 1990 emission level by 2005;

Findings

substantial employment gains; scrapping of old equipment offers productivity gains for manufacturing which will improve(!)

45

competitiveness (Ingham and Ulph, 1990, cited in Pearce, 1991).

F. *Region*
>   Global;
>   *Period*
>   1990s;
>   *Policy*
>   non-specific environmental policy;
>   *Findings*
>   cautious optimism in respect of net employment effect in OECD
>   countries but less optimism for the east of Europe or the former
>   Soviet Union in the short term; unanswered questions in respect
>   of the developing countries (ILO, 1990, pp. 40 ff.).

G. *Region*
>   Western Europe;
>   *Period*
>   1990s;
>   *Policy*
>   non-specific environmental policy;
>   *Findings*
>   net employment effects strongly positive (Kreisky Commission,
>   1989, p. 163).

H. *Region*
>   Europe and the former Soviet Union;
>   *Period*
>   1990s;
>   *Policy*
>   non-specific environmental policy;
>   *Findings*
>   the net effect on employment may be neutral or positive;
>   countries more forward in environmental programmes are
>   expected to develop a comparative advantage, thus gaining
>   relatively more in employment; training programmes are needed
>   to staff an increased number of environmental jobs; public works
>   programmes can be designed to meet both the need for
>   environmental protection and unemployment relief (see also
>   section below on "Public works") (Alfthan et al., 1990).

I. *Region*
>   France, Germany, Italy, United Kingdom;
>   *Period*
>   1988-97;
>   *Policy*
>   installation of sulphur dioxide and nitrogen oxide scrubbers at
>   major electricity and industrial plants to control acid rain;

Findings

boosts in employment and income in the first five years (especially in Germany); continued gains in employment and income in France and Italy but falls in Germany and the United Kingdom in the subsequent three years (Klaassen et al., 1987, cited in Pearce, 1991).

J. *Region*

former Federal Republic of Germany;

Period

1986;

Policy

recycling beverage containers from 10 to 85 per cent;

Findings

gain of recycling-related jobs 90,000; loss in new container production 15,000 to 20,000 jobs (Renner, 1991, p. 36).

K. *Region*

Netherlands;

Period

1985-2010;

Policy

doubling environmental protection expenditures as a proportion of total expenditures from 2 to 4 per cent; including measures of energy conservation, investment in public transport, constraints on private transport, recycling of waste and reduced use of fertilisers;

Findings

GNP grows at 95 per cent (over the 25 years) instead of 98 per cent (in the absence of policy); real wages rise by 59 per cent instead of 61 per cent; employment remains unchanged (Netherlands, Ministerie van Huisvesting . . ., 1989, 1990; cited in Pearce, 1991).

L. *Region*

Sahel countries;

Period

1980s;

Policy

failure to limit over-usage of agricultural lands;

Findings

inadequate employment opportunities for rising levels of population (Perrings, 1991).

M. *Region*

European Communities countries;

Period

mid-1980s;

Policy

energy conservation and use of renewable energy sources;

Findings

gain of 3,800 jobs per million tons of oil saved with a total saving of 34 million tons achievable (Hohmeier et al., 1985, in Renner, 1991, p. 28).

N. *Region*

Europe;

Period

1980-2000;

Policy

broad spectrum environmental policy;

Findings

the integration of environmental policy into future development is necessary to avoid the loss of markets and jobs, as it is to protect human and ecological well-being; the need for training is emphasised in order to minimise shortages of skills, e.g. in waste management, water treatment, pollution control and conservation programmes (CEC, 1990, pp. 82 and 83).

O. *Region*

Netherlands;

Period

1979-87;

Policy

doubling of annual environmental expenditure during the period 1979-85 to 5 billion guilders;

Findings

depending on environmental policies of other countries, GDP falls by 0.3-0.6 per cent; consumer prices rise by 0.8-4.3 per cent; the trade balance declines by around 1 billion guilders; employment effects range from a fall of 10,000 to a rise of 6,000, the latter being achieved in the event of vigorous environmental programmes abroad (and an absence of wage indexation) (Netherlands, Centraal Planbureau, 1975, in OECD, 1985).

P. *Region*

Austria;

Period

1979-85;

Policy

implementation of "necessary" environmental expenditure between 1.7 and 2.5 per cent of GDP (the actual percentage for the period was around 1 per cent);

Findings

drag on annual growth rate between 0.35 and 0.57 per cent; employment effect not specified; annual inflationary effects of 0.1-0.2 per cent (Austria, Bundesministerium für Gesundheit und Umweltschutz, 1980, in OECD, 1985).

Q. *Region*

United States;

Period

1979 onward;

Policy

increased reliance on solar energy and energy conservation measures;

Findings

employment losses 1 million jobs; employment gains 4 million jobs (Rodberg, 1979, cited in Renner, 1991, p. 27).

R. *Region*

Finland;

Period

1976-82;

Policy

a FMk 2.5 billion water protection programme (1975 prices);

Findings

GDP levels rise from 0.3 per cent in 1976 to 0.6 per cent in 1982; inflation rises by 0.2 per cent; employment rises from 3,500 to 7,500; wages rise; the effect on the current and capital balance of Finland is adverse (Finland, National Board of Waters, 1978, cited in OECD, 1985).

S. *Region*

Norway;

Period

1974-83;

Policy

assessment of private sector cost increases related to growing environmental expenditure;

Findings

the level of GDP rose by 1.5 per cent owing to multiplier effects given slack in the economy; prices by 1983 rose by 0.1-0.9 per cent; unemployment fell by 25,000 (Forsund and Tveitereid, 1977, and Forsund and Waage, 1978, in OECD, 1985).

T. *Region*

United States;

Period

1973-85;

Policy
United States environmental policy enacted;

Findings
GDP annual growth has been slowed by 0.19 per cent; *ceteris paribus*, employment would have suffered correspondingly (Jorgensen and Wilcoxen, 1990, cited in Pearce, 1991. Similar low results are reported by Pearce from a conference paper by Nordhaus, 1991).

U. *Region*
United States;

Period
1970-87;

Policy
additional federal environmental programmes implemented for the period 1970-80;

Findings
(main variant) the GNP level of 1987 falls by 0.7 per cent; the price level rises by 7.4 per cent; unemployment falls by 0.4 per cent of the labour force; the trade balance first loses, then improves to a gain of US$1.6 billion (1979 prices) (Data Resources Inc., 1981, in OECD, 1985).

V. *Region*
France;

Period
1965-74;

Policy
stepping up pollution control expenditure to FF3.3 billion instead of an actual figure of FF2 billion (and other retrospective scenarios);

Findings
the GDP level grows by 0.25 per cent in 1974 (deflated); consumer prices rise by 0.1 per cent over the period; the peak of the fall in unemployment was 43,500, in 1974 (France, Ministère de l'Environnement et du Cadre de la vie, 1980, in OECD, 1985).

The evidence presented is not without ambiguities. None the less, most of the findings indicate that environmental policy will add to employment and detract from income. The first finding is encouraging while the latter is not. Income effects, in line with other macro-economic effects, appear to be weak, however. Moreover, as will be explored in the next subsection, income falls may be assumed to have been overstated in the evidence.

Appraisal of findings

Environmental policy has been seen to have a favourable impact on aggregate employment in the short run, as against a possible modest loss of income and growth in the long run. Employment gains arise from policy-induced environmental protective efforts. In the short run, these gains are amplified by the need to build up a capacity for such efforts. For example, pollution control measures require investments in the manufacture of pollution abatement equipment. This amplification of activity at an early stage of implementation may actually give rise to additional economic buoyancy and an increase in incomes which — as the cited studies indicate — reverses in the long run. The eventual fall in income resulting from environmental policies warrants special comment. It may be the case that the falls recorded are in fact more apparent than real.

Additional employment and other factor inputs that are called for to meet higher environmental standards are entered as additional costs in the accounts of private and public enterprises. Such additional costs will be passed on through higher charges. Environmental policy therefore holds an inflationary potential, which has the effect of reducing real income for those affected. In practice, the inflationary potential has proved not to be serious.[4] In any event, it does not seem to present a good explanation of why incomes should fall as a result of the introduction of environmental policy. Not only does inflation depend on an accommodative monetary policy, it is also interpreted more easily as a mechanism of income redistribution than as one of income reduction.

To find a more plausible basis for the recorded falls in incomes following the introduction of environmental policy, let us assume for a moment that the economy fully employs the available means of production. In that case, a call for additional environmental efforts will put a claim on labour and capital already otherwise committed. The effect is one of "crowding out" other production. Loss of income, regardless of its transmission process, therefore directly relates to the loss of production surrendered on behalf of new environmental priorities. In turn, the loss of income can be projected into the future because it would imply a fall in savings and investment. However, the validity of this view can be challenged if the environmental protection activities responsible for the loss of income have productive value themselves — an issue to be addressed below.

The assumption of the full employment of production factors need not be met, of course. In that case, "crowding out" would be limited to the factors, if any, which remain in short supply. It is conceivable therefore to

---

[4] See OECD (1985) covering Austria, Finland, France, the Netherlands, Norway and the United States, which reports an inflationary potential of 0.3-0.5 per cent. UNECE (1988, Ch. 5) writes that inflationary fears have been misplaced.

mount additional environmental efforts without a fall in income, or with a limited fall. For instance, an environmental public works programme built around the use of unemployed workers could, in principle, generate the sought environmental results without loss other than the loss of involuntary leisure.

Having contended that an adverse effect of environmental policy on income may be mitigated by the availability of surplus labour and other production factors, we may advance a further reason which casts doubt on the findings that suggest such falls. The reason relates to flaws in the measurement of income. The traditional income measure is an indicator of welfare based on purchasing power, i.e. measuring access to goods and services supplied by the (market) economy. The quality of the environment provides an input of welfare too, in the form of psychic income and health. However, since environmental welfare is not usually obtained by purchase, economists have chosen to neglect this aspect in the past. The current interest in environmental or "green" accounting derives precisely from a desire to overcome this shortcoming.[5]

Unfortunately, the findings reported on in the previous section are based on economic models in which income still remains conventionally defined. Therefore, when examining claims of moderate falls in income following the introduction of environmental measures which have the effect of diverting labour and capital, one must bear in mind that only the costs of the policy are being considered, and not the benefits. Granted a measure of income which incorporates the non-monetary gains from environmental policy, one would expect income to rise on the premise that environmental policy benefits have been considered to outweigh policy costs.

Indeed, environmental accounting points to a conceivable *increase* in the conventional income measure following the introduction of environmental policy. This is possible because the neglect of the environmental dimension has affected traditional economic and econometric models such as were used in the studies quoted. Besides yielding non-monetary income through satisfaction and physical well-being, the environment offers the resources on which the production of marketable goods and services depends. Economic models have taken these natural resources too much for granted, concentrating on the constraints of labour and capital instead. As a result, these models have not come to grips with the issues of sustainability. It follows that such models would have ignored the drag on marketable production that might

---

[5] For an overview see, for instance, Peskin and Lutz (1990). Recently, the World Resources Institute (1991) called on the United Nations to use its World Conference on Environment and Development in Brazil to initiate changes to national accounting practices to bring these in line with sustainable development. Using the case of Costa Rica, the Institute argues that a 4.6 per cent annual economic growth rate between 1970 and 1989 is overstated by more than a quarter, on account of income forgone because of the loss of forests, soils and fisheries.

Table 10. Environment-protective activities — Selected criteria

Sector	Labour intensity	Balance of payments	Main focus of action
Pollution abatement	Moderate	Negative potential [1]	Private
Agricultural rehabilitation	High	Favourable [2]	Private and social
Soft energies/ energy conservation	Improved Variable	Negative first; positive [1] Negative first; positive [1]	Private Private
Transport and communications	Low	Favourable [3]	Private and social
Water and sewage works	High	Negligible	Social
Recycling, waste management	Variable	Favourable [4]	Private
Conservation and forestry	High	Favourable [5]	Private and social
Environmental R & D/training	High	Negligible	Private and social
Environmental administration	High	Negligible	Private and social

[1] Import of necessary materials and/or equipment but subsequent savings on fuels, especially LDCs. [2] Reduced reliance on imported chemicals. [3] Reduced reliance on imported cars and fuel, especially LDCs. [4] Comparative advantage in labour cost in LDCs. [5] Tourism potential.

ensue in the absence of environmental policy, owing to natural resource constraints. It also follows that such models would then fail to observe falls in the traditional measure of income, as they would fail to register when the continuity of economic growth might be in environmental jeopardy.

So far the discussion has centred on the employment and income effects of environmental policy. A further important macroeconomic aspect concerns the effect that environmental policy may have on the balance of payments. Unfortunately, the review of studies does not offer conclusive evidence in this regard. Besides, as will be examined in Chapter 7, balance-of-payments consequences depend on the level of international coordination of environmental policy. International coordination, inter alia, ought to minimise the distortion of international competitiveness as a result of environmental policy. This issue will also be addressed in the next chapter, where the position is adopted that environmental policy as a cause of competitive differences must be seen in the context of many other factors affecting competition, and that countries may choose to provide industries unfairly affected by national environmental policies with fiscal or other offsets. In fact, within the bounds of sustainability, different environmental preferences between rich and poor countries would seem to form a legitimate basis for trade.

Some speculative observations on the balance-of-payments effects of environmental policy in relation to the environment-protective sector will be presented in the subsequent section (see table 10). For example, environmental policy may call for the importation of sophisticated pollution abatement equipment which less developed and indebted countries can ill afford. In such cases, aid and technology transfer may have a prominent role to play.

Employment in the environment-protective sector

Environmental policy encourages environment-protective activities which create more jobs than will be lost in adversely affected sectors. This repeated message is summed up by the Worldwatch Institute: "Renewable energy employs more workers than coal or oil; recycling employs more than landfilling; and railroads more than cars" (Renner, 1991, p. 17). Here we offer a sectoral picture of the economic activities which stand to gain as a result of environmental policies. The downside of the equation will be presented in the subsection "Sectoral setbacks" below.

Before we set out to predict the areas in which environmental policy will have an expansionary effect, the speculative nature of this exercise must be acknowledged. At present, no established classification of environment-protective activities is available. Accordingly, existing sectoral economic models have problems in separating the positive and negative impacts of environmental policy on production and employment.[6] In any case, the complexities of adding environmental policy changes to an already exceedingly dynamic economic system are baffling and probably cannot therefore be mathematically programmed into a model which yields reliable sectoral prognoses.

None the less, the subject of environment-protective activities has produced a variety of ideas and expectations in the literature and media. In what follows, a short sketch of these ideas has been organised around a classification of the environment-protective sector into nine subsectors. Table 10 sets out these subsectors and indicates, for an expansion in the activities of each of these, the potential labour intensity; the expected balance-of-payments effect, which is especially relevant for less developed countries; and the level at which government might be involved. Brief indicative notes on the prospects of each of the subsectors follow.

Pollution abatement

Pollution control in respect of air, water and soils constitutes a major area of environment-protective activity. During the 1980s public and private expenditure on pollution control in OECD countries ranged between 1 and 2 per cent of GDP and around 2 per cent of total employment.[7] This is expected to rise steeply. For instance, by the year

---

[6] Work is under way to develop environmental input-output models; see Duchin et al. (1991), for example.

[7] Lower estimates have also been presented. For example, Bezdek, Wendling and Jones (1989), cited in Pereira (1991), arrive at 176,000 jobs in pollution abatement and control in the United States in 1985, on a turnover of US$20 billion and investments of US$8.5 billion.

2000 the United States hopes to raise its expenditure of US$115 billion to US$171 billion in real terms, or 2.8 per cent of GDP. The National Environment Protection Plan of the Netherlands even projects a figure going to 4 per cent. What is noteworthy is that countries that are ahead in pollution control in industry, e.g. the former Federal Republic of Germany and Japan, are net exporters of control equipment, while other countries, including the United Kingdom and the United States, are net importers (Renner, 1991, pp. 22 ff.).

Pollution control is of particular concern for the less developed world because, more than other environment-protective activities, it draws on scarce capital and technical know-how and because it is potentially costly in terms of foreign exchange. Concern for a reliable environmental performance of industry in developing countries may therefore help to strengthen the case for international aid and for pollution-abatement technology transfer in order to avoid a systematic excess of industrial pollution — as found also in the former Eastern European countries — as well as to avoid failures of safety which could bring a repetition of tragic occurrences such as the Bhopal disaster in India.

Agricultural rehabilitation

The need to rehabilitate agricultural lands illustrates that the costs of environmental programmes are linked not merely to the psychic income of already affluent communities but also to employment and productivity. In the case of economies mainly dependent on agriculture, the link is vital. It extends also to fisheries. In spite of this, degradation and erosion of agricultural lands are commonplace. Contributing factors include overcropping, mono-cropping, overgrazing and the use of technologies relying on short-term equations, such as those involving a heavy dosage of chemical fertiliser (a prime source also of water pollution) and the use of unsafe herbicides and insecticides.

The recycling of organic material to the land, the building of wind-breaks, the prevention of run-offs, crop rotation and fallow periods are amongst the measures that are important in safeguarding the continuity of production. Often, the collective organisation of these measures is proving to be a greater barrier than the labour required or the production to be sacrificed in the short run.[8] In some of the poorest countries, an explanation is found in part in the necessity to maintain food production for populations doubling almost every 25 years. The situation in the Sahel countries, for example, has become critical (see box 3 below). Other parts of the world also offer a worrying picture. Recently, the National Conservation Strategy for Pakistan has suggested employing

---

[8] Project work may help to overcome organisational bottlenecks. For instance, the ILO is assisting in two projects of wasteland development by women's groups in India. The work is assisted by the Governments of Denmark and the Netherlands.

underutilised military staff in land rehabilitation and reclamation (cited in Markandya, 1991, p. 35).

Soft energies [9]/energy conservation

The wholesale price of fossil fuels predominantly reflects the low costs of extraction and distribution. Across the mining sector, new technologies have offered major savings in costs over recent decades. The price of fossil fuels does not, at present, reflect their environmental cost in terms of air pollution and global warming. Nor does it reflect the need to preserve oil and gas and (to a lesser extent) coal for the requirements of centuries to come. As a result, we have seen that renewable energy alternatives have been systematically disadvantaged. Nuclear energy, on the other hand, has in the past attracted extensive state support for a variety of reasons. However, the environmental hazards of this technology have, until recently, also been poorly assessed.

A policy of energy pricing which takes account of undesirable environmental spillovers is likely to reduce the reliance on fossil and nuclear fuels, as it is likely to reduce energy consumption. The labour demand implications of reduced consumption levels are negative. However, a shift in emphasis to renewable energy generation technology will benefit employment. The labour input of 1,000 gigawatt-hours of energy is currently estimated at 100 work-years in nuclear plants, 116 work-years in coal-fired stations, and 248 and 542 work-years respectively on solar and wind farms (Renner, 1991, p. 25).

The competitiveness of solar and wind technology following energy price reforms is not expected to extend to countries in which people may spend a major part of their day collecting scarce firewood for cooking. In these countries, tree planting with suitable fast-growing species such as eucalyptus or acacia may offer a partial remedy. Furthermore, the production of biogas presents a soft-energy alternative that remains relatively underdeveloped. In addition to biogas, the manufacturing of biofuel from suitable crops will increase as a result of price reforms. Brazil already produces a significant part of its petrol requirements in this way.[10] Fuel crops, however, require an abundance of cheap land with low opportunity costs and should not become a threat to food production or remaining wilderness areas. In other words, an environmental policy based on the removal of price distortions ought not to stop at energy but ought to include, inter alia, the value of land and of wilderness. In some cases, the

---

[9] After Lovins (1977).

[10] By 1980, in response to the oil crisis of the 1970s, the Brazilian National Alcohol Programme produced 3,500 million litres of biofuel, mainly from sugar cane. This created 41,000 permanent jobs and 83,000 seasonal jobs. The programme saved US$520 million in foreign exchange. At a production cost of US$0.57 per litre, however, the economies of the programme have been diminished by low world market prices for mineral fuel (Pereira, 1986).

interests of indigenous people who still live in harmony with wilderness areas also need to be taken into account.

If the cost of energy rises because environmental spillovers are taken into consideration and because of a need to provide energy on a sustainable footing, the conservation of energy will gain in attractiveness. Even today, the consensus of research in the developed economies is that energy conservation measures offer a better return on expenditure than any other energy investment. It is thought that the consumption of electricity in the European Communities, for instance, can be as much as halved simply by designing better buildings and electrical equipment. This level of reduction in energy consumption is confirmed while projecting per capita income growth to continue (see Goldemberg et al., 1988). Naturally, developing countries cannot be expected to achieve comparable savings of what they have little of. Nevertheless, they stand to gain from new knowledge on energy conservation.

An awareness of the advantages of energy conservation measures in countries with high levels of consumption has already led to many improvements since the so-called energy crisis of the 1970s. These include double-glazing, thermal insulation in walls and ceilings, low wattage lights, solar hot-water systems, etc. In fact, the rate of growth of electricity consumption declined in affluent countries during the 1980s. Yet there is still scope for further improvement. Higher energy costs would stimulate the implementation of such further improvements while also stimulating research and development in energy efficiency. As an illustration of the significance of prices, compare the difference in the price of petrol in the United States on the one hand, and the European Communities and Japan, on the other. In mid-1991 the price of petrol in the United States stood at US$0.40 per litre, as against between US$0.90 to US$1.40 in the European Communities and Japan. This price difference is reflected in more frugal engine design and car use, which accounts, partly at least, for the fact that petrol consumption per car in the United States is, at just under 3,000 litres per annum, more than double the consumption in Europe and Japan.

Investment in energy conservation contributes to employment. Whereas US$1 million spent on American energy production represents 12 jobs, three different studies showed that the same amount spent on conservation represented 18 jobs (Alaska), 35 jobs (Oregon) and 60-80 jobs (New York State) (Renner, 1991, pp. 25 ff.). Given the capital intensity of energy production, similar findings are likely to emerge in many other countries.

Transport and communications

In Box 3 the environmental costs of motor vehicles are detailed. These non-private cost details are coupled with the recommendation that the full costs of motoring, be it in cars, buses or trucks, should be charged to the motorist. This approach, shared by many environmentalists, indicates a desire to reduce the growing dependence on private transport and to divert money away from the construction of more roads and highways to rail transport. Likewise, other modes of transport might be required to pay for environmental or social costs. Airlines, for example, are not charged for noise and air pollution.

Box 3. Environmental costs of motor vehicles

Environmental costs of motor vehicles not, or not fully, paid by the vehicle's owner

— Risk of death and injury. Globally, it is estimated that 400,000 persons are killed on the roads per year. Many times this number suffer permanent injuries.

— A variety of pollution costs, including emission of greenhouse gases, lead, asbestos and noise; producing direct adverse consequences on health in the urban environment and also affecting plants, animals and produce.

— Congestion costs due to loss of land for roads, road exchanges and parking. In urban areas, cars may take up as much space as is available for people to live in. Alternatively, the space requirements of cars contribute to urban sprawl.

— Roads constitute a source of visual damage to the environment; in conjunction with the danger, pollution and congestion already cited, they act as spoilers of the quality of communal (and private) spaces in towns and neighbourhoods.

— Roads connect people but also divide the area they traverse. Accordingly, the more important traffic arteries have become social and physical barriers separating neighbourhoods.

— The car consumes materials and there is insufficient thought to recycling; graphic reminders are piles of burning tyres and abandoned vehicles (sometimes in places of scenic beauty).

— The car consumes energy but there is little thought about renewal.

Raising the price of private motoring does not imply that subsidies for public transport should be increased. A system of public transport that has long been in decline, however, could be ill-equipped to cope with a renewed interest in its facilities. The answer which has been suggested is to inject more competition into the operation of public transport and to widen the spectrum of services and charges.[11]

---

[11] Examples of new services include taxi concessions at railway stations and the carrying of trucks by rail to cover long distances.

Higher transport prices which fully reflect the costs incurred in movement on the road, by rail, in the air or on water may bring a number of beneficial developments. Economising on transport, as with the use of energy, yields savings as well as environmental benefits. It may also help to boost the development of promising substitutes. One of these is a future age of electronic communication in which the exchange of information will be cheap, remote decision-making convenient, and home production (particularly in the tertiary sector) practicable. Another development, for short trips, relates to a rediscovery of the bicycle. However, this choice is commonly constrained by the absence of structural provisions which afford cyclists levels of safety similar to those for motorised road users.

Comparative data on the distribution of transport modes provide an indication of the scope for environmental policy in this sector. The share of private car transport in urban passenger trips in what used to be Eastern Europe (excluding the former German Democratic Republic) and the former Soviet Union ranges from 11 to 15 per cent. In Western Europe the figure is around 45 per cent. In the United States it is 82 per cent. Pedestrian and bicycle trips vary between 30 per cent and 50 per cent in all countries except the United States, where the figure is 10 per cent. Public transport accounts for 3 per cent of trips in the United States, 5 to 19 per cent in Western Europe and over 50 per cent in the former Eastern Europe (figures are for 1978-87; see Pucher, 1990).

In this spectrum, the developing countries would generally be the least car-dependent. Furthermore, these countries offer, on the whole, poorer public transport facilities than those of the former Eastern Europe and Soviet Union. Therefore, developing countries are in a position to avoid the perceived mistakes of the West and place a higher priority on public transport. By a reduced reliance on private motorised transport, it seems possible to avoid some of the privately, socially and environmentally high costs of a transport solution which would also prove a drain on both savings and foreign exchange. Such savings, in turn, could be put to investment in human and physical capital and provide additional productive opportunities for employment.

Water and sewage works

The over-use of water resources, coupled with unsatisfactory sewage treatment and disposal, pose major environmental concerns in a rapidly urbanising world. The upgrading of the water supply system, the treatment of sewage and the development of recycling (conceivably using dual-piping systems) are high on the environmental agenda in rich and poor countries alike. Such projects may also offer additional unemployment relief (see section on "Public works" below) in activities already providing much employment. Figures for the European Communities suggest that the water sector employs around 0.5 million people (Alfthan et al., 1990).

Realistic water pricing provides an important tool for achieving economies in consumption, the upgrading of production facilities, and the containment of disease. The impact of higher water prices can be severe, however, particularly for the urban poor and for the farmers who, sometimes unwisely, have come to depend on large quantities of undervalued water (for example see Jonish, 1992).

Recycling and waste management

As with other environmental policies, a policy to encourage recycling and to help to place waste generation on a sustainable footing can be built around environmental price reform. For instance, domestic and enterprise waste is collected at a flat fee which offers little incentive for recycling. Without an incentive, the quantities of waste going into landfills or being incinerated have risen disturbingly. The elaborate packaging requirements of trade with distant lands and modern retailing are adding to the strain. These requirements are also incompatible with traditional approaches, e.g. refundable bottle deposits or the private supply of containers. For these reasons, schemes have been suggested that encourage households and enterprises to sort their waste before disposal and thereby to make recycling a better proposition. The sorting is done according to a system of debits or credits which depend on the amount of each type of waste collected, reinforced by penalty rates on unsorted waste.

The sorting of waste is one way of encouraging recycling. The levying of premiums on virgin materials — where these are exploited on an unsustainable basis — is another way of improving the recovery rate of materials. Furthermore, it has been suggested that governments may require enterprises to take financial responsibility for the disposal costs of their products in order to incorporate this consideration at the design stage.

Recyclable materials include glass, metals, paper, many plastics, tyres, compostable matter, etc. Water and heat also lend themselves to recycling. In all cases, recycling generates much more employment than disposal. Estimates for the United States suggest that for every million tons of waste, recycling offers 2,000 jobs, incineration (which can be combined with electricity generation) 150-1,100 jobs, and landfills 50-360 jobs (Renner, 1991, p. 34). This comparison does not take into account the number of jobs in "new" material extraction. The mining sector, however, has become one of the most capital-intensive economic sectors.

Estimates of total employment in waste management in the European Communities indicate 2-2.5 million jobs, a number that is expected to grow by 1.2 million during the 1990s (Euroconsult, 1989). For the whole of Western Europe, the estimate rises to a total of 3-3.5 million jobs (OECD, cited in Lewis, 1991, p. 18). Compared to the United States, these figures are high on account of higher labour intensities in Europe, i.e. 12,000-15,000 jobs per US$1 billion in Europe against 7,000 jobs in the

United States (Lewis, 1991). They may be higher again in Third World countries, where the economics of recycling are favoured by low wages and a high opportunity cost (in terms of capital and foreign exchange) of materials. In Shanghai, for instance, the public administration employs 29,000 full-time workers for recycling activities; many more are employed in the production of equipment for collection, sorting and processing (Gaudier, 1991). Numerous other examples suggest the special viability of recycling projects in developing countries (e.g. see Johnson Cointreau et al., 1984).

Conservation and forestry

The conservation of remaining wilderness areas and the rehabilitation of land into parks and natural reserves serve a number of important environmental functions, which include the preservation of biodiversity, the protection of our natural heritage, and the maintenance of safe water quality. Wilderness areas may also have a beneficial impact on the quality of air, on the microclimate and, through locking up carbon, on the macroclimate. In addition, conservation offers economic opportunities related to the increased demand for recreation in natural surroundings. Associated with this growing demand for recreation, tourism has expanded more quickly than any other economic sector in developed economies during recent decades. Tourism is labour intensive and generates jobs in industrialised and developing economies alike. Other economic opportunities to which conservation gives rise relate to the (sustainable) harvesting of plants and animals found only in more complex ecosystems; to research in respect of the potential of species and biochemistry as yet commercially undiscovered; and to the harvesting of indigenous timber.

Wilderness areas provide the traditional source of supply of timber. However, timber is commonly extracted on an unsustainable basis, with irreversible losses or severe degradation of unique native forests. After harvesting (or without), land can be ecologically reduced to the demands of agriculture or silviculture. In 1980, forests covered some 27.5 per cent of the world land mass. About half of these forests were native, located mainly in the tropics of South America, Africa and south-east Asia. The tropical forests form the richest ecosystems on earth and play a perhaps critical role in climate formation. None the less, they are being lost at a rate of nearly 1 per cent per annum (UNEP, 1992).

Environmental R & D/training

Environmental R & D is of paramount importance if the economic aspirations of growing populations are to be fulfilled on a sustainable basis in the framework of a finite biosphere. Fortunately, the potency of R & D has been amply demonstrated by a remarkable rate of technical progress in modern times. Technical progress, however, has been aimed more at maximising economic output than at minimising inputs drawn from the natural environment. To overcome this bias, the approach following the "polluter-pays-principle" (PPP) can be used. The PPP approach can give impetus to environmental R & D, most notably at the level of private enterprise.

Government itself also has a role to play in environmental research and development. It may pursue this role in conjunction with its responsibilities in the area of education and training. This aspect deserves emphasis because the prospect of shortages of appropriately qualified staff in environment-protective activities looms large (Alfthan et al., 1990; Gaudier, 1991). Clearly, environmental education and training programmes (or components in programmes) are in urgent need of expansion, especially where lead times are long. To meet such shortages will not only require new or additional environmental study openings for school-leavers but also on-the-job educational programmes to help suitable staff to gain the necessary environmental knowledge and skills.

The shortage of environmentally qualified staff is illustrated by indicative estimates for the waste management sector in Western Europe: 77,000 professional/managerial positions; 94,000 technical and administrative positions; and 141,000 skilled positions (Lewis, 1991). Unmet training needs are also reported for the water sector and other environment-protective activities in Europe (Alfthan et al., 1990).

Environmental administration

Inevitably, environmental policy initiatives will involve administrative machinery concerned with planning, training, research, monitoring and enforcement. Such administrative tasks will require additional staff for the regulatory agencies at governmental level, as well as for people in private industry at the management level to direct and oversee the environment-protective activities examined above. In some cases, environmental work may be absorbed within existing structures of responsibility. In other cases, functions are being created which call for environmental knowledge or environmental skills of a newly emerging variety of types.

The requirement to train people at the environmental management level is the more pressing given the time and experience necessary for managers to develop informed and balanced judgement. If, for lack of qualified candidates, key positions were filled on a less than discriminating basis, there would be considerable scope for one-sided and counterproductive decision-making in weighing the long-term economic and environmental imperatives for modern societies.

Public works

The above discussion of the environment-protective sector indicates that a range of environment-protective activities depend on government action through its public works programme. That is not to say that such programmes must actually be carried out by government. On the contrary, private contractors might be as well or better equipped for the planning and managing of public works. The point is that the work must be financed collectively on account of the "public good" nature of the environmental provisions sought.[12]

Environmental public works programmes may be undertaken with the further objective of providing employment. This multiple-objective approach has been followed in a number of European countries. For instance, in the early 1980s the Government of Sweden ran a counter-cyclical public works employment programme involving 21,000 jobs, one-third of which were allocated to environmental projects, comprising water and sewage works; forest management; the upkeep of nature parks; and the maintenance of historic monuments. With the exception of water and sewage works (which require special skills, equipment and fittings), environmental projects have become a permanent feature of Swedish job-relief programmes.

In 1984 a similar scheme was begun in France under the name "Travaux d'utilité collective" (TUC). By 1987 the scheme offered half-time work, in conjunction with training and jobsearch assistance, for 700,000 otherwise unemployed young persons. Initially the environmental component in the work undertaken was around 10 per cent. This percentage was boosted in 1987 by two new initiatives, i.e. a programme to reduce the incidence of forest fires in the south of the country and another to rehabilitate the foreshores of a number of river systems (see Alfthan et al., 1990, and Pereira, 1991).

In developing countries too, governments and aid agencies are no longer occupied solely with the economic and social benefits of publicly sponsored projects but have become increasingly sensitive to environmental ramifications. Indeed, many new projects seek to enhance the sustainability of development through environmental initiatives. The World Bank alone has at present over 100 projects on its books which envisage significant environmental benefits in conjunction with developmental benefits, such as the maintenance of employment, the improvement of productivity, or the protection of health (World Bank, 1991, Appendix). These projects, in some 60 countries, involve the promotion of environmentally sound agricultural practices (e.g. the use of organic fertilisers, the planting of wind-breaks, the construction of irrigation systems, biological pest control, etc.), the improvement of urban communal services (e.g. water supply, drainage and waste handling), the encouragement of forestry, the control of floods, and so on. Likewise, the

---

[12] Public goods are goods that offer non-exclusive benefits. Unlike private goods, the consumption of a public good by one person does not detract from the consumption of the same public good by another person. As a textbook rule, private initiative by itself will supply less than optimal quantities of a public good.

ILO is engaged in environment-related project work, albeit on a more modest scale.[13]

The coming together of environmental aims, unemployment relief and communal initiative is opening up new avenues for rewarding action and participation. The preparation of the ground for these initiatives lies in the recognition of environmental and social needs in addition to commercial success. If progress on all three fronts is taken into consideration — as it is in cost-benefit analysis — a range of environmental recovery programmes may be found to offer social returns that are well in excess of commercial norms.

ADJUSTMENT AND ENVIRONMENTAL POLICY

Economic adjustment capacity

Environmental policy is rightly perceived as a possible threat to jobs and profits, even though new environment-related opportunities may abound. Both these possibilities are reflected in the heading to a recent current affairs article on the subject: "California cashes in on cleaning up." — "California's tough environmental laws have forced many companies to flee the State. But these laws may also give California a head start in one of tomorrow's fastest-growing industries: environmental services" (*The Economist* (London), 16 Nov. 1991). Having elaborated on the positive side of the employment balance, we now turn our attention to the negative side. The importance of doing so should not be underestimated. Those who stand to lose as a result of the introduction of environmental policies could, if overlooked, prove to be a formidable political stumbling-block. Perhaps surprisingly, small groups — but ones in which members each have a substantive interest in the outcome of a policy — are generally seen to be disproportionately effective in the political process, even when the overall public interest is vastly superior in weight. The explanation has been advanced that this is because individual stakes in the wider public interest are normally unsubstantive (see Olson, 1982).

The problem of distributional opposition by those affected adversely in the transition following the introduction of environmental policy is not, of course, beyond resolution in constructive debate. Such debate may take place in a tripartite forum of workers, employers and government and begin with the premise that environmental policy is justified in the public

---

[13] Examples include forest management around Addis Ababa to increase fuel wood returns, coupled with the development of employment alternatives for the women who now carry the wood for up to 15 km; employment and urban renewal in Uganda; the reintegration of the economic needs of local villages with the management of protected natural reserves in Mali (possibly extended to Niger and Burkina Faso in future); and wasteland development in India.

interest when the value of the common environmental good pursued exceeds the costs involved. When this premise is met, it follows that society, as the policy beneficiary, is in a position to alleviate the policy cost. In other words, the excess of environmental policy benefits over policy costs allows sectors that are set to decline as a result of environmental measures to be compensated. Such compensation will ensure that, while society is better off, none of its members is worse off.

Naturally, the payment of compensation must be conditional on the intended adjustments taking place. This is to emphasise the transitional basis of compensation and to help to avoid confusion between the case for compensation, on the one hand, and the practice of environmental subsidies, on the other hand. Environmental subsidies have a tendency to become entrenched and to foster economically and politically unattractive dependencies between enterprise and government. For that reason, a clear preference will be expressed in the next chapter for the use of environmental taxes, charges or permits. This preference is not incompatible with proposing temporary assistance to the economic sectors adversely affected by the need for adjustment.

Adjustment signifies the scaling down of environmentally unsound production capacity, while directing new investment to more environment-compatible purposes. Scaling-down costs include job losses and loss of profitability, which, when inevitable, can be met through redundancy payments and dividend offsets funded from the public purse. A probable source for such funding is found in the revenue to which environmental policy may give rise. Such revenue may also fund the redeployment of labour through retraining and mobility allowances as well as provide support in the redeployment of capital. In the case both of labour and of capital, redeployment could be directly aimed at building up the environment-protective sector. However, a measure of flexibility in this respect would enable adjustment to take place via indirect routes also.

Redundancy payments and allowances facilitating the redeployment of labour and other resources constitute costs to be managed within acceptable levels. A priority in the management of such policy transition costs is to ensure that environmental policy is introduced in accordance with a well-balanced time schedule which: (a) does justice to the urgency of the environmental problems addressed, yet (b) moves as gradually as possible in order to exploit the natural adjustment capacity of the economy.

Two matters may be brought up with regard to the exploitation of the natural adjustment capacity of the economy. First and ideally, the schedule for the introduction of environmental policy needs to be firmly and unambiguously announced and adhered to. Many decisions have forward implications which can be aligned with a clear policy timetable, thereby minimising the scope for friction. Second, the policy timetable needs to utilise the pace of the natural turnover of resources against the backdrop of the dynamics to which sectors are subject in any case. For instance, a policy threat to employment can be countered by not replacing staff resigning or retiring. This device offers particular leverage in a context of economic growth. If the economy grows at, say, 2 per cent per year and a sector's normal labour turnover rate is, say, 7 per cent, then, as a first approximation, that sector is capable of absorbing a decline in demand of 9 per cent per year without needing to dismiss staff. (The calculation assumes that labour is homogeneous and that technology remains unchanged.) Given a setting of economic growth, sectoral setbacks resulting from environmental policy may therefore be limited to a decline in relative terms.

Sectoral setbacks

As with economic predictions in general, it is hazardous to forecast the sectors that will suffer employment losses as a result of the introduction of environmental policy. If it were high-sulphur coalmining, highway construction or cattle ranching, it would also be hazardous to tell by how much. In part, a policy response depends on the type and speed of environmental policy. It also depends on the context, e.g. on which sectors are experiencing a rising trend and which sectors are caught in decline. Traditional core industries such as iron and steel and metal processing, for instance, are meeting with inelastic demand, while computers, communications and biotechnology are rapidly expanding. Moreover, policy response depends on the ability of each sector to transform itself and, perhaps particularly, on the ability to capture part of the foreseen growth in demand for environment-protective products and services.

Notwithstanding the above qualifications, problem areas have been widely recognised. These areas relate to: (a) fossil fuel and (given the present state of knowledge) nuclear fuel dependency in energy generation and fossil fuel dependency in transport: environmental policy is therefore expected to affect power plants and the mining of fossil fuels, as well as the motoring industry and road construction; (b) the pollution arising in manufacturing; (c) the extraction rate of mineral resources where viable recycling opportunities can be developed; and (d) the extraction rate of biological resources at unsustainable rates. This last requirement has a wide variety of implications for agriculture (and forestry and fishing) in cases where practices and/or technologies are unduly geared to short-run exploitative results.

The problems in agriculture alluded to under (d) are of particular importance for developing countries. This is so not only because the sustainability of the agricultural sector is pertinent to the need to provide food for growing populations, but also because agriculture is the major provider of employment. Environmental policy calls for a transformation

Table 11. Energy use, pollution and employment by manufacturing activity, United
States, 1987/88 (percentage of all manufacturing)

Industry	GDP	Employment	Energy use	Toxics release
Refining and coal products	3.9	0.8	31.2	3.7
Chemical	9.0	5.5	21.2	58.4
Primary metal	4.3	4.0	14.0	12.5
Paper	4.6	3.6	11.5	13.6
Food products	8.7	8.4	4.8	1.4
Stone, clay and glass	3.2	3.1	4.7	0.5
Lumber and wood products	3.2	3.9	2.0	0.2
Transportation equipment	5.8	10.6	1.7	1.6
Fabricated metal	7.1	7.4	1.7	1.5
Non-electrical machinery	9.5	10.7	1.4	0.4
Electrical machinery	10.0	10.7	1.1	1.4
Printing and publishing	6.8	8.0	0.6	0.3
Other manufacturing [1]	23.8	23.3	4.1	4.2

[1] Tobacco, textiles, apparel, furniture and fixtures, rubber and miscellaneous plastics, instruments, leather, and miscellaneous manufacturing.
Source: Reprinted from Renner, 1991, table 2, p. 14.

in agriculture, forestry or fishing, instead of a reduction (which is perhaps less the case for the sectors mentioned under (a), (b) and (c)). It calls for production methods to become environmentally sound in the move towards sustainability. Indeed, the sustainability of the sector is to ensure the continuity of employment.

The continuity of employment in mining and the industries affected by environmental policy warrants the most concern in industrialised countries. The concern for labour, however, is mitigated by high capital intensities. For instance, figures compiled by the Worldwatch Institute for the United States suggest that, per US$1,000 value added, "non-metallic minerals" call for 19 hours of labour, US$1,830 of capital and 33.1 million BTU of energy; for "metal mining" these figures are 15 hours, US$2,970 and 25.8 million BTU; for "oil and gas extraction", 5 hours, US$340 and 17.3 million BTU; for "coalmining", 15 hours, US$1,550 and 9.6 million BTU. For "all manufacturing" the figures are 21 hours, US$791 and 12.1 million BTU (see Renner, 1991, table 1).

The Worldwatch Institute provides a breakdown of the manufacturing figures, as reproduced in table 11. From this table it can be seen that, in relation to their contribution to GDP, the chemical industry, followed by the primary metal and paper industries, are the major polluters and users of energy. Refining and coal products also use a great deal of energy. Both pollution and energy use are expected to become more costly as a result of environmental policy.

As indicated above, adverse environmental performance does not necessarily signify plant closures and retrenchments. Given time and support, the capacity of producers to adopt new methods and designs may prove considerable. In the short run, furthermore, price rises need not bring about a strong response in demand. The record on plant closures over recent years confirms a weak relationship between closures and the introduction of environmental regulations.[14] On the other hand, the sectoral interdependence of the economy determines that sectors which perform well in environmental respects can also become depressed as a result of environmental policy. Care must be taken, therefore, to extend policy assistance to those sectors indirectly affected and suffering set-backs.

Growth, employment and leisure

Environmental policy involves a variety of measures that deal with environmental costs at the point of incidence. Such measures are of a partial or micro type, and are meant to take effect on a specific problem of pollution, congestion, depletion or erosion, one at a time. In addition to this approach, other forms of environmental policy have been proposed which take on a macro dimension. Two of these forms deserve especial mention because, apart from their environmental significance, both forms impinge directly on the labour market. The policies concerned involve the population growth and the regulation of working hours. Population policy, which is examined in more detail in Chapter 5, is of particular concern to low-income countries, while a discussion of the regulation of working hours is principally relevant to high-income countries.

Labour conditions and population growth

Environmentalists share the general concern about the historically explosive rate of global population growth. Notwithstanding recent declines in the birth rate in industrialised countries especially, their categoric opinion is that the environmental stress of current population levels is abundantly apparent already. Moreover, the need to overcome the unsatisfactory level of economic development of many nations is expected to raise the level of environmental stress further.[15] The concern is echoed by the South Commission's warning that "... Lastly, the environmental impact of uncontrolled population growth has to be fully appreciated both

---

[14] Obsoleteness of plant is the main cause of closures: see Alfthan et al. (1990). Renner (1991), p. 22, reports that, of 224 plant closures in the United States between 1980 and 1986, only 5 per cent were caused by inability or unwillingness to meet environmental requirements.

by government and by society at large" (South Commission, 1990, p. 280).

Population growth is not only a source of concern for the environment; it also places considerable demands on the labour market. Many of the least developed economies are debt-ridden and unable to accumulate enough savings to keep up with population growth. These countries therefore do not maintain the necessary level of per capita provision in terms of the means of production, education, infrastructure, and so on. What little capital is available is not evenly spread, because of tendencies towards economic and social dualism. This means that more and more workers are virtually excluded from the distribution of capital and become marginalised, with little but their own hands to fend for survival. These people make up the informal sector and live predominantly in the (fast-growing) shanty towns fringing many of the Third World megacities (see Chapter 6; and Rodgers, 1989). As the informal sector lacks adequate means of production or skills to match, its productivity is condemned and poverty assured.

When savings and the accumulation of human and physical capital do not keep up with population growth, development fails. When they do keep up, on the other hand, success in development is not guaranteed. Development requires a complex set of conditions to be met by difficult decisions on the mix between private and public undertaking, rural and urban investment, simple and "high" technology, present and future needs, and natural resources and sustainability (e.g. see Markandya, 1991). Once development *does* take place, however, the labour market is expected to produce wage levels that, other things being equal, are inversely related to the rate at which population grows. This standard economic finding does not rule out development at rates well in excess of population growth or with rapid rises in the real value of wages. Instead, it suggests that population growth will make developmental results more difficult to attain.

Working hours and environment

As with population growth, environmentalists have been critical of economic growth once consumption may be considered affluent.[16] It is noted that in industrialised countries in particular, considerable sums are

---

[15] A low level of development will restrict choices. Accordingly, poverty may lead to unsustainable environmental practices and a relatively high level of environmental stress. Under those circumstances, economic development becomes an important requirement to relieve environmental stress. The harmony between the economic and environmental purpose, however, cannot mask the existence of a basic conflict between economy and environment.

[16] Daly (1991), an advocate of a stationary economy, puts the view uncompromisingly: "It is impossible for the economy to grow its way out of poverty and environmental degradation ... but it is precisely the non-sustainability of growth that gives urgency to the concept of sustainable development".

expended on the promotion of consumption. This promotion finds support because of a concern to stimulate employment. Unfortunately, political attitudes on this point are mainly governed by a desire to reduce unemployment quickly (i.e. before election time) while perhaps insufficient thought is being given to a long-term analysis of technological change and its effect on the role of work in the society of the future (Stewart, 1983, Ch. 8). The long-term analysis, however, raises critical issues, including the issue of leisure (see, for example, Jones, 1982, or Gorz, 1982).

Extending leisure, it is suggested in industrialised countries (not in developing countries), offers better prospects for welfare than an ongoing expansion of production, given continued technological progress. Extending leisure may also be expected to assist in reducing unemployment. The point has further merit in the eyes of environmentalists, who see in the trade-off between extended leisure and reduced production an opportunity to save on natural resources and to cut down on pollution (e.g. confirmed by Schorr, 1991). The environmental interest in leisure is part of the debate on the natural resource limits of economic growth. This debate has wider ramifications because the development of poorer countries is likely to be affected by choices over work and leisure in richer countries. Although money income in affluent countries would fail to grow if more leisure were preferred, developing countries would stand to gain by becoming more competitive and because of a global lessening of natural resource constraints.

When the proposition that there be more leisure was put to a major test in the United States, it was found that up to 40 per cent of workers would choose to trade a loss of income for a gain in leisure (Best, 1980). Increased levels of leisure do not of themselves deliver environmental advantages, however. Many production activities are environmentally benign while a range of leisure activities (e.g. travel and tourism) can pose problems for the environment.[17] None the less, the environmental balance is likely to be favourable. The welfare balance of more leisure, on the other hand, remains the subject of some dispute. Only recently, arguments for-and-against stalemated the Kreisky Commission (Kreisky, 1989, p. 139) in its report on European employment issues.

A policy of work-hour flexibility could offer a way out of the Kreisky stalemate.[18] Under work-hour flexibility, the key to a solution on the desirable number of working hours is not found in a rigid national determination but with the grass-roots preferences of employers and workers. Barriers to flexibility are currently found in legislation and trade

---

[17] The reader may be reminded here that the principle of pricing environmental costs is meant to apply to consumers as it does to producers.

[18] For a detailed treatment of the subject of work-hours, see White (1987). Encouraging accounts of recent experiences with flexible work schedules in a number of countries can be found in the *Social and Labour Bulletin* (Geneva, ILO), various issues.

union concern that a work package involving less than a standard number of hours could be used to put full-time positions at risk and to erode supplementary conditions in respect of illness, pension rights, maternity leave, redundancy, etc. To overcome these barriers, it appears important therefore that the principle of proportionality of rights to hours worked is defended and that the possibility of being made partially redundant be subject to safeguards similar to those applying under full redundancy.[19]

Failing of environmental policy

One's enthusiasm to attend to an ailing environment may engender a temptation to belittle the economic adjustments necessitated by environmental policy. A recognition of the difficulties of adjustment, even if transitional, will contribute to environmental policy design and help to overcome political resistance. On the other hand, the recognition of transitional difficulties does not in itself justify a blockage of environmental policy. Care is needed to compare the structural adjustment costs of environmental policy with the benefits to be obtained.

A number of arguments can be brought to bear on such a comparison. First, as shown above, steps can be taken to minimise and alleviate the cost of adjustment and to furnish compensation. Second, policy costs occur "up front" while environmental policy benefits may be a long-term prospect. This calls for caution in applying a high rate of discount, which might lead present generations to make decisions which are biased against future generations. In particular, current income and employment could be pursued with insufficient regard to the need to sustain the resources on which future employment will depend. Third, the benefits of environmental policy can no longer be measured in positive terms only. A worsening of the environmental predicament over recent decades has meant that the benefits of policy action must now often include allowances for the avoided costs of not having an environmental policy. Against a global perspective of increasing and cumulative demands on the natural environment, the option not to act no longer remains neutral. This deserves to be emphasised, because environmental inaction could well contribute to a loss of productivity and employment, to poverty and, in extreme cases, to human displacement and starvation.

Environmental failure as a cause of unemployment and a force in population displacement can occur in a number of ways, including the desertification or erosion of lands; the pollution of natural resources; the depletion of water supplies; flooding following deforestation or wetland filling; over-harvesting, over-grazing, over-fishing; salination; plagues of

---

[19] The principle of pro rata maintenance of primary and secondary conditions for part-time workers, was confirmed at the Maastricht Meeting of the European Communities (December 1991) as a part of EC social and employment legislation.

71

introduced weeds or pests;[20] damaging levels of ultraviolet radiation resulting from ozone depletion; and the prospect of human-induced climatic change. An example is found in the disastrous economic effects of the depletion of the Aral Sea and the salination of the agricultural lands irrigated by its waters. Unfortunately, similar mistakes are being made in other places in the world. Another example relates to the process of desertification affecting the Sahel countries. Details of this instance of environmental breakdown are given in box 4. Further analysis of desertification and other cases of environmental breakdown appears in Chapter 5.

Environmental failure, be it due to unsustainable levels of economic activities, to environmentally unsound technology or to unsustainable population pressure, must be distinguished from environmental failure resulting from natural disasters in which humans have no hand. Our concern is with the first type of failure and the fact that greater numbers of people are falling victim to it.[21] The rising incidence of environmental failure is measured in terms of additional mortality, greater poverty and increased migration. In the past, international migration numbers have been made up of an involuntary flow of refugees caught up in war and suppression and a largely voluntary and regulated stream of economic migrants. In recent decades, however, the flow of migrants has swollen through the displacement of people by developmental breakdown and associated catastrophes such as famine, floods or disease. Increasingly these people are labelled "environmental migrants" (see Kritz, 1990). The movement of these migrants is governed by desperation more than choice and is marked by irregularity more than order.

Box 4.   Desertification and loss of livelihood

Nearly 650,000 km2 of land (an area bigger than Spain and Portugal) have turned into desert during the last 50 years in the Sahel region. Up to 75 per cent of the population in the region depend on agriculture for subsistence and income. During this century, the area has been hit by three major droughts (1910-14, 1940-44, and in the early 1970s). Nevertheless it seems that the ecological, social and economic catastrophe of desertification is caused primarily by human activity rather than by dire rainfall patterns.

Foremost among human factors in desertification is population growth, with present rates between 2.7 and 3.3 per cent per year. The growing

---

[20] New fears in this respect have been expressed on account of genetically altered species.

[21] Von Weizsäcker (1990) cites a rate of increase of 350 per cent per decade in the number of victims of environmental failure. A similar increase is reported in the *Süddeutsche Zeitung* (Munich), 13 Dec. 1991.

population has increased the demand for food, energy and land. Areas once forested have been cleared for agriculture. In recent times, these new agricultural lands have been converted to a more intensive usage for cash crops. Fallow periods have shortened and mono-cropping has become more commonplace. New technologies, such as mechanisation and fertilisers, have failed to halt a decline in yield. In Senegal a peasant with traditional tools could produce as much as 1.5 to 2.0 metric tons of groundnuts from 2 to 3 ha a few decades ago. One generation later, using a plough and chemical fertiliser, the yield is less than 1.0 metric ton from 8 ha. The decline in yield has been accompanied by falling international prices, leading to the abandonment of land. Through wind erosion, the abandoned land quickly falls prey to desertification.

The loss of agricultural livelihood is causing poverty and out-migration while impeding rehabilitation. Compounding the problems is a growing scarcity of firewood. Firewood and charcoal are replaced by cattle dung and agricultural waste, leaving little organic manure and protective soil cover on harvested fields.

Apart from the Sahel, other parts of the world are vulnerable to desertification. Such areas include Botswana and Namibia; the Andean region; substantial areas of the West and Mid-West of the United States; Central Asia and Mongolia; the Middle East; major parts of Afghanistan and Pakistan; and most of the Australian land mass.

Source: Lo and Sene (1989).

CONCLUSIONS

In addition to prospects of forced migration on environmental grounds, there is an emerging anticipation of the possibility of armed conflict between nations over environmental resources (see Gleick, 1991). Recently, the Executive Director of UNEP has spoken in this vein, identifying present and foreseeable disputes over water resources as being of particular concern. Clearly, such concern underlines the need for environmental policy. It also underlines the importance of international cooperation and of a global responsibility to provide aid. Without aid, the neediest of countries do not appear to have the capacity to implement the environmental protection measures necessary to ensure sustainability and to avoid the risks of human deprivation and displacement.

We have seen that the risk of environmental breakdown is pronounced in a number of the least developed economies. However, low levels of income hinder action on environmental priorities, even though livelihoods may be more intimately connected with the condition of the natural environment. Likewise, poverty stands in the way of efforts to raise financial and technical resources to respond to an environmental breakdown when it occurs.[22]

In the industrialised countries, fears of job losses may prove to be misguided in the aggregate, while policy features such as compensation and graduality may offer protection of the interests of those who will be caught up in adjustment. In addition, fears of income losses are misplaced if environmental policy is cost effective. This conclusion rests on the new ideas promoted by environmental accounting, which allow for non-monetary income and which consider also the need to preserve the sustainability of the natural resource base.

The advent of environmental policy is giving rise to an environment-protective sector covering a multitude of new activities. Part of this sector can be driven by private initiative while another part requires collective undertakings. A range of collective environmental initiatives offer the further advantage of being labour intensive. In less developed countries where, as a norm, labour is in greater surplus, such initiatives therefore promise high rates of social return. High rates of social return are now attracting government interest in combining environmental and employment policies. The same applies to project work based on international aid.

The difference between social and commercial rates of return, as reflected in concern for the environment or for employment, constitutes a government concern. Government policy must try to ensure that decision-making, be it by households, enterprises or its own agencies, bridges this difference. If, for instance, the environmental effects of a production process are "external" to the decision-making of the producer, i.e. not (or not sufficiently) accounted for, policy must try to ensure that such effects are "internalised" into the decision-making process. The instruments required to achieve this are the subject of the next chapter.

References

Alfthan, T. et al. 1990. *Employment and training implications of environmental policies in Europe.* Training Discussion Paper No. 52. Geneva, ILO.

Austria, Bundesministerium für Gesundheit und Umweltschutz. 1980. "Studie über die Auswirkungen des Umweltschutzes auf Motivation und Innovation" [Study on the effects of environmental policy on incentives and innovation], in *Beiträge zu Umweltschutz, Lebensmittel-angelegenheiten und Veterinärverwaltung* (Vienna), No. 4.

Barker, T.; Lewney, R. 1991. "A green scenario for the UK economy", in Barker, T. (ed.). 1991. *Green futures for economic growth: Britain in 2010.* Cambridge, Cambridge Econometrics.

---

[22] The problems of implementing environmental policy in conditions of poverty are not dissimilar from the problems of structural adjustment in less developed economies. Therefore lessons can be borrowed from the structural adjustment experience. For example, see van der Hoeven (1991).

Best, F. 1980. *Exchanging earnings for leisure: Findings of an exploratory survey on work time preferences.* Research and Development Monograph No. 79. Washington, DC, United States Department of Labor.

Bezdek, R. et al. 1989. "The economic and employment effects of investments in pollution abatement and control technologies", in *Ambio* (Stockholm, Royal Swedish Academy of Sciences), Vol. 18, No. 5.

Cairncross, F. 1991. *Costing the earth.* London, Economist Books.

Commission of the European Communities (CEC). 1990. *Employment in Europe.* Brussels.

Daly, H. E. 1991. "Sustainable growth: A bad oxymoron", in *Grassroots Development* (Rosslyn, Virgina, Journal of the Inter-American Foundation), Vol. 15, No. 3.

Data Resources Inc. 1981. *The macro-economic impact of federal pollution control programs: 1981 assessment.* Washington, DC.

Duchin, F. et al. 1991. *Strategies for environmentally sound economic development.* Mimeographed. New York, Institute for Economic Analysis.

Euroconsult, 1989. *Structure and socio-economic significance of the waste mangement and recycling industry of the European Communities.* Mimeographed. Brussels.

Finland, National Board of Waters. 1978. *Final report for the International Bank for Reconstruction and Development of the research project carried out in 1975-78 by the National Board of Waters.* Helsinki.

Forsund, F. R.; Tveitereid, S. 1977. *Price and income effects of environmental investments in Norwegian mining and industry.* Article No. 93. Oslo, Central Bureau of Statistics.

———; Waage, P. 1978. *Pollution abatement in Norwegian mining and manufacturing industries: Goals, principles, measures, economic instruments and macro-economic effects.* Oslo, Ministry of the Environment.

France, Ministère de l'Environnement et du Cadre de la vie. 1980. *Les impacts macro-économiques de la politique de l'environnement.* Paris, CEPREMAP.

Gaudier, M. 1991. *Environment — Employment — New industrial societies: A bibliographic map.* Bibliographic Series No. 15, Geneva, ILO/International Institute for Labour Studies.

Gleick, P. H. 1991. "Environment and security: The clear connection", in *Bulletin of the Atomic Scientists* (Chicago, Illinois, Educational Foundation for Nuclear Science), Vol. 47. No. 3.

Glomsrod, S.; Vennemo, H.; Johnson, T. 1990. *Stabilisation of emissions of CO_2: A computable general equilibrium assessment.* Discussion Paper No. 148. Oslo, Central Bureau of Statistics.

Goldemberg, J. et al. 1988. *Energy for a sustainable world.* New Delhi, Wiley Eastern.

Gorz, A. 1982. *Farewell to the working class.* London and Sydney, Pluto Press.

Hohmeier, O., et al. 1985. *Employment effects of energy conservation investments in EC countries.* Luxembourg, Commission of the European Communities.

ILO. 1990. *Environment and the world of work.* Report of the Director-General (Part I), International Labour Conference, 77th Session, Geneva, 1990.

75

Ingham, A.; Ulph, A. 1990. *Carbon taxes and the UK manufacturing sector.* Mimeographed. Southampton (United Kingdom), University of Southampton, Department of Economics.

Johnson Cointreau, S. et al. 1984. *Recycling from municipal refuse: A state-of-the-art review and annotated bibliography.* UNDP Project Management Report No. 1, Washington, DC, World Bank.

Jonish, J. 1992. *The river as an international environmental resource — The case of the Colorado.* Mimeographed WEP working paper (WEP 2-22/WP.221). Geneva, ILO.

Jones, B. 1982. *Sleepers, wake: Technology and the future of work.* Oxford, Oxford University Press.

Jorgensen, D.; Wilcoxen, P. 1990. "Environmental regulation and US economic growth", in *Rand Journal of Economics* (Washington, DC, Rand Corporation), Vol. 21, No. 2.

Klaassen, G. et al. 1987. *The macro-economic effects of the large combustion plants directive proposal: Economic aspects of controlling acid rain in Europe.* Amsterdam, Instituut voor Milieuvraagstukken.

Kreisky, B. 1989. *A programme for full employment in the 1990s: Report of the Kreisky Commission on Employment Issues in Europe.* Oxford, Pergamon Press.

Kritz, M. M. 1990. *Climate change and migration adaptations.* Working Paper 2.16. Ithaca, NY, Cornell University, Population and Development Program.

Lewis, K. 1991. *Employment and training implications of the waste management industry.* Mimeographed. Geneva, ILO.

Lo, H. M.; Sene, A. 1989. "Human action and the desertification of the Sahel", in *International Social Science Journal* (Paris, UNESCO), Vol. XLI, No. 3, pp. 449-457.

Lovins, A. B. 1977. *Soft energy paths: Towards a durable peace.* Harmondsworth (United Kingdom), Penguin Books.

McGavin, B. 1991. "Going green — But what about the workers?", in *Employment Gazette* (London), Jan.

Markandya, A. 1991. *Technology, environment and employment: A survey.* Mimeographed WEP working paper (WEP 2-22/WP.216). Geneva, ILO.

Medhurst, J. 1990. *The impact of environmental management on skills and jobs.* Birmingham (United Kingdom), ECOTEC Ltd.

Netherlands, Centraal Planbureau. 1975. *Economische gevolgen van bestrijding van milieuverontreiniging* [Economic consequences of environmental pollution control measures]. Monograph No. 20. The Hague.

———; Ministerie van Huisvesting, Ruimtelijke Ordening and Milieu. 1989, 1990. *National Environmental Plan of the Netherlands.* Amsterdam.

Nordhaus, W. D. 1991. *Economic growth: Limits and perils.* Paper presented at the International Congress on Environment, Ethics, Economics and Institutions, Milan, March 1991.

Olson, M. 1982. *The rise and decline of nations.* New Haven, Connecticut, Yale University Press.

Organization for Economic Co-operation and Development (OECD). 1978. *Macro-economic evaluation of environmental programmes.* Paris.

———. 1985. *The macroeconomic impact of environmental expenditure.* Paris.

Pearce, D. 1991. "Growth, employment and environmental policy", in *Economic Report* (London, Employment Institute), Vol. 6, No. 1.

Pereira, A. F. 1986. *Ethanol, employment and development: Lessons from Brazil.* Geneva, ILO.

———. 1991. *Technology policy for environmental sustainability and for employment and income generation: Conceptual and methodological issues.* Mimeographed WEP working paper (WEP 2-22/WP.215). Geneva, ILO.

Perrings, C. 1991. *Incentives for the ecologically sustainable use of human and natural resources in the drylands of sub-Saharan Africa: A review.* Mimeographed WEP working paper (WEP 2-22/WP.219). Geneva, ILO.

Peskin, H.; Lutz, E. 1990. *A survey of resource and environmental accounting in industrial countries.* World Bank Environment Department Working Paper No. 37. Washington, DC.

Pucher, J. 1990. "Capitalism, socialism and urban transportation", in *Journal of the American Planning Association,* Summer.

Renner, M. 1991. *Jobs in a sustainable economy.* Worldwatch Paper No. 104. Washington, DC, Worldwatch Institute.

Rodberg, L. 1979. *Employment impact of the solar transition.* Washington, DC, Congress of the United States, Joint Economic Committee.

Rodgers, G. (ed.) 1989. *Urban poverty and the labour market: Access to jobs and incomes in Asian and Latin American cities.* Geneva, ILO.

Schor, J. B. 1991. "Global equity and environmental crisis: An argument for reducing working hours in the North", in *World Development* (Oxford, Pergamon Press), Vol. 19, No. 1.

Sondheimer, J. 1991. "Macroeconomic effects of a carbon tax", in Barker, T. (ed.). 1991. *Green futures for economic growth: Britain in 2010.* Cambridge, Cambridge Econometrics.

South Commission. 1990. *The challenge to the South: The report of the South Commission.* Oxford, Oxford University Press.

Stewart, M. 1983. *Controlling the economic future: Policy dilemmas in a shrinking world.* Brighton (United Kingdom), Harvester Press.

United Nations Economic Commission for Europe (UNECE). 1988. *Overall economic perspective to the year 2000.* New York.

United Nations Environment Programme (UNEP). 1992. *Saving our planet: Challenges and hopes.* Nairobi.

Van der Hoeven, R. 1991. *Adjustment with a human face? Still relevant or overtaken by events?* Mimeographed. Geneva, ILO.

Von Weizsäcker, E. U. 1990. *Erdpolitik: Okologische Realpolitik an der Schwelle zum Jahrhundert der Umwelt* [Earth politics: Ecological decision-making on the threshold of the century of the environment]. 2nd ed. Darmstadt (Germany), Wissenschaftliche Buchgesellschaft.

White, M. 1987. *Working hours: Assessing the potential for reduction.* Geneva, ILO.

World Bank. 1991. *The World Bank and the environment: A progress report.* Washington, DC.

World Resources Institute. 1991. *Accounts overdue: Natural resource depreciation in Costa Rica.* Baltimore, Maryland, WRI Publications.

ON INSTRUMENTS OF ENVIRONMENTAL POLICY *

J. A. Doeleman **

4

It is now commonly acknowledged that, without appropriate intervention, markets are failing to take proper account of a wide range of environmental costs, such as those associated with pollution, resource depletion (both mineral and biological), farmland degradation, waste disposal, urban congestion and loss of wilderness areas, and biodiversity. This failure has contributed to placing an undue burden on the environment, causing economic losses shouldered, involuntarily, by the community at large as well as damage to the environment itself. Accordingly, environmental policy designed to correct for market failure has become a matter of priority.

Having considered employment, as well as other effects that are expected to follow the introduction of environmental policy, we now propose to look more closely at the types of instrument that constitute such policy, their functioning and their relative merit. Most instruments fall broadly into two categories: namely, "economic" or "market-based" instruments, and "command and control" instruments (see, for example, Eskeland and Jimenez, 1991). The first category makes use of incentives — normally of a financial type — while the second category relies on regulation by command (permission, prohibition, condition). Both the economic and the command approaches are associated with environmental policy operating at the micro level, that is, where measures are designed to tackle specific or selected environmental problems, e.g. urban congestion, industrial pollution, land erosion, ozone depletion, and so on. It is on these measures that we intend to concentrate. Such measures are different from those that may be introduced at a macro level and which are accordingly aimed at producing environmental results in a more

---

* This chapter is an abridged version of a larger study prepared for the ILO World Employment Programme.

** ILO, Geneva; and University of Newcastle, Australia. With research assistance by P. Haag.

general way, e.g. population control, land tenure legislation,[1] technological support, or policies seeking to determine the agricultural/industrial or rural/urban mix of the economy. The distinction between micro and macro policies is, however, somewhat ambiguous. The choice between an economic and a regulatory approach is relevant also to the implementation of environmental policy at the macro level. For instance, population control can be placed on an economic basis, using incentives; or legislation can lay down a permissible family size.

In the past, the regulatory or command approach to environmental policy has prevailed. With this approach, the emphasis has been on centralised control, devolving from governmental bureaucracy. However, the growing interest in environmental policy that has been shown in recent years has brought economic instruments to the fore. By relying on financial incentives, economic instruments shift the control of environmental impacts directly to the economic agents responsible, e.g. farms, business, industry, government agencies, or households. The ways in which economic incentives can be employed to achieve environmental aims have been pioneered in recent decades. In practice, however, the use of economic instruments of environmental policy is not yet widespread. This could well change during the 1990s, especially in the developed economies. Notwithstanding the prospect of such change, the role of command solutions would not thereby be forgone, because regulation will continue to offer a broad range of advantages.

Against this background of new, emerging, economic-type environmental instruments, we begin with a short presentation of the common features of these instruments. The chapter continues with a survey of the different types of economic instrument, looking at their use or intended use. The survey is followed by a section dealing with "command and control" instruments, in which the advantages and disadvantages of the command and economic approaches are also compared. The final section examines the choice of instruments of environmental policy in the context of developing countries, finding that more, and better analysed, experience is needed before firm recommendations can be put forward.

INSTRUMENTS AND STANDARDS

Before we look at the ways in which new environmental instruments are put into practice, a brief comment on the nature of these instruments may help to clarify how they function. The aim of both economic instruments and command and control instruments of environmental

---

[1] Not necessarily a decisive factor (Perrings, 1991) but considered important by, for instance, the Asian Development Bank (1991).

policy is to achieve one or more environmental standards (norms or targets) in a large and expanding set of environmental standards, now seemingly requiring intervention if they are to be accomplished. Instruments are the means to achieve the standards. Both traditional and new instruments of environmental policy merely provide methods — not all if which are equally effective or equitable — in order to attain environmental ends. In other words, they do not as yet provide a formula to determine such ends or goals.

The determination of environmental goals is, of course, a political problem, albeit based on scientific inputs from a number of disciplines. If the political process is weak or unrepresentative, or both, the setting of environmental goals (the standards) could reflect this. Accordingly, environmental policy may falter — but not because of the instruments applied. Alternatively, a weak political process may set ambitious environmental goals and adopt imaginative instruments, yet fail to apply these instruments with determination. Problems of this kind, however, are not our concern here: we are concerned basically with the relative merit of different instruments and the implementation of the newly proposed economic instruments.

Economic instruments of environmental policy rely on financial incentives to achieve a given environmental standard. They do this by enabling what have been called "missing markets" (see Chapter 2). An example may illustrate the simplicity of the idea of the missing market. Consider, for instance, the pollution tax. The problem facing the policymaker is to decide what is an appropriate level of taxation. This problem is solved by seeing that a predetermined pollution standard is met. The mechanism works by a reduction in the tax following overachievement of the target and a rise in the tax following underachievement (Baumol and Oates, 1979). Likewise, an environmental standard can be enforced by a system of permits. Permits are auctioned by the authorities to prospective detractors from the standard. The total supply of permits is in harmony with the environmental standard, and the price of a permit is determined as by normal market interaction between supply and demand (Dales, 1970).[2]

The theoretical ease of the solution to deciding upon an appropriate charge for environmental costs should not mask the difficulties of its implementation in practice and, more importantly, of determining the environmental standards that are to generate the solution. In principle, the determination of environmental standards should reflect environmental preferences — which are expected to differ according to the stage and type of economic development, and the natural resource endowment of a country. The probable constraint on the expression of these preferences,

---

[2] The two examples of creating a missing market follow the widely supported "polluter-pays-principle" (see, for example, WCED, 1987, p. 221).

however, is that environmental standards must be compatible with long-run sustainability and responsibility as regards future generations.[3]

The new economic instruments, unlike the command and control instruments, do call for overall environmental standards to be explicit rather than implicit. Other features include the flexibility of standards, which would not only vary between countries and within countries but also vary over time. For example, it may be desirable to move gradually towards an environmental target that is considered to be demanding in terms of adjustment cost.[4] Alternatively, new scientific knowledge may indicate a need to tighten or relax standards. Moreover, standards make it possible for minimum environmental safeguards to become operational. This is particularly important in order to ensure the sustainability of environment-dependent economic activities, and also relates to aspects of international environmental trade and investment issues (see Chapter 7). Finally, the use of environmental standards creates a record of achievement. A record makes it possible to compare trends between countries, cities or regions, thus providing feedback of progress and a recognition of problems.

THE EMERGENCE OF NEW ENVIRONMENTAL INSTRUMENTS

Economic instruments of environmental policy, as we have seen, rely on incentives which are financial in nature. They seek to enforce the discipline of the price mechanism in preference to adopting the command approach. A number of useful references may be drawn upon for a discussion of economic environmental instruments. Two of the most detailed studies are restricted to OECD countries (OECD, 1989b and 1991; see also Bernstein (1991), which includes minimal information on developing countries). More recent surveys take a global view by considering possible applications of economic mechanisms through which a number of countries could achieve their environmental objectives, notably to control the emission of greenhouse gases (see, for instance, United Kingdom Government, 1990; UNCTC, 1991; UNCED, 1991; and European Parliament, 1991). Little research has been undertaken, however, in respect of the applicability of economic instruments of environmental policy in developing economies. This issue will be taken up below (see the subsection "Developing countries" below).

In what follows, five groups of economic instruments of environmental policy have been distinguished. In use or under consideration, they are: fiscal measures; permits or licences; swaps; bonds and insurance; and aid.

---

[3] Given a responsible setting of environmental standards, a noteworthy feature of economic instruments is that the recognised failure of the market to take either environmental costs or the future sufficiently into account can be amended by the market.

[4] This was foreseen, for example, in the proposal for a carbon dioxide target by UNECE (1990), pp. 13ff.

Fiscal environmental measures

Fiscal environmental measures involve governments in "green" taxes or subsidies, charges or bonuses, aimed at improving the environmental behaviour of firms, individuals, and the departments and agencies of the government itself. As the environmental costs of economic activities often spill over on to the community at large, fiscal environmental measures are designed to correct a tendency at the grass roots to reflect private interests and to underestimate the costs to the community.

Pollution taxes (on numerous undesirable emissions); congestion charges (e.g. to control peak traffic or, conceivably, to control the distribution of city size); royalties in mining, stumpage fees in forestry, grazing tolls; recycling charges (e.g. on virgin pulp in the paper industry) or the proposed differentiation (by bulk and by type) of charges on waste disposal — all serve as examples of environmentally based taxes. Environmental subsidies are also common, such as depreciation and loan allowances for pollution abatement equipment. Other examples include provisions for erosion control and pest management in the agricultural sector and subsidies for public transport systems.

Environmental taxes or charges normally involve a correction of the market that involves the very parties who detract from environmental resources to make appropriate additional payments. In some cases it may be better not to speak of correction, because a genuine market is as yet not in place. A surprising number of countries, for instance, charge flat rates for water use, regardless of consumption levels. Similarly, waste collection is as a rule based on fixed charges. Charging in these cases is perhaps different from the levying of an environmental tax.

Different, too, is the not uncommon incidence of taxes and subsidies that (although this is unintended) carry counter-environmental incentives. For instance, mining attracts fiscal bonuses in many countries, thereby inhibiting recycling or, in the case of fossil fuels, contributing to global warming. Likewise, fertiliser usage is commonly subsidised (see Chapter 5). For that matter, the wider picture of agricultural protection is regarded as an environmental anomaly. Of course, this is not to suggest that environmental aims should necessarily prevail over the aims that have given rise to those fiscal measures which carry counter-environmental impacts. It is merely to say that environmental aspects are important and ought not to be neglected, just as it is important, for instance, to ensure that the other aims for fiscal measures serve a general rather than a sectional interest.

The choice between taxes and subsidies

Subsidies may be preferred to taxes when, politically, it is easier to draw from general revenues than to draw from the interests vested in a particular economic sector. This condition is not limited to developing

Figure 1. Financial (economic) environmental instruments in operation (1987)

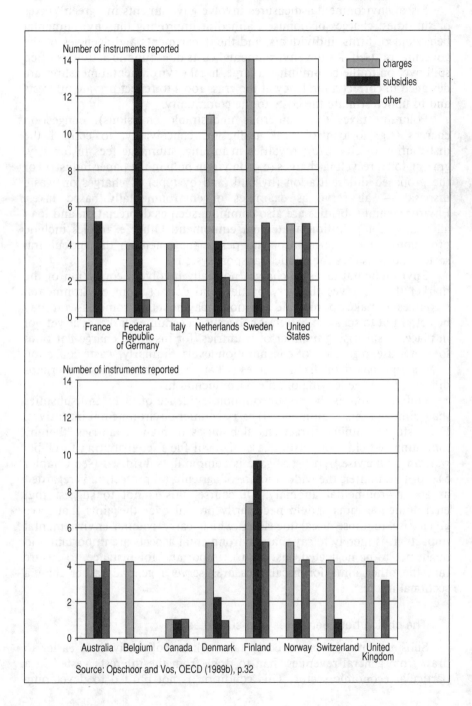

Source: Opschoor and Vos, OECD (1989b), p.32

countries as the use of subsidies as environmental instruments is omnipresent. Figure 1 illustrates the extent to which OECD countries have actually relied on positive financial inducements for producers to act in accordance with a variety of environmental aims. The reason lies in the political expediency offered by the subsidy approach. As a rule, subsidies are paid by the general public, whose per capita interest in such payments is generally diffuse. On the other hand, interest in the choice between taxes or subsidies by the very economic sectors to be affected by environmental policy will not be diffuse but intense. Such intense interest, as is to be expected, does not normally remain passive but expresses itself in lobbying.

Superficially, the choice to subsidise environment-friendly behaviour as distinct from penalising environment-unfriendly behaviour appears to have similar effects in terms of efficiency.[5] Although conceivably true in the short run, the tax, charge or penalty approach offers promising long-run benefits which subsidies are not likely to yield. These benefits particularly relate to the incentive to develop and implement *new* environmentally sound technology.

Furthermore, a choice in favour of subsidies has implications for equity. Although it may be considered politically opportune to improve environment in a particular economic sector while avoiding the perceived costs in terms of employment and profits by the use of subsidies, the avoidance of costs is apparent only. Subsidies have to be funded. This raises questions of fairness. Is it right that below-par environmental behaviour in farming or industry should be rewarded with financial or other assistance, and that the tax-paying general public should be asked to make the necessary sacrifices to provide that help? Besides, the sacrifices by the general public that are necessary to fund the subsidies have adverse effects on employment and profit elsewhere in the economy.

The choice between charges and subsidies is not limited to fiscal environmental controls. Similar concerns arise in the consideration of environmental swap arrangements (see below).[6]

Environmental permits or licences

The concept of environmental permits or licences has evolved with the notion of emission trading schemes. In trading schemes, permits giving an

---

[5] In a seminal paper on social (environmental) cost, the recent Nobel laureate R. H. Coase (1960) argues that both taxes and subsidies may produce the same result. Indeed, his argument goes further, claiming that neither taxes nor subsidies are a necessary condition for an optimal result in trading off commercial, social and environmental interests. He states that, if environmental interests were neglected, those who are adversely affected thereby could, depending on practicality, seek to induce (bribe) the agents of adverse environmental effects to reduce those effects to more economic levels. This conclusion has been much criticised in the literature both on dynamic grounds (incentives for technological development) and on grounds of equity. For example, see Mishan (1971).

[6] For instance, the debt-for-nature swaps have the drawback that the threats to the world's natural heritage may become a political tool.

entitlement to produce environmentally undesirable emissions can be bought and sold in a market according to the requirements of firms operating production processes which pollute. Trading can take place around an initial allocation of pollution quotas determined by the authorities. Firms able to contain pollution within their quota of permits can sell permits to firms less able to do so; or, as has been a practice, can "bank" permits for later use.

A more ambitious version of this scheme is one in which the polluting firm is not provided with an initial permit allocation, but must purchase the whole of their requirements of permits in the market or from the issuing authority. In both models, the number of available permits is consistent with the maintenance of a specified pollution standard as defined for a delineated area or "bubble". The standard in turn is produced by a political determination which has gained the necessary political support.

The idea of emission trading schemes has been pioneered in the United States but experience to date remains limited (see Dales, 1968; Tisdell, 1983; and Tietenberg, 1990). Outside the United States, pollution or other overall environmental standards are not generally on the official record, as governments have been content to control the environmental spillovers of different economic sectors on an ad hoc negotiated basis. On this basis, the responsible bureaucracies have "settled" with industries what are acceptable emission levels, being guided more by available technology and costs of implementation than by the economy-wide environmental outcome.

Today, interest is particularly strong in the international community because emission trading offers a promising means to control national contributions to global environmental problems. Without control the global environment stands to deteriorate rapidly, offering an additional source for international conflict capable of damaging the fragile progress towards greater harmony which has marked recent times. Emission trading offers not only an efficient and non-discretionary means of achieving a range of global environmental standards, but also redistributional prospects through revenue generation, which are likely to favour the developing economies in particular (see, for example, United Nations Centre on Transnational Corporations, 1991; Dudek, 1989; Dasgupta and Maler, 1990).

Environmental swap arrangements

Environmental swap arrangements refer to settlements involving offsets for environmental damages or, conversely, offsets in exchange for undertaking environmental rehabilitation or protection. As in the case of fiscal measures, the offsets being swapped have the character of either a charge or tax, or of a subsidy or inducement. The latter is illustrated by the debt-for-nature swaps currently in the limelight.[7] Offsets which impose rather than induce, on the other hand, are associated with the provision of compensation for environmental damages incurred. Compensation would normally involve a financial transfer but may also be paid in kind. The payment of compensation would be preferred to the mitigation or prevention of environmental damage when the amount of compensation required will be less than the cost of avoiding the damage.

Recently, two new power stations in the Netherlands have been estimated to emit 6 million tons of carbon dioxide. The offset proposed in compensation is the reafforestation of 10,000 hectares of land per year for 25 years. This reafforestation, however, will not be undertaken in the Netherlands but in Latin America, saving approximately 90 per cent of the costs.[8] An example of an environmental offset of the subsidy type is found in the US$750 million programme designed to upgrade environmentally two nickel smelters near Murmansk. The programme is financed by the governments of Finland, Norway and Sweden. Likewise, Bulgaria currently receives EC assistance to improve the safety of two of its nuclear reactors, of the Chernobyl type.

The examples indicate that the use of environmental offsets currently arises on an incidental basis. It may be true to suggest that the international interest in offset arrangements is greater than the domestic interest. Domestically, the environmental costs of economic development have generally been accepted without compensation, provided: (a) that such costs were justified by the developmental benefits; (b) that the environmental costs could not easily (economically) be avoided; and (c) that the attribution of the costs would not strongly discriminate against the interests of a limited set of persons but be shared broadly. In other words, the emphasis has been on a positive cost-benefit ratio for the community as a whole, while less attention has generally been paid to the distribution of developmental costs and benefits. It is conceivable, however, that offsets or compensation will become more widely practised domestically.[9]

---

[7] In 1987, an American non-governmental organisation (Conservation International) bought US$650,000 of Bolivia's commercial debt at an 85 per cent discount in exchange for a promise of the creation and management of a 3.7 million acre buffer around the Bino Biosphere Reserve. Since then, other such swaps have been completed in a number of countries, including Costa Rica, Ecuador, Madagascar and the Philippines. A survey of details of recent debt-for-nature swaps is found in UNCTC (1991), pp. 22ff. Other offset examples are also reported by this source. Recently, European Communities talks with Poland and other eastern and central European countries have centred on debt relief in exchange for pollution controls.

[8] The reafforestation programme will be financed from "carbon taxes" instituted early in 1990.

[9] Environmental legislation can be envisaged that requires the voluntary cooperation of parties adversely affected environmentally by defined economic activities, i.e. granting citizens what have been called "environmental amenity rights".

Environmental bonds and insurance

Environmental bonds rely on the price mechanism to influence environmental behaviour at some time in the future. Environmental insurance makes provision for liabilities that could arise following the materialisation of environmental risks. The deposit and refund arrangements for food and beverage containers are familiar. With new and cheaper packaging materials, however, deposit schemes are more widely preached than practised. Other examples include refunds on old car bodies (Sweden and Germany) and deposits on batteries (under consideration). On a different plane, mining projects are now often approved under environmental bond arrangements in addition to pollution and other controls. These arrangements stipulate the rehabilitation of the landscape and vegetation after the abandonment of the mine. The enforcement of compliance by bonds in environmentally sensitive projects is attractive because of the risk that penalties cannot be enforced in cases of business failure or fraud.

Insurance against environmental risks is in its infancy. The need to insure, especially against major environmental disasters, can implicitly be waived by a government authorising an economic development. The government will then have considered the risks to be those of the community, judging them justifiable in view of the beneficial consequences of the development as well as of the reasonable precautions taken.

The transfer of environmental risks from developer (sometimes the government) to the community (sometimes including future generations) leads to an erroneous appraisal of the true cost of economic initiatives. The problem has been strongly canvassed by critics of the nuclear industry. Following the Three Mile Island emergency in the United States and the Chernobyl disaster in the former USSR, as well as many lesser mishaps, it has been found that the environmental insurance costs associated with the nuclear industry would significantly alter the competitive position of nuclear energy, all the more so if financial provisions were to be made for the safe decommissioning of the plant in due course. Comparable lessons are being learned from regular accidents in oil production and transport. Fortunately, there is a growing acknowledgement of the value of ascribing the liability for environmental risks to the source.[10]

Environmentally based aid

The stark features of the distribution of income between nations raise questions concerning the adequacy of aid, the problems of development

---

[10] In Germany, insurance groups are formulating a set of packages for companies seeking cover against environmental liabilities. Premiums are not currently available. See *Süddeutsche Zeitung* (Munich), 21 Oct. 1991.

and, of late, associated environmental considerations. In conditions of poverty it is more difficult to attach priority to the safeguarding of the environment and to act within the long-term framework necessary for the sustainable use and enjoyment of that environment. Poverty calls for aid, including environmentally based aid. Recently, a new source of environmentally based aid was created in the Global Environment Facility, a multilateral fund of US$1.3 billion (see Chapter 7). This amount is extremely modest when compared with the estimated US$1,288 billion needed to implement the World Environment Plan to the year 2000 [11] or with an annual military expenditure of the order of US$900 billion.

Environmentally based aid has been differentiated from debt-for-nature swaps. The latter might be considered a form of trade, with benefits not necessarily restricted to the recipient. The distinction, however, is probably more apparent than real. The debt-for-nature swap does not involve the "export" of nature. Moreover, funds earmarked as aid are routinely used in ways directly or indirectly benefiting the donor country. For that reason, multilateral aid may be preferred to bilateral aid. As noted, it is possible to find a new source of multilateral aid by using economic mechanisms to control global environmental problems. It must be noted also that the poorest countries carry the least responsibility for these problems.

THE COMMAND APPROACH AND COMPARISON

Economic instruments of environmental policy such as have been described above have so far not been thoroughly tested, considering the range of possible applications. With lessons yet to be learned, the advantages of economic environmental instruments over command instruments therefore remain uncertain. They are likely to depend on the type of environmental problem, the stage of development of a country and the nature of its economy. Time and experience are needed, it seems, before the respective roles in environmental policy of economic instruments and of command and control measures can be clarified. It is probable, however, that with the ascendancy of environmental policy both approaches will gain in importance.

A number of environmental problems will continue to call for regulation by command on several grounds. First, an economic instrument may be impractical to administer and thus unattractive in terms of expense. Second, economic instruments may be perceived as inequitable

---

[11] This plan allots US$270 billion to stabilising the world population; US$52 billion to the protection of forests and biodiversity; US$60 million to tree planting; US$ 417 billion to energy conservation; US$189 billion to soil protection; and US$300 billion to the retirement of Third World debt. See IUCN/UNEP/WWF (1991).

and therefore become politically unacceptable, given an unequal distribution of income. For instance, rights of access to basic environmental amenities can be considered non-negotiable just as (environment-related) safety and health issues are. Other grounds include cases where natural environmental assets are so fragile that no dealings over them are desirable (e.g. endangered species), or an ethical principle is involved, as has been raised regarding selected genetic experiments.

The command approach is exemplified by the Montreal Protocol, under which the use of chloro-fluorocarbons (CFCs) will be banned after the expiry of the phase-out period (a period recently brought forward by some countries on a voluntary basis) (see Chapter 7). Similarly, a range of pesticides and insecticides has been outlawed in developed and developing countries alike. The planning of land use will continue to rely on zoning regulations. Wilderness areas and wildlife, in a number of cases, need unconditional forms of protection. Dynamite fishing is banned in most countries. Dragnet fishing and whaling are currently being phased out by international agreement. And so on . . .

On the other hand, in the control of many aspects of pollution, of congestion, of mineral and biological resource use, and of land and water management, the role of environmental policy based on economic incentives appears set to expand. There is evidence of disenchantment with the command approach to environmental policy. Environmental command measures depend on a centralised setting of environmental standards, common to all without discrimination. Typically, such measures impose uniform technical solutions to cope with environmental spillovers. The choice of solution is summed up by the acronym BATNEEC, used in the United Kingdom, which stands for "best available techniques not entailing excessive costs". The choice, however, applies to the regulator. Those subject to the outright regulation may find it inflexible and offering no inducement to improve their environmental performance. Moreover, depending on varying abilities to observe environmental regulations, the cost of compliance may be anything but equal for those affected.

The inflexibility of the command approach in respect of technology perhaps represents the most decisive disadvantage. Economic instruments requiring payments for environmental costs incurred are thought to provide a powerful financial stimulus for enterprises and households to find ways to reduce those costs (and thus to avoid environmental payments).[12] Accordingly, a strong boost would be given to the implementation of environment-friendlier technology as well as to research into environmentally successful technology. Put in different

---

[12] Ideally, environmental payments are tied to levels of spillover and not to the activity giving rise to the spillover. Sometimes the ideal is not practical and environmental payments are sought in product charges. For example, the motorist may be asked to pay an environmental levy on petrol instead of on noxious exhaust gases.

words, the need to pay for environmental costs mobilises the profit motive in determining both the choice of available technologies and the shape of new technologies to be developed.

Command measures are also associated with a high level of bureaucratic involvement in key economic sectors. The discretion of this involvement poses a moral danger of the "capture" of the regulator by the regulated. Fines for non-compliance have generally been low and detection has not been vigorous. Economic instruments do not have the same discretionary element. Besides, they may be more cost effective by being less vulnerable to the tendency of budget maximisation common to bureaucracies.

What both the command and the incentive approaches have in common is that the use of economic instruments will require adjustments in those sectors of the economy affected by environmental policy. If the cost of adjustment is not sufficiently taken into account, resistance to the policy will make itself felt at the political level. This resistance — which may concern loss of employment (see Chapter 3) or concern over international competitiveness (see Chapter 7) — is independent of the overall justification of policy in terms of benefits and costs. It requires attention not to the totals but to the distribution of the benefits and costs. Sectional economic interests may hold considerable political power, as witness the protective policies even in those countries considered most pluralist.

Notwithstanding sectional opposition, the justification of environmental policy in terms of benefits and costs is becoming easier. First, pressures on the environment have, on the whole, been increasing with time, thus raising the benefit level of intervention. Second, modern technology, especially in electronics and communications, is reducing the cost of policy. For instance, the idea of electronic (peak) pricing and billing for road use no longer seems far-fetched. Third, once new environmental policies are adopted, opportunities may be found for cost pooling between different environmental policies of the same class. For example, monitoring and billing on several polluting emissions can be undertaken in a simultaneous operation.

DEVELOPING COUNTRIES

The need for developmental policies is much better articulated in the literature than the comparatively new demands for environmental policies in the context of development. None the less, the South Commission (1990, pp. 134ff.) offers a concise appraisal of both the environmental problems of developing countries and the policies needed to alleviate these problems. Although this appraisal tackles the questions "what to do" and "why", it does not provide us with clues on "how", i.e. what instruments of environmental policy are to be preferred. Conversely, the recent OECD guide *Environmental policy: How to apply economic instruments* (OECD, 1991) offers no guidance concerning the use of economic instruments in developing countries.

Nevertheless, questions over the choice of environmental instruments are very much part of the current debate, as is echoed in the papers prepared by the Secretariat for the 1992 United Nations Conference on Environment and Development: "This fundamental issue of the relationship between the environment and our economic life will . . . be the prime focus of the 1992 Conference. A key challenge in this context will be to determine how taxes, incentives, subsidies and other instruments of economic and fiscal policy can be re-examined to ensure that they meet both environmental and economic objectives" (UNCED, 1991, para. 7).

Reasons have been advanced to suggest that, generally speaking, the role of economic instruments is comparatively limited in the developing countries. Amongst these reasons is the expectation that, other things being equal, a lower priority applies for the environment in developing economies and a higher priority for productive employment (Koo, 1979, p. 25); although this is not unambiguously supported by the evidence.[13] Moreover, the reason implies that a lower priority for the environment suggests forgoing policy altogether when, in fact, the use of policy instruments can be tuned to any desired standard of environmental protection.

A second, and important, reason derives from the constraint that, in subsistence conditions, economic disincentives to incur environmental costs might impose a burden on the poor which they cannot reasonably be expected to meet. A remedy to this predicament can, at least partially, be found in the recycling of environmental revenue generated by the economic instrument (see box 5). A remedy can also be found in aid from inside or outside the developing country. A further reason is that countries at a low stage of development where the institutional framework is weak are ill-equipped to organise the monitoring, collection and enforcement of such economic instruments. These problems would be similar in kind to those hindering more sophisticated forms of tax collection in these countries.

---

[13] In an early study on the location of pollution-intensive industries in countries including Malaysia, the Republic of Korea and Brazil, Leonard and Duerksen (1980), for example, found no evidence that these countries offered themselves to multinational enterprises as "pollution havens".

Box 5. Allocation of revenue of economic instruments

A feature of economic instruments of environmental policy is their capacity to generate revenue. The distribution of such revenue follows a number of options which, in turn, are significant for the relevance of these instruments in the context of development.

1. The collection of revenue implies that environmental costs have actually been incurred. It has been suggested therefore that revenues might be spent on efforts designed to abate or counter the environmental costs.

2. A second suggestion is that the revenue collected against environmental costs incurred must be allocated to those suffering the environmental costs. This is the notion of revenue as compensation.

3. An important variant on the above notion pertains to the application of economic instruments of environmental policy in conditions of poverty. Although it may be harsh to collect revenues in payment for unenvironmental practices in conditions of poverty, the revenue collected can be channelled back to the parties affected by the environmental policy. For instance, subsistence farmers, presented by government with a fee per head of cattle designed to limit overgrazing, might demand that the revenue so collected be recycled, avoiding a net transfer to the group.

4. It has been further suggested that environmental revenue might be employed to maintain the international competitive position of a sector adversely affected by the introduction of environmental charges.

5. Lastly, revenue can be used on a transitional basis to cushion losses of employment and other adjustment costs following the introduction of economic instruments of environmental policy (see Chapter 3).

In spite of reservations concerning the introduction of environmental policies in developing economies, support for the use of economic environmental policy instruments is encountered in many sources. For instance, the United Nations Workshop on Creative Financing Mechanisms for Environmentally Sound Technologies (held in Belém, 1990) favours the adoption of economic schemes of environmental policy in developing economies. Likewise, support is found in the preparatory documents for UNCED 1992 (e.g. UNCED, 1991)). A similar line is taken also in the United States Congress Office of Technology Assessment (1991) and Panayotou (1991, pp. 83-132). Panayotou, who supplies a wealth of pertinent evidence, is particularly persuasive on the relevance of economic instruments in developing countries.

Economic instruments have been included in the programmes of the World Bank (1990) and the Asian Development Bank (1991). The World Bank writes in this respect that the scope for "command and control" environmental instruments in developing countries is more limited. However, it sees scope for environmental trading schemes in the same light. On the other hand, the Bank identifies a role for fiscal intervention or "green taxes" as well as effluent charges and stumpage fees. The Asian Development Bank explicitly discusses the demerits of the "command" approach in the Asian context.

In fact, support in the developing countries for the use of economic instruments has already been translated into action. Albeit on a small scale, it can be said that practice precedes theory. In China, for instance, certain industrial pollutants are subject to emission fees which are collected by local Environment Protection Bureaux (cited in Bernstein, 1991). Revenues are placed in banks and used subsequently for borrowings by firms for pollution control investments, covering 20-25 per cent of the needs for this purpose. Environmental measures undertaken or considered in India are set out in box 6.

Box 6. Economic instruments of environmental policy: Industrial pollution control in India

In India, the Environment Act and Rules of 1986 establishes a set of Minimum National Discharge Standards which compare satisfactorily with industrial pollution standards in use in developed countries. States are allowed to tighten these standards further. Economic instruments used to achieve environmental standards include:

Charges:

— effluent charges on the consumption of water (Rs.0.01-0.03 per kilolitre);

— pollution consent fees (Rs.200 — 10,000);

— monitoring fees for review of compliance.

Subsidies:

— excise tax on pollution control equipment reduced from 25 per cent to 15 per cent;

— depreciation allowance accelerated from 30 per cent to 50 per cent;

— maximum customs duty reduced from 80 per cent to 40 per cent;

— soft loans and grants for financing equipment;

— removal of subsidies on fertilisers (with exemptions for small farmers).

Measures envisaged are:

— further easing of repayments on loans related to pollution control or waste minimisation;

— additional grant programmes for effluent treatment plants;

— gradual increase of effluent charges to match treatment costs of effluents;

— charges for handling and disposal of solid wastes;

— widening of minimum environmental standards to cover all industrial sources.

Source: World Bank, 1991.

The pricing of environmental resources by economic policy instruments need not be the *first* economic priority in developing countries. Almost invariably, the complaint encountered is that a variety of tax credits, investment subsidies and related measures are at present in place which are actually counter-environmental and encourage deforestation, unsustainable agricultural practices, overuse of water supplies etc.

Under the circumstances, it has been argued that the policy-based environmental disincentives currently in place might be overcome as an initial step (Kosmo, 1989, p. 39). This more cautious approach would fit the reservation also expressed in Chapter 2, which warns that policies appropriate in the context of an advanced economy may not be so in the context of underdevelopment.

In this respect, the Asian Development Bank (1991) reports on the amendment of Thailand's policy of "free" access to hilly terrain, which has encouraged overexpansion of rubber on steep slopes, leading to catastrophic landslides and floods in 1988. In recent years, furthermore, Nepal, Pakistan, Indonesia and the Philippines have all agreed to reduce substantially their subsidies on pesticides and fertilisers as part of their structural adjustment programmes. Similarly, subsidies on farm equipment and land-clearing machinery are being questioned, as well as fiscal incentives which in fact promote deforestation or forest "mining". Finally, the Bank points out that the agricultural use of water in many countries is commonly subsidised to a high degree.

CONCLUSIONS

The current upsurge of interest in environmental policy is reassuring from the point of view of the environment. It is also reassuring from the point of view of sustainable development, in which the economy draws on environmental resources on a renewable basis and in which productive employment and physical well-being can be safeguarded for present and future generations. On the other hand, our sense of reassurance may be moderated by the knowledge that the growth of interest in environmental policy finds its roots in a setting which, by a range of measures, shows a net environmental deterioration at the global, regional and local levels; and in both rich and poor countries.

This chapter has emphasised new environmental instruments of the economic type and also highlighted the existence of counter-environmental price distortions. The attention given to economic instruments of environmental policy has been particularly pronounced in the developed economies. However, their relevance is not restricted to developed economies. Moreover, economic instruments may prove to be of special significance to developing countries in the control of global environmental problems, on account of the redistributive possibilities they offer.

Although the emergence of new instruments of environmental policy is clearly in evidence, this does not detract from the continuing importance of "command and control" measures. Neither economic nor command instruments alone can achieve the range of environmental standards necessary to place economies on a sustainable footing. A package is needed which exploits the advantages of costs, effectiveness and equity that are particular to each method and environmental problem. Given a growing body of experience with environmental policy, lessons in this respect might be learned quickly. Especially in developing countries, however, insufficient experience is available at this stage.

Finally, we note a basic limitation regarding the environmental instruments reported on in this chapter. The measures entertained, it has been said, operate at a micro level. They are designed selectively to contain specific environmental problems. As part of the design, these measures seek to establish a (willingness-to-pay) trade-off between economic and environmental aims. The trade-off perceived as optimal is established pragmatically, given the particular set of environmental circumstances of the day and place.

If, however, the circumstances of the day were changing for the worse with the passing of time — in line with a historical decline of the environmental record — the optimum trade-off would deteriorate accordingly. Time, in other words, may undermine progress in spite of seemingly rational environmental choices at the grass-roots level. Preventing this problem will require environmental policy to become more responsive to the wider pressures resulting from economic and demographic momentum and the role of technology as the mediator between the economy and the environment.

References

Asian Development Bank. 1991. *Asian Development Outlook.* Manila.

Barrett, S. 1991. "Soil conservation and agricultural pricing policies", in *Journal of Development Economics* (Amsterdam, Elsevier), Vol. 36, pp. 167-187.

Baumol, W. J.; Oates, W. E. 1979. *Economics, environmental policy and the quality of life.* Englewood Cliffs, New Jersey, Prentice Hall.

Bernstein, J. D. 1991. *Alternative approaches to pollution control and waste management.* Discussion Paper. New York, UNDP.

Coase, R. H. 1960. "The problem of social cost", in *Journal of Law and Economics* (Chicago, University of Chicago Press), Vol. 3, No. 1, pp. 1-44.

Dales, J. H. 1968. *Pollution, property and prices.* Toronto, University of Toronto Press.

Dasgupta, P.; Maler, K. 1990. "The environment and emerging development issues". Paper presented to the World Bank Annual Conference on Development Economics, 26-27 April 1990, pp. 1-39.

Doeleman, J. A. 1985. "Historical perspective on cost-benefit analysis", in *Futures* (Guildford, United Kingdom), Vol. 17, No. 2, pp. 149-164.

Dudek, D. 1989. *Marketable instruments for managing global environmental problems.* Vancouver, Western Economics Association.

Eskeland, G.; Jimenez, E. 1991. "The environment: Curbing pollution in developing countries", in *Finance and Development* (Washington, DC), Vol. 28, No. 1, pp. 15-19.

European Parliament. May 1991. *On economic and fiscal instruments of environmental policy.* Report of the Committee on the Environment, Public Health and Consumer Protection. Doc. EN/RR/109943.

Hardin, G. 1968. "The tragedy of the commons", in *Science* (Washington, DC), Vol. 162, pp. 1243-1248.

International Union for Conservation of Nature/United Nations Environment Programme/World Wide Fund for Nature (IUCN/UNEP/WWF). 1991. *Caring for the earth: A strategy for sustainable living.* Gland (Switzerland).

Koo, A. Y. C., et al. 1979. *Environmental repercussions on trade and investment.* East Lansing, Michigan, Michigan State University, on behalf of the ILO.

Kosmo, M. 1989. *Economic incentives and industrial pollution in developing countries.* World Bank Environment Department Working Paper No. 2. Washington, DC, World Bank.

Leonard, H. J.; Duerksen, C. J. 1980. "Environmental regulations and the location of industry: An international perspective", in *Colombia Journal of World Business* (Bogotá), Summer, pp. 52-68.

Markandya, A.; Pearce, D. W. 1988. *Environmental considerations and the choice of the discount rate in developing countries.* World Bank Environment Department Working Paper No. 3. Washington, DC, World Bank.

Mishan, E. J. 1971. "The post-war literature on externalities: An interpretative essay", in *Journal of Economic Literature* (Nashville, Tennessee), Vol. 9, pp. 1-21.

Organization for Economic Co-operation and Development (OECD). 1989a. *Environmental policy benefits: Monetary valuation.* Study carried out by D. W. Pearce and A. Markandya. Paris.

———. 1989b. *Economic instruments for environmental protection.* Study carried out by J. B. Opschoor and H. B. Vos. Paris.

———. 1991. *Environmental policy: How to apply economic instruments.* Paris.

Panayotou, T. 1991. "Economic incentives in environmental management and their relevance to developing countries", in Denizhan Eröcal (ed.). *Environmental management in developing countries.* Paris, OECD.

Pearce, D.; Markandya, A.; Barbier, E. B. 1989. *Blueprint for a green economy.* London, Earthscan.

Perrings, C. 1991. *Incentives for the ecologically sustainable use of human and natural resources in the drylands of sub-Saharan Africa: A review.* Mimeographed WEP working paper (WEP 2-22/WP.219). Geneva, ILO.

Pigou, A. C. 1920. *The economics of welfare.* London, Macmillan.

South Commission. 1990. *The challenge to the South: The report of the South Commission.* Oxford, Oxford University Press.

Teitenberg, T. H. 1990. "Economic instruments for environmental regulation", in *Oxford Review of Economic Policy* (Oxford, Oxford University Press), Vol. 6, No. 1, pp. 17-33.

Tisdell, C. A. 1983. "A further review of pollution control", in *Journal of Environmental Systems* (Farmingdale, New York), Vol. 12, pp. 363-380.

United Kingdom Government. 1990. *This common inheritance: Britain's environmental strategy.* White Paper. London, HMSO.

United Nations Conference on Environment and Development (UNCED) Preparatory Committee, Third Session. July 1991. *Utilisation of economic instruments (cross-sectoral issues).* Doc. PC/50. Geneva.

United Nations Economic Commission for Europe (UNECE). 1990. *Sustainable development: Framework for discussion of selected issues.* Doc. EC.ADR.48, 13 Mar. 1990. Mimeographed. Geneva.

United Nations Centre on Transnational Corporations (UNCTC). 1991. *Options to increase transfer of environmentally sound technologies to developing countries on favourable terms.* Draft document. New York.

United States Congress, Office of Technology Assessment. 1991. *Energy in developing countries.* Washington, DC.

World Bank. 1990. *The World Bank and the environment: First Annual Report.* Washington, DC.

———. 1991. *India: Industrial pollution control project.* Staff Appraisal Report No. 9347-IN. Mimeographed. Washington, DC.

World Commission on Environment and Development (WCED). 1987. *Our common future.* Oxford, Oxford University Press. (Also known as the Brundtland Report.)

ENVIRONMENTAL DEGRADATION IN RURAL AREAS

P. Bifani *

5

The interrelationship between the exploitation and degradation of environmental and natural resources, on the one hand, and development and poverty, on the other (discussed in Chapter 2), is particularly relevant in the rural areas of developing countries, which account for the bulk of the labour force in most of these countries. Also, the larger percentage of the poor of the world live in rural areas suffering from serious environmental degradation. Besides, despite the successful economic performance reported in terms of growth of output (mainly in Asia), the growth of employment opportunities in these rural areas continues to lag behind.

Until the early years of this century, almost all increases in agricultural production occurred as a result of the expansion of the area cultivated. However, by the middle of this century and particularly in the past 20 years, growth in agricultural production has been made possible almost entirely by the more intensive cultivation of land already in use. The continuing trend towards intensive agriculture raises a number of important questions with respect to resource use. Intensification means increasing the use of mechanisation and high-yielding varieties, agro-chemical applications and irrigation. Increasing environmental problems such as pollution and the overexploitation of natural resources, associated with intensification, are becoming quite serious in many developing countries. Of particular concern is the growing loss of arable land owing to erosion and salinisation, the deforestation of the tropical rain forest, the over-exploitation of rangelands (particularly in semi-arid zones), the increasing cultivation and intensification of hillsides, the depletion of groundwater, and so on. These issues are discussed in the following section.

Our second concern in this chapter is to examine the causes of environmental degradation in developing countries, e.g. population

---

* Universidad Autónoma de Madrid.

pressures, poverty, consumption patterns and technology. What is the nature of the poverty-environment linkages? Is the mere coexistence of rural poverty, large populations and environmental degradation a sufficient reason to establish a simple unidirectional cause-and-effect relationship? Is it possible to provide for environmental protection while overcoming poverty? These questions are discussed in the section "Causes of environmental degradation" below.

Our third concern in this chapter is an examination of suitable policy measures that are necessary for checking "forced environmental degradation" discussed in Chapter 2. Agriculture in developing countries has traditionally benefited from support policies facilitating the use of particular technologies, e.g. mechanisation, pesticides and fertilisers, or the intensive use of land and water. Government intervention has tended to distort prices and induce an overuse of natural resources. These policy issues are discussed in the final section of the chapter.

RURAL ENVIRONMENTAL DEGRADATION: SOME EVIDENCE

Evidence on the degradation of environmental resources in Third World agriculture has been accumulating rapidly over the past two decades. Deforestation, soil erosion, desertification, soil salinisation, alkalinisation and waterlogging form the different but often interrelated aspects of soil degradation. The empirical evidence presented in various studies often paints an alarming picture of the scale and the intensity of these processes at work in Third World agriculture. Some of this evidence surely has not remained uncontroversial and has been challenged recently. (see, for example, Nelson, 1988). Our purpose here is not to enter into such controversies, which in any case have been largely about the degree and scale of the processes at work rather than about their overall tendency and direction.

There are many manifestations of environmental degradation affecting different agricultural systems and directly related to the technology in use. Among the processes of environmental degradation affecting rural areas, the most important are those associated with soil erosion, resulting from excessive and inadequate mechanisation; salinisation and waterlogging due to inefficient irrigation systems; and chemical pollution caused by the excessive use of agrochemicals. Some of these disruptive processes are closely linked with particular ecological areas such as arid lands, mountain foothills and humid tropical forests.

Degradation of arid lands

Tropical arid and semi-arid lands are those with an average of 100-400 and 400-800 mm of rainfall a year, respectively. The former cannot be

cultivated without irrigation, while the latter can be cultivated — although the quantity of rainfall, its concentration in only a few months of the year and its spatial, seasonal and year-to-year variability limit the range of crops that can be grown, as well as their productivity. In arid lands, nomadic or semi-nomadic pastoralism is the main activity. In semi-arid areas the growing of rain-fed crops such as millet, sorghum, groundnuts and legumes, together with animal husbandry, are the major activities.

According to a recent UNEP report, "more than 6.1 billion hectares, nearly 40 per cent of the Earth's land area, is dryland. Of this about 0.9 billion hectares are hyper-arid deserts. The remaining 5.2 billion hectares are arid, semi-arid and dry sub-humid lands, part of which have become deserts through human degradation. These lands are the habitat and the source of livelihood for about one fifth of the world's population." (UNEP, 1992a, p. xiii). As noted in Chapter 3, the majority of the poor living in arid and semi-arid regions are victims of population displacement and unemployment. These people are among the poorest in developing countries.

According to the FAO, in sub-Saharan Africa 65 million hectares of grazing land have been turned into desert during the past 50 years, affecting the livelihood of nearly 100 million people (FAO, 1986). At the peak of the crisis in 1984 and 1985, 30 to 35 million people in 21 African countries "were seriously affected by droughts. Approximately 10 million were displaced and become known as environmental refugees" (UNEP, 1992a, p. 12).

In arid and semi-arid zones the possibilities for diversifying and intensifying production are quite limited. Commerce and handicrafts are some of the activities that provide additional income and employment with which to import basic goods from outside the region during the drought periods. However, the extra income is generally insufficient to compensate for the losses caused by lengthy drought seasons, with a resulting increase in poverty and environmental degradation, including labour out-migration. In the absence of any significant non-farm employment opportunities the out-migration often becomes inevitable.

The economies of arid and semi-arid areas have evolved towards cash crop production. To give an example, in the Sudano-Sahelian region millet and sorghum for consumption have been replaced by groundnuts for export. In the case of pastoralists, the external dynamic factor has been the increasing urban demand for animal products, including the replacement of the traditional subsistence herding system by the raising of animals for marketing.

A specialisation in cash crops tends to lead to an intensification of cultivation, particularly if the crop faces declining international prices. Without adequate replenishment of fertilisers and organic material, the intensification leads to loss of fertility and eventually to erosion. It also implies mechanisation, with a serious impact on land due to increasing erosion and compaction of soils, which also affects groundwater. In the case of the new market-oriented animal raising, the impact on the environment can be considered positive, since it tends to reduce the animal population: herders can survive with fewer animals, since the sale of their products generates a reasonable level of income. However, the market orientation also induces changes that do not suit local environmental conditions, as happens with the composition of the herds: camels and goats are replaced by cattle and sheep, which are more in demand, fetching much higher prices. Yet cattle and sheep are more vulnerable to drought and other hazards of arid areas. Moreover, they also consume much more water, which is indeed a scarce resource in these areas.

The expansion of cash crops implies a reduction of land for food crops, which are then increasingly cultivated in more arid marginal land with lower productivity.

In an effort to raise productivity, such technological innovations as the improvement of crop techniques, mechanisation and fertilisers have been introduced. However, semi-arid crops have not yet been the subject of a "Green Revolution", although the development of high-yielding varieties of sorghum has been promising (Swindale, 1985). In the case of animal husbandry, efforts have been made to reduce the vulnerability of the newly introduced species to the hazards of arid areas. For example, in West Africa the introduction of the vaccine against rinderpest has been extremely important in reducing cattle losses caused by this disease; however, this also contributes to overstocking and overgrazing.

Deterioration of mountain foothills

Other areas with severe degradation are hillsides and the slopes of mountains. There are no statistics on the highlands: nor do they represent a well-defined ecosystem. The deterioration of hillsides affects such areas as the Himalayan foothills, including Nepal's Terai, the West Himalayas in India and the non-Hindu-Kush Himalayan mountains of China; the highlands of Mexico and Central America; the Andean region of South America; Central Africa and Ethiopia; Central Myanmar; and the island mountain regions of Indonesia, the Philippines and the Caribbean.

Nearly 56 per cent of the population and 68 per cent of the total arable land of Nepal are in the hills, which nevertheless produce only 30 per cent of food supplies. In Latin America and the Caribbean, nearly one-third of the population and half of the farms are located in sloping areas; their contribution to the food supply of the respective countries fluctuates between 40 and 80 per cent of the total.

The best-known case is that of the Himalayan foothills. The pattern of poverty and environmental degradation here is indeed very similar to that of the arid and semi-arid lands. Economic activities were traditionally centred on forest exploitation, agriculture and animal raising. It is generally believed that population growth leads to increasing pressure for food production and fuelwood. Further, the encroachment on the hillsides results from the expansion of agriculture.

The productive system of hillsides is formed by a cultivated area and a non-cultivated or supporting area. The latter is supposed to produce the organic matter needed by the former, where it is transferred by animals that also contribute to the recycling of nutrients from crop residues to cultivated land. The forests of the supporting area are also supposed to provide fuelwood, ensuring that dung is not removed and contributes to the replenishment of organic matter and soil nutrients. If agricultural expansion, deforestation and erosion lead to a reduction of the supporting, non-cultivated area, the system is increasingly exposed to degradation. There is less organic matter available, animal wastes are used to provide energy, thus breaking the nutrients cycle, while organic material does not return to the natural system. The fertility of the land declines. The declining productivity of the natural system contributes to migration (in the case of the Himalayan foothills it is mainly male out-migration). The migration of the male labour force has no negative effects on the local economy since local employment opportunities are scarce. On the contrary, an economic advantage of out-migration is that it brings additional monetary income to the region in the form of regular remittances.

It is estimated that in the hill areas of Uttar Pradesh in India as much as one-third of the total income originates in cash remittances (Khanka, 1985). Although this out-migration is beneficial to the rural environment, it may have adverse effects on the urban environment which should also be taken into account.

As the forests retreat, more labour is needed for gathering fuelwood and for animal herding. These tasks are performed more and more by women and children. It is reported that in Nepal women spent as much time in fuelwood gathering as they did in farm activities (Kumar and Hotchkiss, 1988).

Deforestation

Deforestation and, more specifically, the conversion of tropical rain forests, has received wide coverage in the media and is a frequent item on any agenda on environmental issues. The debate concerning the warming of the planet and the build-up of atmospheric carbon dioxide has added a new dimension to this most controversial environmental issue.

There is no doubt that the conversion of the tropical rain forest has accelerated. The available data on the annual rate of tropical forest conversion is estimated between $113,000 \text{ km}^2$ and $205,000 \text{ km}^2$, depending on the source used (FAO, 1988).

Deforestation for cropland expansion and human settlement is certainly not a new phenomenon. In fact it is a long-term process which started in colonial times with the discovery of the economic possibilities of timber production. It is in this long-term perspective that the economic, social and environmental effects of deforestation should be assessed. For example, the Asian Development Bank (1991) notes that in Malaysia the more intensive deforestation process occurred in the years since 1900 when crop land covered 5,640 km^2; during the century cropland expanded to 48,060 km^2 in 1980, with a reduction of closed forests from 240,000 km^2 to 154,000 km^2. Deforestation is caused by various activities, ranging from agriculture and ranching to industrial projects. In most countries, one, or just a few, factors are at the origin of deforestation. However, in the Amazon, almost all the major causes concur to make the problem very serious (see box 7).

Box 7. The Brazilian Amazon: A case study

It is possible to classify the motives for a conversion of the Brazilian Amazon into five main types: (a) frontier expansion — migrants coming mainly from the Nordeste region, landless workers or people displaced by the technological modernisation of agricultural activities in other areas of the country; (b) the opening of the forest for economic purposes, such as ranching or industrial development. This type of conversion is based on the use of rich resources and fertile land; (c) the state colonisation programmes in the context of the governmental control of the Amazon, the expansion of agricultural land and the opening of new employment opportunities; (d) conversion due to infrastructural development; and (e) the conversion of forest for pure speculation through the sale of land acquired cheaply from the Government.

During the 1960s and early 1970s the idea of the colonisation of tropical forests received serious attention from governments and international organisations. It was viewed as a solution to growing population pressure associated with the low job creation capacity of the economy, and as a solution to resettling landless people without having to implement more troublesome agrarian reforms. It was also seen as a mechanism to expand the agricultural frontier and to increase agricultural production through the incorporation of new land. This solution, by reducing the migration to cities, would alleviate the pressure on the urban labour market.

Colonisation has two well-differentiated phases: spontaneous colonisation, and planned and promoted colonisation. The former is associated with the development of the large highways completed by the end of the 1960s (e.g. the Belém-Brasilia and the Cuiabá-Santarém highways, among others) that made possible the occupation of virgin land at low or even zero cost. This opportunity came at a very particular moment that was marked by demographic explosion in the centre-south of Brazil and the Nordeste, a lack of employment opportunities in the new industrial areas and a rapid technological change in the centre and south of the country that displaced large numbers of workers.

The second era of colonisation started with the "Operaçao Amazônia" in 1966. This was the government-promoted colonisation of the tropical Amazonian rain forest, based on a programme of regional development with fiscal incentives and facilities for private investment to resettle the excess population of the Nordeste on the new land. The experience was negative: migrants from the Nordeste did not adapt to the conditions of the Amazon, lacked technology and resources; the technical assistance provided by the Government proved to be insufficient; and the fertility of the land for the colonists was extremely poor.

Pasture development has been estimated to account for nearly 60 per cent of tropical forest conversion in Brazil. Not only does this conversion have an enormous environmental impact, but also from the social perspective it generates very little employment and tends to lead to concentration of land.

The facts relating to deforestation in the Amazon are more or less the same as in other developing areas of the world, be it the timber exploitation in Western Africa or Borneo or the expansion of plantation agriculture in Asia. For example, in Thailand the high value of teak motivated its predatory exploitation nearly to depletion. Moreover, in Thailand cropland tripled between 1950 and 1988 as a result of the expansion of the cassava-growing area for the export of pellets to feed cattle in Europe. The area planted with cassava increased from 64,000 hectares in 1960 to 1,042,000 hectares in 1980, becoming the second largest crop in the country after rice. In 1964, the forested area of Thailand represented 53 per cent; by 1979 this was reduced to 38 per cent. The environmental impact is serious in terms of increasing soil erosion. On the other hand, the economic benefits have been only temporary.

Deforestation has caused massive displacement of people forced to seek livelihoods elsewhere. It is estimated that in Haiti, more than 100,000 people have migrated as a result of deforestation. In Indonesia, more than a million people are reported to have moved out of deforested areas of Java, and migrated to Borneo and other islands (cited in UNEP, 1992b).

CAUSES OF ENVIRONMENTAL DEGRADATION

What causes such degradation? In this section the importance of five major causal factors, i.e. poverty, population pressures, consumption patterns, energy and technology, are examined.

105

Poverty

Poverty in the Third World has been a major development concern (Sen, 1987; World Bank, 1990; UNDP, 1990). In many parts of the world, particularly in Latin America and Africa but also in other regions, poverty has actually increased (Cornia et al., 1987). The links between poverty and the environment remain unclear, however, and at best the subject continues to be shrouded in controversy. The interrelationship between poverty and the environment has been recognised by the World Commission on Environment and Development report in the following words: "Poverty is a major cause and effect of global environmental problems. It is therefore futile to attempt to deal with environmental problems without a broader perspective that encompasses the factors underlying world poverty and international equality" (WCED, 1987).

To define poverty solely in terms of deprivation is inadequate for an understanding of its implications for development and its impact on the environment. The concept needs to be supplemented with its related aspects, such as marginalisation and vulnerability. Poverty is linked with the process of development, the rate of economic growth, the uses of resources and the distribution both of resources and of the income generated in the production process. But much of the work on development, as noted by Bhagwati, has been considered mainly as an objective in itself rather than as a process to overcome poverty (Bhagwati, 1988).

The linkage between poverty and the environment defines particular characteristics of environmental disruption. In general, it can be said that, while in rural areas these linkages materialise through the overexploitation of resources and their consequent decreasing productivity, urban poverty encounters environmental problems typical of the man-made environment (see Chapter 6).

The association between poverty and unsustainable agricultural practices is nowadays referred to as a stylised fact in almost all the studies on environment and agriculture in developing countries (see, for example, Eckholm, 1976; United Nations Conference on Desertification, 1977; Leonard et al., 1989; Myers, 1989; Jagannathan, 1990; Jagannathan and Agunbiade, 1990; Dasgupta and Maler, 1990; and Perrings, 1991). Perrings (1991, p. 1), for example, begins his extensive review of the subject in relation to sub-Saharan Africa by maintaining that "one of the most striking coincidences of the last decade has been that between deepening poverty and accelerating environmental degradation in . . . the drylands of sub-Saharan Africa". Drawing on a number of empirical case studies on other parts of the Third World (mainly India and Latin America), Dasgupta and Maler (1990, p. 22) also confirm the close association between poverty and environmental degradation.

The pressure by the increasingly marginalised poor rural population on common lands is identified as an important link between socio-economic development and environmental degradation, especially in dry-land agriculture in arid and semi-arid areas. It is important to note that in establishing this link none of the authoritative sources in the literature identifies the source of the problem in the traditional communal nature of landownership on common lands, or with the "tragedy of global commons" à la Hardin (1968, pp. 1243-1248). On the contrary, it is precisely the breakdown of the traditional control mechanisms resulting from the commercialisation of agriculture and the growing pressure of the marginalised poor that is said to be the cause of environmental degradation, as the communally owned and controlled land turns into "free access" land (see Repetto and Holmes, 1983; Dasgupta and Maler, 1990; Perrings, 1991). In fact, Perrings even goes a step further in identifying the cause of unsustainable development on privately controlled landholdings in sub-Saharan Africa with the poverty of owner-occupiers of such lands. The risk-averse attitude of poor peasant households and their conservatism in the choice of asset holdings, which is a direct result of their poverty, Perrings maintains, block the adoption of new land-augmenting and land-conserving innovations and lead to environmental degradation.

Of course, one should distinguish between proximate and ultimate causes of environmental degradation. Poverty in itself cannot be regarded as an exogenous cause of environmental degradation. Poverty is rather a "condition of being" of the economic agents caused by a complex set of socio-economic and physical processes, including the environment itself.

Poor people are pushed towards the exploitation of marginal areas of low productivity; lacking resources and technology, they tend to overexploit the natural resources (e.g. land, water and wood) with a consequent decline in productivity. A process of cumulative causation is set off, reinforcing poverty, which in turn exerts more pressure on the environment, and so on. An increasingly deteriorating environment is not only less productive but also more vulnerable to unexpected social and natural events, making poor societies also prone to disasters. The problem is accentuated by institutional factors such as the increasing fragmentation of landholdings, land conflicts, or a lack of access to capital, technology and other necessary inputs.

Recently some studies have attempted to establish correlations between poverty and environmentally vulnerable and/or disrupted areas. It is noted that nearly 80 per cent of the poor in Latin America, 60 per cent in Asia and 51 per cent in Africa are living in marginal areas characterised by low productivity and high vulnerability to environmental degradation (Leonard et al., 1989, pp. 12-22). In 1984, the FAO noted a coincidence of poverty with areas seriously affected by deforestation, erosion and desertification. It is now frequent to find references to the geographical coincidence of poverty in environmentally degraded areas, such as the

Brazilian Nordeste, Haiti, the Andean countries, some regions of India, Nepal and various parts of Africa.

Bryer (1991) notes that growing poverty is a major reason why the number of disasters has been increasing. According to his report most disasters happen in countries of the "poor South and most are of their own making". The interesting aspect is that disasters show that there are strong links between environmental degradation and poverty. Environmental degradation has significantly contributed to famines in Ethiopia, the Sudan and Mozambique; the lack of adequate infrastructure and widespread poverty made the people of Bangladesh highly vulnerable to natural events such as cyclones and the consequent floods; conditions in poor, unhealthy and degraded man-made environments of Latin America favoured the spread of cholera. The report notes that there were 523 disasters in the 1960s, 767 in the 1970s and 1,387 in the 1980s. Yet the report notes that, although these disasters are the most conspicuous, there are everyday disasters associated with poverty.

Poverty is also believed to account for a great deal of deforestation and for much of the expansion of subsistence agriculture in which the traditional shifting cultivation pattern is associated with the conversion of forest to cropland by immigrants and new settlers. It has been estimated that between 200 and 250 million subsistence farmers and land-hungry migrants are causing the destruction of nearly 51,000 km^2 of tropical forest every year.

Is poverty really the main underlying cause of environmental degradation or is it rather a sort of catalytic or disabling factor (Lanly, 1982)? The hypothesis that poverty by itself is a cause of environmental degradation has not been empirically proved. Furthermore, if the hypothesis is correct, the question is: Does it mean that environmental degradation could decline *pari passu* with increasing income per capita and the decline of poverty? On the other hand, it is also true that some of the most pervasive and serious environmental degradation is closely associated with high incomes (particularly in developed countries), e.g. the depletion of the ozone layer, climatic change, acid rain, and so on.

There are cases, particularly in Latin American countries, where 5 per cent of the farmers own more than 80 per cent of farmland. Therefore, with less than 5 per cent of the land and forest resources of the region, the poor cannot be held responsible for the deterioration of agricultural resources. On the other hand, there is no doubt that the lack of conservation practices, combined with inadequate technology and increasing intensification in small landholdings contribute to accelerated degradation, and consequently to an increase in rural poverty. Thus, poverty is only one of the factors contributing to environmental degradation.

Population

The level of the population relative to the resource base, and the high rates of growth of population in the Third World, are considered to be the fundamental cause of both poverty and environmental degradation. Two versions of the population thesis, often not clearly separated in the literature, could be distinguished. The first is that population growth would directly lead to the marginalisation of labour as the growth of the supply of labour outpaces demand. The second version is that population growth has given rise to a rapid growth of demand for food, which has in turn led to the adoption of policies mainly concerned with the maximisation of food production to the neglect of the environment and adversely affecting poverty through the marginalisation of labour. We may refer to these two versions as the direct and indirect versions of the population thesis.

Both these versions have been criticised in the literature on the grounds that they treat population growth as exogenous to poverty, and by implication to environmental degradation (Dasgupta and Maler, 1990; Perrings, 1991). As Dasgupta and Maler pointed out, under the conditions of destitution, and growing environmental degradation requiring an ever-increasing exertion of labour to scrape a living out of the harsh environment, children are not only a means to old-age security, but are also of current use to parents. However, in both its versions, the population thesis suffers from more fundamental shortcomings because of its treatment of technology and employment in the process of development. In both versions, the link between population, on the one hand, and poverty and environmental degradation, on the other, is mediated through technological change and employment generation. To treat the processes of technological change and employment creation as given, and to concentrate on population as the main exogenous policy tool is misplaced. It is through the analysis of these two mediating links, namely technology and employment (as noted in Chapter 2), that the real policy options for economies or subeconomies undergoing unsustainable development should be sought. It has been the contention of mainstream development economics so far that it is these latter two processes which are more amenable to policy intervention, compared with population whose interaction with economic processes is extremely complex and seems to have very much a momentum of its own. Furthermore, if we adhere to the propositions mentioned above on the endogeneity of population growth to poverty and environmental degradation — which indeed may be too simplistic, as many previous economic theories of population growth have turned out to be — the main burden of sustainable development has to be carried out by technological change and productive employment generation.

This is not to underestimate the importance of population policy in developing countries. Population policy, if successful, is an example of the type of policy which could enhance the achievement of the dual aims of environmental protection and economic growth in a complementary fashion. The point made above is rather that economies with similar population-natural resource ratios and similar population growth rates can experience sustainable or unsustainable development depending on their pattern of employment generation and technological trajectories.

Neither population growth alone nor poverty *per se* can be identified as the only factor or the most important factors responsible for land deterioration. However, it is not only a problem of the absolute number of people using the resource of a given occupied space. If population is seen solely as a number, the result is a quantitative approach in which an increase in the number of people will lead to a proportional increase in the pressure exerted by the population on the natural system, without recognising the elements of differentiation introduced by the development pattern to which this number belongs. Such an approach would be similar to the one used by natural scientists in their studies of animal populations — it is indeed a pure carrying capacity approach (United Nations ECLAC, 1991).

Consumption patterns

To overcome the shortcomings of the above approach, an alternative is to consider the consumption pattern of the local population in relation to the local environment and its resource endowment. Thus, it is estimated that an average American consumes at least 1,500 kg of agricultural produce per year while an average Chinese consumes only 600 kg. In the case of energy, whereas each American consumes every year an amount equivalent to 55 barrels of oil, the consumption of a Bangladeshi is barely three barrels. To understand the pressure on the natural system, it is important to link increasing numbers of people with their respective consumption styles and excessive consumption levels. In a dynamic perspective this means that, while the annual increase in demands on the environment resulting from the population growth in Bangladesh (2.4 per cent) will be the equivalent of approximately 9 million barrels, the resulting increase in the United States (0.8 per cent) will be nearly 110 million barrels. Although the population of developed countries is less than 20 per cent of the world's population, they are responsible for the bulk of the total energy and commercial fuels, wood products and steel consumed in the world. On the other hand, they are responsible for most of the production, trade and consumption of chloro-fluorocarbons (CFC), carbon dioxide emissions and sulphur emissions. It is estimated that Europe and North America account for 80 per cent of the world's emissions of sulphur dioxide, nitrogen oxides, carbon monoxide and hydrocarbons, which are the causes of acid rain and oxidant smog (OECD, 1985). These consumption patterns of less than 20 per cent of the world's population (even if associated with a very low rate of population growth) are likely to exert a far more significant impact on the environment and the use of natural resources than the high rates of population growth of a much larger population with a much lower consumption capacity. In this context, carrying capacity is clearly a misleading concept for the evaluation of the population-environment relationship.

Traditional peoples can clearly adapt their consumption pattern to the local availability of resources. However, these traditional adaptation patterns, still frequent in many areas of developing countries, are rapidly disappearing as a consequence of the adoption of Western patterns of consumption. The population-resources relationship is also modified by the characteristics of the insertion of local communities into the international system. This insertion operates through the production system and consumption patterns. The former tends to subordinate the local natural system to the requirements of the international markets, favouring homogenisation of cultures, modification of traditional exploitation, the adoption of alien varieties of crops and the slow disappearance of local varieties. The growing dominance of cash crop systems tends to reduce the natural resource base of the country. In this case the concept of carrying capacity is inadequate for evaluating the population-resource relationship, because the pressure over the local environment results from the demand originating in populations located in other areas with consumption patterns shaped not by the characteristics of a particular environment and its endowment of resources, but rather by the possibility to enjoy access to any resource available in the world.

Energy

Perhaps the key issue in the context of sustainable development relates to energy. In the past, energy derived from fossil-based fuels has been the main source of economic growth in the developed countries and consequently it accounted for much of the environmental degradation. It is clear that raising the per capita income and standard of living in the Third World would necessarily imply an increase in the demand for energy. If this increase in demand is to be met largely through sources that are not environment-friendly, clearly there would be a negative impact on environment. "The World Energy Conference projects (in its 'moderate' economic growth case) a tripling in consumption of commercial energy in developing countries between now and 2020" (United States Congress, Office of Technology Assessment, 1991, p. 10). This increase is attributed to population growth and economic development. Further, the share of commercial energy in total energy consumption grows as it takes the place of traditional biomass fuels (United States Congress, Office of Technology Assessment, 1991, p. 11). The evidence also suggests that the consumption of commercial energy varies significantly among developing countries because of varying energy intensity. For example, countries emphasising heavy industry and high rates of urbanisation are believed to contribute to high energy intensity. With improved technologies, however, many countries were able to reduce the level of energy intensity. These findings suggest that there is scope for promoting growth and yet restraining the consumption of commercial energy, the feasibility of sustainable development through appropriate policies and measures. This view is also reflected in another recent study which suggests that such a trade-off is more apparent than real. According to this study, "It is feasible with final energy use of approximately 1 kilowatt (kW) per capita — roughly the same as the present level — to provide enough energy services not only to satisfy the basic human needs of the whole population but also to raise their standard of living to the level of Western Europe. Energy need *not* be a constraint on the satisfaction of basic needs or the improvement of living standards in developing countries if available energy sources are used more efficiently and if there is a shift to modern energy carriers, especially electricity and biomass-based gaseous and liquid fuels" (Goldemberg et al., 1988).

In other words, for these policies to be effective, one must identify more efficient ways of using the energy. It is well known that the current practices of energy use are far from efficient because of poor cooking and lighting devices and appliances. Likewise, in agriculture and industry there is also considerable scope for improving energy efficiency. "Integrated iron and steel plants in China and India, for example, use twice as much energy per ton of crude steel produced as integrated plants in the United States and Japan" (United States Congress, Office of Technology Assessment, 1991, p. 18). These findings suggest that an appropriate energy policy in the context of sustainable development should focus not only on the careful selection and development of energy supplies but also on the demand side through proper incentive structures and the diffusion of energy-efficient technologies. As pointed out earlier, the choice of appropriate development strategies also plays a key role in the process.

Technology

Science and technology are indeed the main elements that define the characteristics of the population-environment relationship. In fact, a complete relationship between development and the environment is formed by the application of technology.

In collaboration with the International Institute for Applied Systems Analysis (IIASA), the FAO applied the concept of carrying capacity associated with different levels of technological development, in order to assess the population-sustaining capacity of land resources in 119 developing countries (Parikh and Rabar, 1981). Agro-ecological zones were associated with three levels of technological input: low, moderate and high. The study concluded that with the low level of technological input the carrying capacity of 65 countries with about 1.1 billion people will be largely exceeded by the year 2000.

The environmentalists argued that the results of the above study largely understated the real situation of food production and that the cost of the different technological levels was not determined. This was considered a serious shortcoming, particularly in assessing the viability of technological inputs. On the other hand, the study referred only to the soil characteristics of the different countries: it did not consider the impact that international demand exerts on the natural environment.

A more recent study along similar lines, focusing on fuelwood and food production, was undertaken by the World Bank (1985) for seven West African countries. The study concluded that none of the countries will have the capacity to sustain their future populations.

An important general conclusion of these studies is that, in many cases, carrying capacity can be raised through investment and technological development, as was also noted in Chapter 2. However, a basic limitation is the profitability of technological applications in many areas of the world. For the Sahelian region, the World Bank concluded that to increase carrying capacity through the application of available modern intensive production techniques had not proved to be sufficiently remunerative.

National experiences of developing countries have also been documented to show the negative environmental impact of modern agricultural technologies (the Green Revolution and Biorevolution). The heavy use of fertilisers and pesticides, for example, leads to adverse environmental effects, e.g. in Bangladesh (see box 8). Indonesia is another example of a country where the overuse of agricultural biological technology (fertilisers and pesticides) leads to environmental degradation. Indonesia's impressive agricultural performance — from the largest importer of rice to a net exporter in less than 20 years — has been achieved with a substantial use of fertilisers and pesticides which were heavily subsidised by the Government. The indiscriminate use of chemicals caused serious ecological problems, e.g. pollution of coastal waters and poisoning of the areas used for breeding fish and shrimps. Furthermore, it has eliminated the predators of the brown plant-hopper, encouraging the growth of this insect and its resistance to chemicals. The negative effects of this environmental degradation took the form of damage to the rice crop.

There are also output and employment implications arising from the overuse of agricultural technology. However, data on the quantitative employment impact of changes in fertiliser and pesticide prices, for example, are quite rare. One would need cross-price elasticities between fertilisers, machinery and labour (see Markandya, 1991, pp. 14-16). An increase in the price of fertiliser may lead to a decline in the use of labour,

Box 8. The impact of the Green Revolution on employment, income and environment in rural Bangladesh

Recently, three surveys were undertaken in rural villages in Bangladesh to examine the impact of the so-called Green Revolution on environment and employment during the 1970s and 1980s. Findings confirmed that new seed varieties have more than doubled riced yields per hectare while increasing employment by 6-13 per cent. None the less, per capita incomes from market exchange have fallen in real terms and agricultural productivity gains are lagging behind a 2.5 per cent rate of population growth per annum.

Income available from non-exchange sources has also declined. This trend is a sequel of deforestation and the replacement of orchard trees owing to the demand for additional land for the cultivation of rice (Bangladesh is a rice importer). The loss of trees has reduced access to fuelwood, wild honey, fruit and herbal medicine. Moreover, livestock and poultry numbers have declined with the greater scarcity of land.

The Green Revolution has relied heavily on the use of (imported) inorganic fertilisers and pesticides, which are now recognised to bring adverse environmental effects. Water pollution has resulted in a decline of 60-75 per cent of the amount of fish raised in rice paddies. Other aspects of environmental degradation are reduced soil fertility, soil erosion, and a narrower genetic diversity (most rice farmers now depend on only two varieties).

It seems that with time the vulnerability of small farmers has increased. The sale of smallholdings is a common event, and an increase in landlessness has been observed.

Source: Alauddin et al. (1991).

as seems to be the case in Thailand (with tractor farming systems), India, Egypt and Taiwan, China. However, the demand for labour rises in the Philippines, Thailand (with animal power farming) and India (with paddy and cotton) (see Alicbusan and Sebastian, 1989; Markandya, 1991).

The above examples do not suggest that the agricultural technology *per se* was bad or environmentally unfriendly. What they do show is that a misuse or excessive use of certain technologies can cause environmental degradation. This misuse of technology can often be attributed to wrong policies, which is the subject of the following section.

SOME POLICY ISSUES

In developed countries, where one of the main environmental problems so far has been one of pollution, the main policy instruments used are: a broad set of economic instruments, regulations, and specific programmes and projects, for the achievement of specific environmental objectives. These are discussed in Chapter 4. All these instruments are designed to compensate for a particular aspect of market failure vis-à-vis the environment and to ensure that environmental issues will be duly considered by individuals and firms in the market-place as well as by governments.

In developing countries with predominant agricultural and rural non-farm sectors, the situation is more difficult since markets operate less efficiently than in developed countries, or they are simply missing (see Chapter 2). Government intervention, which is often widespread, may tend to increase rather than reduce market failures and the misuse or misallocation of resources. For example, we noted above that in Indonesia the use of fertilisers and pesticides was heavily subsidised by the Government. The Indonesian farmers paid only about 10 to 20 per cent of the total cost of these inputs. A severe loss of rice production alone led to a shift in government policies. The Indonesian Government has now banned the use of most of the chemicals. Only four chemicals are approved for distribution to the farmers. The agricultural subsidy policy has also been revised. This Indonesian experience suggests that both economic and non-economic instruments may need to be introduced in combination to check environmental degradation.

Government tax policies have also encouraged deforestation, for example. In the case of Nepal, prior to 1950, the peasants were forced "to clear large areas of upland Nepal" (Metz, 1991, pp. 805-820). Policy measures led to similar situation in the Palawan region in the Philippines (Lopez, 1987). For several decades, resettlement on reclaimed lands has been a part of the agrarian policy in the Philippines.

The above cases show that neither population pressures nor poverty can be blamed wholly for the deterioration of agricultural land. Often the process of deterioration is set off by specific policies that are sometimes part and parcel of agrarian strategies devised to promote large-farm agriculture (as in Latin America and the Philippines). In all the cases, the original balance between population and resources was disturbed. Indeed, in the Philippines it has been noted that the expelled indigenous communities of Palawan had developed sustainable agricultural practices which were suited to their original location but which in fact became lost with the resettlement programme and the arrival of immigrants (Lopez, 1987).

One specific policy that has encouraged the misuse of resources is agricultural price policy. Price support measures are usually introduced to ensure an adequate food supply at low prices for the urban population. When agricultural production is oriented towards export markets, export taxes are generally used to generate additional government revenue. These measures have often led to market distortions and damage to the environment. It is therefore crucial to aim at a consistent integration and compatibility of environmental and agricultural policies.

Support measures and mechanisms which promote the use of environmentally harmful practices or which lead to the overuse and/or misuse of technology, causing major environmental disruptions, will need to be revised. In other words, a first step towards an environmental policy in the rural areas of developing countries should be a reduction in price distortions. Although in the short run these distortions may promote an increase in production, in the long run they tend to damage the environment with negative consequences in terms of declining productivity and falling production. However, it must be recognised that these corrections, which were designed to reduce the negative impact of the application of technology and the intensity of land use, can result in increasing costs to the farmer and eventually to lower levels of production.

As noted in Chapter 4, economic instruments can be used to promote some activities or to discourage others. Thus, charges can be levied in order to prevent the conversion of land to agricultural uses which lead to environmental degradation. Similarly, subsidies or other incentives can be applied to speed up the adoption of environmentally sound agricultural practices and technology.

The targeting of economic measures for environmental purposes can be relevant both for the preservation of the environment and for increasing production. A uniform charge on fertiliser use will obviously have completely different effects on intensively exploited lands and marginal lands. For example, although in highly intensive farms a charge on fertilisers will serve the dual purpose of providing governmental revenues and reducing the negative impact of heavy fertilisation (pollution), it should be noted that in developing countries large intensive farms exist side by side with poorly exploited plots where the increasing use of fertilisers is likely to have beneficial effects. Thus, for example, it has been reported that, in the African semi-arid areas, subsidies may be more appropriate than charges, since inputs such as organic fertilisers have positive effects on land productivity. The formulation of policy should therefore be based on a combination of factors, i.e. farming characteristics such as size, crop culture, current level of intensification, ecological aspects such as soil characteristics, and technological features such as current levels of fertilisation, the use of organic versus inorganic fertilisers, mechanisation, etc.

While a considerable amount of research has been devoted to transferring agricultural technology from the temperate regions to the tropics, little attention, if any, has been paid to the techniques of its management. A proper management of agrochemicals in terms of quantity used, placement and time of their application should also form an important part of an environment-friendly technology policy. A suitable

World Commission on Environment and Development (WCED). 1987. *Our common future*. Oxford, Oxford University Press (also known as the Brundtland Report).

approach to integrated pest management, combined with the use of specific crop varieties that are resistant to stress or diseases, can minimise the negative environmental impact.

Technologies should be screened not only in relation to their short-term productivity potentials but also in terms of their long-term environmental implications, and their employment and income generation potential. Thus, the basic criteria for technology choice should include, among others: employment and income generation; the stabilisation of production at a level compatible with the potentialities of each specific environment; the minimisation of the use of non-renewable resources; and increasing efficiency in the use of scarce resources and of technologies that prevent soil erosion, permit the integration of crops with livestock, and preserve biodiversity. As noted in Chapter 2 in the context of sub-Saharan Africa, stagnant technology, inter alia, forces the poor to deplete natural or environmental capital. It should be the objective of technology policy to check environmental degradation through appropriate technological innovations. By making possible greater food production and distribution, and thus the satisfaction of basic needs, higher levels of technology can raise the level of sustainability.

Finally, one should also recognise the role which policies could play in influencing the pattern of consumption and production of agricultural and industrial products. Thus, fiscal policies could be used to restrain the consumption of those products that are not friendly to the environment, to the extent that the consumption of these products is determined by income. By the same token, policies aimed at reducing income inequalities could also discourage consumption (since it is positively correlated with income) of commodities that are not environment-friendly (e.g. automobiles, refrigerators, energy-intensive appliances). Similar arguments can be put forward with regard to the production of commodities that are not environment-friendly. Besides adopting appropriate technologies, one would have to consider policies influencing the scale of production as well as international trade. Clearly, these measures form an integral part of the development strategies which developing countries choose to adopt. It is in this context that one has to examine the compatibility of employment-oriented development strategies with the environmental objectives.

References

Alauddin, M. et al. 1991. *Employment, economic and environmental impact of natural resource utilisation in agriculture and forestry: Case studies from rural Bangladesh*. Draft manuscript. Geneva, ILO.

Alicbusan, A.; Sebastian, I. 1989. *Sustainable development issues in adjustment lending policies*. World Bank Environment Department Working Paper No. 6. Washington, DC, World Bank.

Asian Development Bank. 1991. *Asian Development Outlook*. Manila.

Bhagwati, J. 1988. "Poverty and public policy", in *World Development* (Oxford, Pergamon Press), Vol. 16, No. 5, pp. 539-556.

Bryer, D. 1991. "Oxfam's Overseas Director presenting the last Oxfam Report", quoted in *New Scientist* (London), No. 1789, 5 Oct.

Cornia, G. A. et al. 1987. *Adjustment with a human face: Protecting the vulnerable and promoting growth. A UNICEF study*. Oxford, Clarendon Press.

Dasgupta, P.; Maler, K. 1990. *The environment and emerging development issues*. Paper presented at the World Bank Conference on Development Economics, 26-27 April 1990.

Fearnside, M. 1986. "Agricultural plans for Brazil's Grande Carajas: Lost opportunity for sustainable local development", in *World Development* (Oxford, Pergamon Press), Vol. 14, No. 3, pp. 385-409.

Food and Agriculture Organization (FAO). 1986. *African agriculture: The next 25 years*. Annex II: "The land resource base". Rome.

——. 1988. "Tropical Forestry Plan Action", in *Unasylva* (Rome), Vol. 38, No. 152.

Goldemberg, J. et al. 1988. *Energy for a sustainable world*. New Delhi, Wiley Eastern.

Hardin, G. 1968. "The tragedy of the commons", in *Science* (Washington, DC), Vol. 162.

Hecht, S. 1983. "La deforestación en la Cuenca del Amazonas: Magnitud, dinámica y efectos sobre los recursos edáficos", in ECLA/UNEP/CIFCA: *Expansión de la frontera agropecuaria y medio ambiente en América Latina*. Madrid, CIFCA.

International Union for Conservation of Nature and Natural Resources/United Nations Environment Programme/World Wide Fund for Nature (IUCN/UNEP/WWF). 1991. *Caring for the Earth: A strategy for sustainable living*. Gland (Switzerland).

Jagannathan, V. J. 1990. *Poverty-environment linkages: Case study of West Java*. World Bank Environment Department Divisional Working Paper No. 1990-8. Washington, DC, World Bank.

——; Agunbiade, A. G. 1990. *Poverty-environment linkages in Nigeria: Issues for research*. World Bank Environment Department Divisional Working Paper No. 1990-7. Washington, DC, World Bank.

Jonish, J. 1991. *Sustainable development and employment: The case of forestry in Malaysia*. Draft manuscript. Geneva, ILO.

Khanka, S. S. 1985. "Labour migration and its effects in a low developed region of Uttar Pradesh", in Single, J. S. (ed.): *Environmental regeneration in the Himalaya: Concepts and strategies*. New Delhi, Kay-Kay Printers.

Kumar, S. K.; Hotchkiss, D. 1988. *Consequences of deforestation for women's time allocation: Agricultural production and nutrition in the hill areas of Nepal*. Research Report No. 69. Washington, DC, International Food Policy Research Institute.

Lanly, J. P. 1982. *Tropical forest resources*. FAO Forestry Paper No. 3. Rome, FAO/UNEP.

Leonard, H. J., et al. 1989. *Environment and the poor: Development strategies for a common agenda*. Washington, DC, Overseas Development Council.

Lopez, M. E. 1987. "The politics of lands at risk in a Phili[Little, P. D. et al.: *Lands at risk in the Third W perspectives*. Boulder, Colorado, Westview Press.

Markandya, A. 1991. *Technology, environment and emplc* Mimeographed WEP working paper (WEP 2-22/WP.216

Metz, J. J. 1991. "A reassessment of the causes and se\ environmental crisis", in *World Development* (Oxford, Vol. 19, No. 7.

Myers, N. 1989. "The environmental basis of sustainable c World Bank: *Environment management and econon* Baltimore, Maryland, Johns Hopkins University Press.

Nelson, M. 1983. *The development of tropical lands*. Baltir Johns Hopkins University Press.

Nelson, R. 1988. *Dryland management: The "desertification"* Bank Environment Department Working Paper No. 8. W World Bank.

Organization for Economic Co-operation and Development *The state of the environment*. Paris.

Parikh, K.; Rabar, F. 1981. *Food for all in a sustainable world: 7 and Agriculture Programme*. Conference paper, Internation Applied Systems Analysis/Food and Agriculture Programme Conference. Laxenburg (Austria), 1981.

Perrings, C. 1991. *Incentives for the ecologically sustainable use natural resources in the drylands of sub-Saharan Afric* Mimeographed WEP working paper (WEP 2-22/WP.219). G

Repetto, R.; Holmes, J. 1983. "The role of population in resourc developing countries", in *Population and Development Revie\ Population Council), Vol. 9, No. 4.

Sen, A., 1987. *Poverty and famines: An essay on entitlement and* Oxford, Clarendon Press.

Swindale, L. D. 1985. *Sorghum in Africa: Problems and prospects f advances in production*. Paper presented at the Workshop on A Poverty and Starvation and Improvement of Health, Genev 1985.

United Nations. 1977. *United Nations Conference on Desertificatio and consequences*. Oxford, Pergamon Press.

United Nations Development Programme (UNDP). 199(*Development Report 1990*. New York, Oxford University Press

United Nations Economic Commission for Latin America and the (ECLAC). 1991. *El desarrollo sustenable: Transformación equidad y medio ambiente*. Santiago (Chile).

United Nations Environment Programme (UNEP). 1992a. *desertification and implementation of the United Nations Plan o Combat Desertification*. Report of the Executive Director. Nairc

——. 1992b. *Saving our planet: Challenges and hopes*, Nairobi.

United States Congress, Office of Technology Assessment. 1991. *developing countries*. Washington, DC.

World Bank. 1985. *Desertification in the Sahelian and Sudanian zone Africa*. Washington, DC.

——. 1990. *World Development Report 1990: Poverty*. Oxford York, Oxford University Press for the World Bank.

URBANISATION, EMPLOYMENT AND THE ENVIRONMENT

6

S. V. Sethuraman *
with the assistance of A. Ahmed **

Chapter 5 was concerned largely (though not exclusively) with the degradation of the rural environment in developing countries. This chapter deals with the relationship between the environment and urbanisation in these countries. Rapid growth in urban population and employment in most developing countries has been accompanied by environmental degradation, and it has become increasingly clear that, unless appropriate social, economic and environmental measures are taken now, present trends in urbanisation and urban development in the developing world cannot be sustained for long.

The proximate causes of urban environmental degradation are well known. They include air, water and noise pollution; insufficient sanitary facilities; inadequate liquid and solid waste disposal systems; land erosion; population and traffic congestion; and spatial imbalances in the distribution of urban centres. While there are variations in the levels and patterns of urban development among and within developing countries, most of these problems are common to all such countries. But they differ in magnitude and in the ways in which they become manifest in different developing country situations.

In this chapter, some conceptual issues regarding the relationship between urban development and the environment are discussed first. The patterns and levels of urbanisation in developing countries are then reviewed. The question of urban poverty and employment, which is one of the main reasons for concern in the context of urbanisation and environmental degradation, is discussed next. The chapter also looks at the importance of the urban informal sector in providing employment to growing numbers of the urban poor and the unemployed, and its link with the growing environmental problems that are associated with urban poverty. The regional environmental consequences of urban development

* ILO, Geneva. ** Institute of Development Studies, University of Sussex, Brighton (United Kingdom).

are also examined with particular emphasis on the spatial aspects. Finally, policy issues concerning the urban environment and employment are discussed, with a view to identifying policies that could lead to higher levels of urban employment without compromising the environmental objective.

Urbanisation is not only a process of economic development, but a direct consequence of anthropogenic intervention in natural environments, following which physical space is converted into built environments. Thus, natural systems are turned into human settlements. Urbanisation should therefore be seen to be as much a process of interaction between natural and built environments as an economic process.

It is through the interplay of economic forces that transformation of this kind take place. The market determines the extent to which the transformation is economically feasible and viable. The present concern with sustainable development is an acknowledgement that the current mode, rate and process of exploitation of the natural environment and urbanisation are far from optimal from a social point of view, and hence need to be checked urgently.

It is the market allocation of resources within the economy that often leads to unsustainable patterns of environmental resource use. It is not only the logic of the free market that allows the rich to exploit the environment: the condition of poverty too leads the poor to exploit their surroundings in ways and at rates that are unsustainable in the future. As noted in Chapters 2 and 5, the necessities of the poor, and their living and working conditions, drive them to "overexploit" the environment, leading to "forced" environmental degradation. Since a large proportion of the urban population in developing countries live in a state of poverty, economic and institutional transformation to alleviate poverty could be a first step towards arresting the degradation of the urban environment. By creating employment and income opportunities for the poor and by providing access to essential amenities, the negative impact on the environment could be reduced, if not eliminated. This is not to say, however, that the elimination of poverty would in itself be sufficient to prevent environmental degradation.

PATTERNS AND LEVELS OF URBANISATION IN DEVELOPING COUNTRIES

The report of the World Commission on Environment and Development (1987) labelled this century as the "century of the urban revolution". By 1970, a quarter of the total population in developing countries were living in urban areas. This had increased to over a third by 1990. It is projected by the United Nations, that by the first quarter of the approach to integrated pest management, combined with the use of specific crop varieties that are resistant to stress or diseases, can minimise the negative environmental impact.

Technologies should be screened not only in relation to their short-term productivity potentials but also in terms of their long-term environmental implications, and their employment and income generation potential. Thus, the basic criteria for technology choice should include, among others: employment and income generation; the stabilisation of production at a level compatible with the potentialities of each specific environment; the minimisation of the use of non-renewable resources; and increasing efficiency in the use of scarce resources and of technologies that prevent soil erosion, permit the integration of crops with livestock, and preserve biodiversity. As noted in Chapter 2 in the context of sub-Saharan Africa, stagnant technology, inter alia, forces the poor to deplete natural or environmental capital. It should be the objective of technology policy to check environmental degradation through appropriate technological innovations. By making possible greater food production and distribution, and thus the satisfaction of basic needs, higher levels of technology can raise the level of sustainability.

Finally, one should also recognise the role which policies could play in influencing the pattern of consumption and production of agricultural and industrial products. Thus, fiscal policies could be used to restrain the consumption of those products that are not friendly to the environment, to the extent that the consumption of these products is determined by income. By the same token, policies aimed at reducing income inequalities could also discourage consumption (since it is positively correlated with income) of commodities that are not environment-friendly (e.g. automobiles, refrigerators, energy-intensive appliances). Similar arguments can be put forward with regard to the production of commodities that are not environment-friendly. Besides adopting appropriate technologies, one would have to consider policies influencing the scale of production as well as international trade. Clearly, these measures form an integral part of the development strategies which developing countries choose to adopt. It is in this context that one has to examine the compatibility of employment-oriented development strategies with the environmental objectives.

References

Alauddin, M. et al. 1991. *Employment, economic and environmental impact of natural resource utilisation in agriculture and forestry: Case studies from rural Bangladesh.* Draft manuscript. Geneva, ILO.

Alicbusan, A.; Sebastian, I. 1989. *Sustainable development issues in adjustment lending policies.* World Bank Environment Department Working Paper No. 6. Washington, DC, World Bank.

Asian Development Bank. 1991. *Asian Development Outlook.* Manila.

Bhagwati, J. 1988. "Poverty and public policy", in *World Development* (Oxford, Pergamon Press), Vol. 16, No. 5, pp. 539-556.

Bryer, D. 1991. "Oxfam's Overseas Director presenting the last Oxfam Report", quoted in *New Scientist* (London), No. 1789, 5 Oct.

Cornia, G. A. et al. 1987. *Adjustment with a human face: Protecting the vulnerable and promoting growth. A UNICEF study.* Oxford, Clarendon Press.

Dasgupta, P.; Maler, K. 1990. *The environment and emerging development issues.* Paper presented at the World Bank Conference on Development Economics, 26-27 April 1990.

Fearnside, M. 1986. "Agricultural plans for Brazil's Grande Carajas: Lost opportunity for sustainable local development", in *World Development* (Oxford, Pergamon Press), Vol. 14, No. 3, pp. 385-409.

Food and Agriculture Organization (FAO). 1986. *African agriculture: The next 25 years.* Annex II: "The land resource base". Rome.

———. 1988. "Tropical Forestry Plan Action", in *Unasylva* (Rome), Vol. 38, No. 152.

Goldemberg, J. et al. 1988. *Energy for a sustainable world.* New Delhi, Wiley Eastern.

Hardin, G. 1968. "The tragedy of the commons", in *Science* (Washington, DC), Vol. 162.

Hecht, S. 1983. "La deforestación en la Cuenca del Amazonas: Magnitud, dinámica y efectos sobre los recursos edáficos", in ECLA/UNEP/CIFCA: *Expansión de la frontera agropecuaria y medio ambiente en América Latina.* Madrid, CIFCA.

International Union for Conservation of Nature and Natural Resources/United Nations Environment Programme/World Wide Fund for Nature (IUCN/UNEP/WWF). 1991. *Caring for the Earth: A strategy for sustainable living.* Gland (Switzerland).

Jagannathan, V. J. 1990. *Poverty-environment linkages: Case study of West Java.* World Bank Environment Department Divisional Working Paper No. 1990-8. Washington, DC, World Bank.

———; Agunbiade, A. G. 1990. *Poverty-environment linkages in Nigeria: Issues for research.* World Bank Environment Department Divisional Working Paper No. 1990-7. Washington, DC, World Bank.

Jonish, J. 1991. *Sustainable development and employment: The case of forestry in Malaysia.* Draft manuscript. Geneva, ILO.

Khanka, S. S. 1985. "Labour migration and its effects in a low developed region of Uttar Pradesh", in Single, J. S. (ed.): *Environmental regeneration in the Himalaya: Concepts and strategies.* New Delhi, Kay-Kay Printers.

Kumar, S. K.; Hotchkiss, D. 1988. *Consequences of deforestation for women's time allocation: Agricultural production and nutrition in the hill areas of Nepal.* Research Report No. 69. Washington, DC, International Food Policy Research Institute.

Lanly, J. P. 1982. *Tropical forest resources.* FAO Forestry Paper No. 3. Rome, FAO/UNEP.

Leonard, H. J., et al. 1989. *Environment and the poor: Development strategies for a common agenda.* Washington, DC, Overseas Development Council.

Lopez, M. E. 1987. "The politics of lands at risk in a Philippine frontier", in Little, P. D. et al.: *Lands at risk in the Third World: Local level perspectives.* Boulder, Colorado, Westview Press.

Markandya, A. 1991. *Technology, environment and employment: A survey.* Mimeographed WEP working paper (WEP 2-22/WP.216). Geneva, ILO.

Metz, J. J. 1991. "A reassessment of the causes and severity of Nepal's environmental crisis", in *World Development* (Oxford, Pergamon Press), Vol. 19, No. 7.

Myers, N. 1989. "The environmental basis of sustainable development", in World Bank: *Environment management and economic development.* Baltimore, Maryland, Johns Hopkins University Press.

Nelson, M. 1983. *The development of tropical lands.* Baltimore, Maryland, Johns Hopkins University Press.

Nelson, R. 1988. *Dryland management: The "desertification" problem.* World Bank Environment Department Working Paper No. 8. Washington, DC, World Bank.

Organization for Economic Co-operation and Development (OECD). 1985. *The state of the environment.* Paris.

Parikh, K.; Rabar, F. 1981. *Food for all in a sustainable world: The IIASA Food and Agriculture Programme.* Conference paper, International Institute for Applied Systems Analysis/Food and Agriculture Programme Status Report Conference. Laxenburg (Austria), 1981.

Perrings, C. 1991. *Incentives for the ecologically sustainable use of human and natural resources in the drylands of sub-Saharan Africa: A review.* Mimeographed WEP working paper (WEP 2-22/WP.219). Geneva, ILO.

Repetto, R.; Holmes, J. 1983. "The role of population in resource depletion in developing countries", in *Population and Development Review* (New York, Population Council), Vol. 9, No. 4.

Sen, A., 1987. *Poverty and famines: An essay on entitlement and deprivation.* Oxford, Clarendon Press.

Swindale, L. D. 1985. *Sorghum in Africa: Problems and prospects for significant advances in production.* Paper presented at the Workshop on Alleviation of Poverty and Starvation and Improvement of Health, Geneva, 8-11 July 1985.

United Nations. 1977. *United Nations Conference on Desertification: Its causes and consequences.* Oxford, Pergamon Press.

United Nations Development Programme (UNDP). 1990. *Human Development Report 1990.* New York, Oxford University Press.

United Nations Economic Commission for Latin America and the Caribbean (ECLAC). 1991. *El desarrollo sustenable: Transformación productiva, equidad y medio ambiente.* Santiago (Chile).

United Nations Environment Programme (UNEP). 1992a. *Status of desertification and implementation of the United Nations Plan of Action to Combat Desertification.* Report of the Executive Director. Nairobi.

———. 1992b. *Saving our planet: Challenges and hopes,* Nairobi.

United States Congress, Office of Technology Assessment. 1991. *Energy in developing countries.* Washington, DC.

World Bank. 1985. *Desertification in the Sahelian and Sudanian zones of West Africa.* Washington, DC.

———. 1990. *World Development Report 1990: Poverty.* Oxford and New York, Oxford University Press for the World Bank.

World Commission on Environment and Development (WCED). 1987. *Our common future*. Oxford, Oxford University Press (also known as the Brundtland Report).

URBANISATION, EMPLOYMENT AND THE ENVIRONMENT

6

S. V. Sethuraman *
with the assistance of A. Ahmed **

Chapter 5 was concerned largely (though not exclusively) with the degradation of the rural environment in developing countries. This chapter deals with the relationship between the environment and urbanisation in these countries. Rapid growth in urban population and employment in most developing countries has been accompanied by environmental degradation, and it has become increasingly clear that, unless appropriate social, economic and environmental measures are taken now, present trends in urbanisation and urban development in the developing world cannot be sustained for long.

The proximate causes of urban environmental degradation are well known. They include air, water and noise pollution; insufficient sanitary facilities; inadequate liquid and solid waste disposal systems; land erosion; population and traffic congestion; and spatial imbalances in the distribution of urban centres. While there are variations in the levels and patterns of urban development among and within developing countries, most of these problems are common to all such countries. But they differ in magnitude and in the ways in which they become manifest in different developing country situations.

In this chapter, some conceptual issues regarding the relationship between urban development and the environment are discussed first. The patterns and levels of urbanisation in developing countries are then reviewed. The question of urban poverty and employment, which is one of the main reasons for concern in the context of urbanisation and environmental degradation, is discussed next. The chapter also looks at the importance of the urban informal sector in providing employment to growing numbers of the urban poor and the unemployed, and its link with the growing environmental problems that are associated with urban poverty. The regional environmental consequences of urban development

---

* ILO, Geneva. ** Institute of Development Studies, University of Sussex, Brighton (United Kingdom).

are also examined with particular emphasis on the spatial aspects. Finally, policy issues concerning the urban environment and employment are discussed, with a view to identifying policies that could lead to higher levels of urban employment without compromising the environmental objective.

Urbanisation is not only a process of economic development, but a direct consequence of anthropogenic intervention in natural environments, following which physical space is converted into built environments. Thus, natural systems are turned into human settlements. Urbanisation should therefore be seen to be as much a process of interaction between natural and built environments as an economic process.

It is through the interplay of economic forces that transformation of this kind take place. The market determines the extent to which the transformation is economically feasible and viable. The present concern with sustainable development is an acknowledgement that the current mode, rate and process of exploitation of the natural environment and urbanisation are far from optimal from a social point of view, and hence need to be checked urgently.

It is the market allocation of resources within the economy that often leads to unsustainable patterns of environmental resource use. It is not only the logic of the free market that allows the rich to exploit the environment: the condition of poverty too leads the poor to exploit their surroundings in ways and at rates that are unsustainable in the future. As noted in Chapters 2 and 5, the necessities of the poor, and their living and working conditions, drive them to "overexploit" the environment, leading to "forced" environmental degradation. Since a large proportion of the urban population in developing countries live in a state of poverty, economic and institutional transformation to alleviate poverty could be a first step towards arresting the degradation of the urban environment. By creating employment and income opportunities for the poor and by providing access to essential amenities, the negative impact on the environment could be reduced, if not eliminated. This is not to say, however, that the elimination of poverty would in itself be sufficient to prevent environmental degradation.

PATTERNS AND LEVELS OF URBANISATION IN DEVELOPING COUNTRIES

The report of the World Commission on Environment and Development (1987) labelled this century as the "century of the urban revolution". By 1970, a quarter of the total population in developing countries were living in urban areas. This had increased to over a third by 1990. It is projected by the United Nations, that by the first quarter of the

Figure 2.   Levels of urbanisation in developing countries, 1970-2025

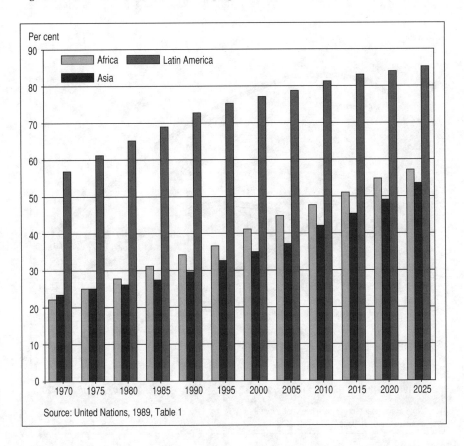

Source: United Nations, 1989, Table 1

next century, over half of the population of developing countries — about 4 billion — will be living in urban areas (see United Nations, 1989b).

While a significant and rapidly increasing degree of urbanisation is projected for the developing world as a whole, there is considerable variation among and within regions, in terms of both the level and the rates of urbanisation. As figure 2 shows, the level of urbanisation in Latin America in 1970 was more than twice as high as that of Africa (22 per cent), and Asia (23 per cent) with well over 50 per cent of the population residing in urban areas. While the level of urbanisation in all regions is projected to rise during the coming decades and beyond, the rate of urbanisation is expected to fall in Latin American countries and rise in Africa and Asia: in Latin America the increase in urban population is estimated at 20 per cent between 1990 and 2000, while for African and Asian countries the corresponding figure is placed at 40 per cent.

Figure 3. Average annual urban growth rate, 1970-2025

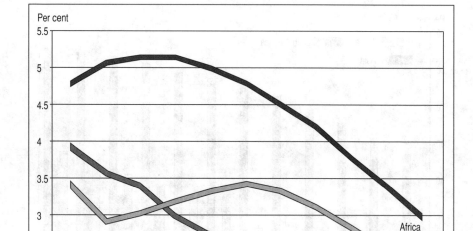

Note: Each year represents a five year interval
Source: United Nations, 1989, Table 3

Figure 3 shows that urbanisation is most rapid in African countries, but that in all regions the rates are expected to decline in the future. However, in absolute terms African and Asian countries should continue to experience rapid urban growth, partly because of the rapid increase in the population. The rapid growth of cities in developing countries means that, of the world's 21 megacities which are expected to expand to have over 10 million people, 17 will be in the developing countries (World Bank, 1991a).

One of the main reasons for the increase in urban population is internal migration. The main causes of rural to urban migration are higher urban wages, the availability of better services such as education and health, and of other amenities in urban areas, and declining rural employment. At present, however, natural increase is a more important reason for urban growth than is migration. With much of the urban population in the reproductive age groups, natural increase will be the main factor contributing to urban population growth in the coming years.

Urban centres account for much of national production and consumption; the very large cities often make a disproportionate contribution to GDP (Singh, 1989): for example, in Brazil, 8 per cent of the country's population lived in Greater São Paulo in 1970, generating 36 per cent of the country's GDP; in India, 20 per cent of the country's population lived in urban areas in 1970-71, contributing 40 per cent to GDP; in China, Shanghai alone accounted for one-eighth of the country's GDP in 1980, even though only about 1 per cent of the population lived there; in Kenya, Nairobi accounted for 20 per cent of the GDP, with only 5.2 per cent of the population living there.

While urban areas in developing countries continue to grow in size and in economic importance, many of these countries, particularly in Africa, have experienced problems from the 1980s onwards. Economic decline and subsequent macro-economic adjustment at a time when the urban labour force was expanding tended to increase urban poverty and unemployment. For example, a recent study on labour in sub-Saharan Africa found that the urban unemployment rate in the region increased from about 10 per cent in the 1970s to about 30 per cent in the mid-1980s (ILO/JASPA, 1988).

Further, as can be seen from table 12, there is a strong correlation between urban unemployment and poverty. However, as the rise and persistence of the urban informal sector shows, the poor cannot afford to remain openly unemployed for long periods of time. According to the World Bank, in 1988 some 330 million urban residents, or about a quarter of the total urban population, lived in poverty. Therefore, if the problems of urban poverty are not addressed now, the Bank predicts that "urban poverty will become the most significant and politically explosive problem in the next century" (World Bank, 1991a, p. 19).

THE URBAN INFORMAL SECTOR AND THE ENVIRONMENT

The growth in unemployment in urban areas has, to a considerable extent, been mitigated by the growth in employment in what is known as the informal sector. An increasing proportion of the urban labour force in developing countries derive their income through employment in this sector. Informal activities range from informal transport and housing construction to manufacturing and the services provided by, for instances, vehicle repairers, shoeshine boys and vendors and hawkers selling a range of agricultural and non-agricultural goods. Food production is also a major source of employment and income for many of the poor in some of the rapidly growing cities in parts of Africa, Asia and the South Pacific.

125

Table 12. Urban unemployment and poverty

Urban area	Poverty or income group			
	Very poor	Poor	Middle	High
Urban Costa Rica, 1982				
Unemployment rate	11.0	6.0	2.0	2.0
Guatemala City, 1980				
Unemployment rate	5.0	2.9	4.7	1.9
Including discouraged workers	10.6	10.8	10.0	7.7
Including estimated under-employment	20.6	19.6	10.0	7.7
Metropolitan Panama, 1983				
Unemployment rate	14.8	11.1	3.8	3.8
Santiago de Chile 1982				
Unemployment rate, heads	50.0	18.3	5.3	5.3
Unemployment rate, spouses	25.5	19.4	6.8	6.8
Santiago de Chile, 1985				
Unemployment rate, heads	23.7	9.1	3.1	3.1
Unemployment rate, spouses	23.4	14.6	4.5	4.5
Urban West Bengal, 1977-78				
Percentage of household members unemployed	9.5	11.4	7.8	6.0
Percentage of unemployed for more than 12 months	74	78	83	84

Source: Derived from Rodgers (1989), p. 17.

ILO studies on the urban informal sector (for example, ILO/PREALC, 1978; Sethuraman, 1981; ILO/JASPA, 1989; ILO, 1991) suggest that anywhere between a quarter and three-quarters of urban employment, especially in large cities, is to be found not in the government or in the large private enterprises but in very small-scale activities, mostly operated by the self-employed, in the informal sector. Micro-enterprises with up to ten workers per enterprise, particularly in manufacturing, also form a significant part of the informal sector.

Besides being small in scale, these informal units tend to employ the workers with very little schooling and skills. They are also mostly poor, lacking the necessary resources for investment. Thus they tend to spend little capital per worker and use simple technologies. What is perhaps more important from the point of view of the environment is that the sector lacks the minimum necessary infrastructure. Studies on the urban informal sector by the ILO and others show clearly that only a fraction of these small vending and production units possess proper business premises in a fixed location, with a permanent structure. Some operate in residential premises, some are itinerant traders and many operate in the open without any fixed location, often on land that does not belong to them.

Since the sector includes at least some activities that are polluting and emit chemical and other toxic substances hazardous to health, clearly they have an adverse effect on the urban environment besides endangering the lives of the workers. A large proportion of employment in the informal sector, especially among women, is in the preparation and vending of food in streets, which has a bearing on public health and hygiene. Informal means of transport, an important component of the sector by virtue of their large numbers, contribute to traffic congestion and to atmospheric pollution from vehicles using leaded fuel. Quite often transport vehicles from the informal sector (such as two- and three-wheelers, a form of motor transport that is highly polluting) are themselves responsible for air pollution in big cities. Finally, another characteristic of the informal sector is that the small units, owing to their limited access to open land, tend to concentrate in and around slum and squatter locations leading to excessive crowding. Crowding in itself is not bad for the environment; what makes it bad is the absence of an adequate support infrastructure, such as drinking water, waste disposal, housing, transport, sewage treatment systems and the like. The concentration of the residential population is in part derived from the concentration of informal sector employment, since most studies show that workers in this sector live and work in the same area.

Several policy implications for the environment emerge from the above. First, uncertainty about the tenure of the premises resulting from the reluctance of city authorities to authorise the business location and to confer legal recognition has prevented the informal units from investing in and improving their business premises. Second, and related to the above, the urban authorities have failed to improve the functioning of the land market, which is riddled with intractable land laws and regulations, and are reluctant to regularise land tenure. Consequently, they have contributed to excessive overcrowding in specific locations where property rights are not well defined. Third, the failure of the authorities to develop an appropriate infrastructure, especially public transport, roads and communications, would also seem to have contributed to overcrowding in selected city locations by discouraging people from moving out. Measures to remedy the above would no doubt form an integral part of the strategy to improve the urban environment. Whether such measures are effective or not depends on the willingness and capacity of the informal sector producers to respond favourably to such changes, as discussed below.

One of the major constraints in this respect is the low income of informal sector producers and workers. Low incomes limit the scope for making additional business investments, improvements in technologies and conditions of work, including the environment. According to an ILO study there is a significant overlap between urban poverty and the informal sector (Rodgers, 1989). Perhaps three-quarters of those in the informal sector earn incomes below what may be considered as the poverty line. Raising the incomes of these workers should therefore be given priority if an improvement in urban environment is to be expected (see section on "Policy issues" below).

It should, however, be noted that certain activities in the urban informal sector, for example the collection and recycling of materials such as paper, plastic, metal, glass, etc., do contribute positively to the urban environment and to the saving of resources. Likewise, in several cities of the developing world, the collection and disposal of garbage is essentially an activity carried out by workers in the informal sector and thus makes a direct contribution to the urban environment. This illustrates the scope for promoting employment in urban areas while at the same time improving the urban environment. What is required to achieve these two objectives is a set of policies that would lead to greater efficiency and equity. For example, is it possible to organise the collection and disposal of garbage in a more efficient way, which would also raise the incomes of the workers concerned? Is it possible to extend such systems to countries where they are not known?

URBAN POVERTY AND THE ENVIRONMENT

As noted in Chapter 5, poverty and environment are closely related. This relationship, in the urban context, may be described as one of mutual causality. Not only does poverty lead to environmental degradation, but the converse is also true. The most obvious example of how the poor contribute to environmental degradation is of course in the use of energy for household consumption, as seen in Chapter 5. The urban poor in developing countries use traditional sources (wood, charcoal, crop and animal wastes) for 80 per cent of their energy consumption (Newland, 1980).

In India firewood accounts for about 50 per cent of the energy used for cooking in cities, especially among poor households. Similarly, in Botswana, for example, fuelwood represents 90 per cent of urban household energy consumption for cooking (World Bank, 1991c). The demand for fuelwood has increased substantially with the growing numbers of poor people in urban centres. One study reports that 223,600 tons of firewood were brought into Delhi during 1981-82 from the forests of Madhya Pradesh, 700 kilometres away (Centre for Science and Environment, 1989). This suggests that some of the most urgent regional environmental problems are directly related to the urban demand for firewood. It also follows that the pollution caused by energy use is particularly serious in slums and squats where population density is high.

The urban poor are mostly housed in slums and squatter settlements, which are by definition characterised by poor housing conditions and insufficient basic amenities such as drinking water and waste disposal and sanitary systems. In the developing countries as a whole, access to safe drinking water for urban residents increased on average from 65 to 75 per cent between 1970 and 1985 (UNEP, 1989). The aggregate picture, however, hides the magnitude of the problem within individual countries. For example, while tap water reaches 80 per cent of homes in Mexico City, in areas with the worst conditions about 40 to 46 per cent of the population lack water services; and although a sewage system reaches 70 per cent of the population, it is estimated that some 3 million people are not served (Schteingart, 1989). Areas or settlements with low-income workers and where infrastructural development is weak and urban population growth is most rapid are the worst served. In India, about 40 per cent of Calcutta's metropolitan population live in slums where "public taps have been dry ever since installation" (Centre for Science and Environment, 1989).

The urban poor who live in shacks built on illegal settlements or in temporary shelters are directly exposed to environmental hazards resulting from poor access to safe drinking water and the absence of sewage treatment facilities and other basic amenities. In their household and working environment, they are consequently exposed to pathogens and other harmful bacteria. Because of the cramped living conditions within such unhealthy environments, they are exposed to serious health hazards.

Exposure to such environmental hazards is particularly severe among households forced to live on the urban fringe where land values are lower. Besides their lack of access to water and sanitation systems, they are also exposed to other hazards: often their dwellings are built near rubbish dumps and sites for industrial wastes or on the banks of polluted rivers, near dangerous slopes or close to railway tracks and the like. Consequently, the poor are subjected not only to health hazards but also to air and noise pollution; they are also vulnerable to environmental disasters such as fire, flooding, landslides, etc.

Thus, not only do the poor contribute to environmental degradation, but deterioration in the urban environment affects them disproportionately. This has also been borne out by recent studies on atmospheric pollution and health carried out by the World Health Organization in selected cities of the developing countries.

One of the consequences of overcrowding in specific locations within urban centres is that people are more vulnerable to contagious diseases and epidemics. Overcrowding is, as observed earlier, in part due to the chaotic regulations affecting the land market: but, more importantly, it is also caused by the poor urban infrastructure, including roads, transport and communications. The absence of such infrastructure or the poor functioning of transport and communications induce firms and households to locate themselves in areas where they have easy access to markets.

URBAN TRANSPORT AND THE ENVIRONMENT

It does not follow from the above that the urban environment-employment nexus can be attributed to poverty alone. According to the *Asian Development Outlook 1991*, vehicle emissions in urban areas of Asia are the major source of air pollution, particularly because of the use of leaded fuel (Asian Development Bank, 1991b). For example, in Indian cities "gasoline-fueled vehicles — mostly two- and three-wheelers — are responsible for 85 per cent of carbon monoxide and 35 to 65 per cent of hydrocarbons, while diesel vehicles — buses and trucks — are responsible for over 90 per cent NO emissions" (United States Congress, Office of Technology Assessment, 1991, p. 15). Since the vast majority of the vehicles are privately owned and many are inefficient in fuel use, it is clear that high-income households also contribute to air pollution. Vehicle-generated emissions are expected at least to double, especially in Bangkok, Manila, Jakarta and Calcutta. The number of vehicles in South and South-East Asia is expected to more than double by the year 2000. Since this growth is rarely accompanied by a corresponding expansion of the network, it is certain to lead to increased congestion. In Bombay, for example, the average speed of vehicles is estimated to be only 13 kilometres per hour (see Deshpande and Deshpande, 1991).

INDUSTRIALISATION AND THE ENVIRONMENT

As noted earlier, urban centres in developing countries are also the major contributors to industrial output. About half the industrial value added in India, Indonesia, the Republic of Korea, the Philippines and Thailand is estimated to come from industries located in their largest urban centres, in and around which industrial pollution is consequently concentrated.

Much of the industrial waste in urban centres is disposed of untreated in rivers, canals and the like (Asian Development Bank, 1991b, pp. 222 and 246; see also HABITAT, 1989). Further, as the industrial structure changes toward industrial chemicals, electroplating and machinery, industrial effluents contain more and more non-degradable toxic or hazardous wastes which pose high health risks, as well as threatening coastal and estuarine fisheries on which the rural population depend for their livelihood. Thus industries not only create jobs but also contribute to environmental degradation. To the extent that this degradation spills over into rural areas and affects employment adversely, it is likely to encourage further rural-urban migration and lead to a vicious circle, thereby aggravating the urban problems.

The implication is that the urban environment in developing countries is likely to get worse with industrial growth if they follow the pattern of the past, i.e. locating industries in and around major urban centres. The remedial policies and measures discussed in Chapter 4 would no doubt minimise, if not eliminate, the harmful effects on the environment. Equally important is the need to consider the spatial dispersal of industrial development away from large urban centres.

POLICY ISSUES

A number of issues that are relevant to policy formulation emerge from the above. First, of course, is the question of population. Some cities in the developing world, especially in sub-Saharan Africa, are growing at an incredible rate of between 5 and 10 per cent per year. This suggests that the urban environment can be expected to deteriorate rapidly unless appropriate remedial measures are taken now. Besides policies to contain population growth in general, one has to deal with rural-urban migration as well. Though the importance of migration as a factor contributing to urban population growth has somewhat diminished in recent years, in many parts of the developing world it is still a major factor. Besides national policies to discourage rural exodus through rural employment promotion, one also has to consider the scope for decentralised urban development. A number of countries have sought to develop secondary cities, regional growth poles and so on, but few of these attempts have been successful. Further, it is not evident that through decentralised development of this kind it is possible to improve both urban employment and the urban environment. To the extent that urban crowding is the result of externalities (both positive and negative), one could attempt to use the economic instruments discussed in Chapter 4 (see the discussion below). If, however, there are large economies of scale in big cities, attempts based on fiscal policies may have only a limited impact on urban growth.

After population one must consider the question of urban poverty. Recent evidence seems to suggest that urban poverty may be increasing, partly owing to the implementation of structural adjustment programmes. In so far as the vast majority of the urban labour force depend on their own labour for income, it is clear that labour market instruments designed to improve efficiency and equity should play an important role in any strategy for urban poverty alleviation. In this context one should also consider the gamut of policies for urban employment promotion in all sectors — most of which are related to the overall economic performance. Since many in the informal sector obtain income from their own business, the strategy should also include interventions to raise the productivity of workers and the returns to investment in this sector. The literature on the urban informal sector suggests a number of ways to reach this goal. Briefly, these include changes in the policy and regulatory framework concerning the informal sector, integrating it into mainstream development, improving access to credit, inputs and product markets by small-scale producers, upgrading their technologies, and so on.

Poverty alleviation strategies, by raising the incomes of urban households, can contribute towards improving the urban environment. With increased purchasing power these households would have the capacity to pay for better urban services and hence generate an effective demand for them. They would also be able to shift towards sources of energy that are less polluting. But with increased incomes one should also expect a higher demand for energy, at both the household consumption and the production levels. Evidence from countries seems to suggest that energy consumption is highly elastic with respect to industrialisation and changes in income. Further urbanisation itself has a statistically measurable and independent impact on energy consumption even when industrialisation and income are held constant. It is estimated that "a 10 per cent increase in the proportion of the population living in cities would increase modern energy consumption by 4.5 per cent or by 4.8 per cent GDP" (Jones, 1991). Because of the high income elasticity of energy consumption, governments need to be sensitive to the patterns of income distribution when devising energy and technology policies. Of equal importance are the energy and pricing policies and the strategies for urban development.

Policies concerning energy use therefore play a vital role in improving the urban environment. Among other sectoral policies one should, of course, include urban transport. Most cities in developing countries are facing serious problems in the area of transport management — especially traffic congestion and air pollution resulting from the use of fossil-based fuels. Are there more efficient ways to organise urban transport? The answer is, of course, "yes". For example, one could consider mass transport systems that are both fuel efficient and at the same time relieve urban traffic congestion. But such a solution also raises questions about employment trade-offs in large- and small-scale transport, management capability and so on (see discussion below).

The provision of urban services, including housing, water supply, sewage treatment facilities, etc., is essentially in the public sector, although there are a few exceptions. One of the key issues in this area is the sector's ability to respond (supply rigidities) to growing demand, which naturally hinges on resource availability and management. Another issue is their ability to provide them at the lowest cost, so that such services become widely accessible to the poor. As one author observed, "urban areas are outgrowing their governments' capabilities. Local governments have inadequate authority to coordinate activities beyond their own boundaries, and their political power and resources are inadequate for project implementation" (Renaud, 1989). It would be important to strengthen the capacities of city governments to carry out regulatory and institutional reform. Their regulatory capacities are important in reforming the laws and regulations relating to informal and formal sector activities. Most of all, an enabling strategy would involve strengthening the financial capacities of city governments and municipalities by creating additional tax and revenue bases (partly by redesigning the existing ones) or through external borrowing. Whilst recognising the limitations of the public sector to do this, one notes a growing pressure to find alternative solutions such as the greater involvement of the private sector and community-based self-help organisations.

Localised micro-economic policies are also important in promoting employment at the sectoral level. In the present context of the environment it should be noted that, apart from the living and working environment, one of the most direct ways in which informal employment and the environment are related is through waste recycling and reuse. For example, the Zabaleen community in Cairo, located on the fringe of the old city, uses labour-intensive methods to recycle a range of rubbish items ranging from paper, plastic, metals, glass and textiles to bone. Using modernised equipment with the help of a newly formed Environmental Protection Agency, the community's activities are now systematised. This has drastically improved the employment and income opportunities of the people (UNDP, 1990).

PROMOTING URBAN EMPLOYMENT AND THE ENVIRONMENT ON A SUSTAINABLE BASIS: SOME PROMISING APPROACHES

Urbanisation in developing countries is playing an important role in allocating labour and other resources and is thus contributing to efficient economic growth. People migrate to cities because that is where income and earning opportunities are available and that is where wealth is created. Empirical studies also show that the productivity of both labour and capital is higher in large cities than in small towns (Townroe, 1979). The issue is then whether this process can continue without harming the urban environment. In spite of the growth in urban employment, particularly in the informal sector, urban poverty persists. What policies are required to make the progress of urban development more efficient and equitable? Since the urban environment is also influenced by industrialisation, another question for consideration is whether industries should be allowed to continue and expand in urban centres, and if so under what conditions. Urban development would no doubt increase the demand for energy and transport; one issue then is whether this demand can be met without causing environmental degradation. Finally, there is the question of improving shelter and other urban services to match the projected needs of the growing urban population; for if they fail to match, the result would be environmental degradation.

The discussion in the preceding section suggests that there are indeed key areas in which policies need to be so designed as to take environmental concerns into account. Besides policies and measures to raise incomes of the urban poor, a major area for policy is to improve the physical environment in which the poor live. This calls for substantial investment in infrastructure such as housing, roads, water supply, waste disposal mechanisms, and so on. To the extent that these services are provided on a cost-effective basis, they have a greater chance of being within the reach of the poor. Besides appropriate technologies, innovative mechanisms such as community participation have been tried (for example, the Kampong Improvement Programmes in Jakarta and self-help organisations in shelter construction in Lusaka); lessons based on such experiences may be relevant and useful to other countries. Finding the resources for the initial investment in infrastructure development has proved to be a major obstacle in many developing countries. A number of studies, especially by the World Bank and HABITAT, have examined the issue of city revenues to meet development expenditures. Deficiencies in the capacity of the public sector to supply such services have led to a search for alternatives, in particular greater participation by the private sector, including the informal sector.

Perhaps the major challenge is in the area of regulations as they affect the functioning of markets. Certain regulations, especially in shelter construction, have been modified in the past two decades with a view to lowering the standards and hence the costs. But such efforts to deregulate in the context of urban land and housing rent control have been slow to come about, owing to severe legal problems, e.g. in modifying legal instruments and institutions. This suggests that the solutions to these problems are essentially of a long-term nature.

Improvements in the physical environment in which the urban poor live may not be sustained if the population-infrastructure balance deteriorates over time, owing to unchecked rises in population density (i.e. the number of persons per square kilometre of floor area of living accommodation). Not only have many cities in the developing world shown variations in population density within the city but also the rate of change in density is uneven. To ensure that attempts to improve urban environment in developing countries are sustainable, it would seem necessary for the city authorities to find ways to control population densities. As in some developed countries, it would seem important to fix some "norms" with regard to acceptable levels of population density. Densities in excess of such norms may prove to be counterproductive; every increase in population density may be followed by a decrease in social benefits in terms of the environment. The marginal cost of improving the physical environment may well exceed the marginal benefits to society. Needless to say, the norms are likely to vary between countries. Viewed in this optique the urban authorities should consider fixing a norm beyond which population density may not be allowed to rise. Given the seriousness of urban poverty, the availability of land and so on, the authorities may not be in a position to change the density from its current level except in the long term. What they can attempt in the short term is to "seal" the density in specific locations at its current level and aim at a gradual reduction over the years through appropriate policies and instruments. The implementation of this idea no doubt poses a number of practical problems, including institutional capacity, and is consequently less appealing. But it is also a known fact that in some cities in developing countries there already exists a system of identification based on work permits, stay permits, ration cards and so on which could serve as a basis for experimenting with this idea. For the choice of the instruments many of the principles discussed in Chapters 2 and 3 would seem to be relevant. For example, to avoid excessive crowding the city authorities could explore the idea of imposing a tax on property owners (or lessees in cases where the property is leased out) when the norm of density (x number of persons per square metre of living space) is not respected. Such a tax would not only discourage property owners from contributing to an increase in population density; it would also raise the revenue of the city authorities. It goes without saying that this approach would be successful only if accompanied by other policies. For example, the authorities might have to develop alternative residential locations for new entrants, taking employment and other linkages into account, to develop more efficient transport and communication facilities, etc., so that the costs of moving out of crowded locations are fully compensated by benefits in other forms.

The second area for policy measures is concerned with energy. Although it is defined at the national level in most countries, especially through pricing, the city authorities would seem to have a role to play too. They may have to develop the appropriate infrastructure as well as use fiscal instruments to bring about a shift in the pattern of energy consumption by poor households. Such measures complement the poverty alleviation strategies: higher incomes would help the poor to change the pattern and sources of energy consumption. In some cases it may be possible to promote initiatives at the community level, e.g. community biogas plants to recycle organic wastes. Electricity derived from hydroelectric sources (which are considered environment friendly) could play an important role. Since much of the atmospheric pollution in Third World cities is caused by vehicles using leaded fuel, traffic congestion and obsolete vehicles that are inefficient in fuel use, there is an urgent need to review the transport systems and their efficiency, with a view to finding solutions to the problems of the environment.

Regional or city governments can influence the volume and pattern of traffic through appropriate instruments, with a view to minimising the impact on the environment. For instance, the State may wish to promote mass transport systems which are considered to be less costly, less energy intensive and less polluting per passenger transported; but it would imply a heavy initial investment and the loss of jobs in the informal petty transport sector. All the above measures may therefore involve some trade-off between the environment and employment. In bringing about these changes the principles discussed in Chapter 3 become relevant. For example, should there be a tax to reduce peak hour traffic, as was done in Singapore? Or should there be a tax on road users? Should the tax vary as a function of energy consumed per head? Singapore, which in 1975 introduced what is known as the "area licensing scheme" whereby the Government levied a charge on road users (vehicles) during peak hours in order to reduce traffic congestion and pollution, there was a substantial reduction in the volume of traffic — about 73 per cent in the zone concerned during peak hours (Asian Development Bank, 1991b, p. 250).

The next major area for policy innovations pertains to industrialisation. Industries influence the urban environment partly through energy consumption and partly through atmospheric and water pollution by virtue of the chemical, toxic or other substances they use. In order to reduce, if not eliminate, such pollution, the policymakers could no doubt rely on national energy policies or on economic instruments to contain pollution as discussed in Chapters 3 and 4. These comprise regulatory instruments, including standards, permits and licences, and direct controls on resource use; economic instruments, including charges on pollution, subsidies and other market-oriented instruments; and "command or control" approach. The "polluter-pays-principle" is clearly relevant in improving the urban environment. However, one should take due notice of the institutional capacities of developing countries for the enforcement of market-based instruments. Since some of the activities in the informal sector also contribute to pollution, the measures suggested above also apply to this sector: but in view of the very small scale of these activities and the low incomes of those working in them, the approach to implementation would probably require some changes. For instance, one might explore ways of avoiding pollution through collective efforts by organising the small units into clusters. What the city authorities can do, in addition to the above, is to develop their own industrial location policy. For example, the State can manipulate the pattern of industries in urban areas by discriminating against the polluting industries — forcing them to locate themselves elsewhere through manipulation of the incentive structures or through direct contacts.

One of the major consequences of industrial development within the metropolitan regions, often not visible, is that it gives rise to an expansion of economic activities elsewhere in the urban economy through backward and forward linkages. It is therefore argued that, in order to slow down or arrest urbanisation, industries should be discouraged from locating in large urban centres. To put it in more general terms, one way to avoid the undesirable consequences of urbanisation is to decentralise employment and development geographically, i.e. to encourage the growth of small towns. There are indeed a number of controversial policy issues in pursuing this idea. Industries choose to locate in large metropolitan areas because they reap what are known as "agglomeration economies" (see Townroe, 1979). Other factors such as centralised bureaucracies have also played a role in the choice of location. Notwithstanding this, attempts have been made to decentralise development by providing investment incentives (taxes/subsidies, pricing of utilities, subsidised infrastructure, etc.) but they have not yielded the desired results (Hardoy and Satterthwaite, 1988). The failure can often be traced to the inappropriate pricing of utilities and various services in metropolitan areas. Also, the authorities have failed to take into account negative externalities imposed by industries in applying the fiscal instruments. The upshot of the above discussion is that, while efforts to disperse development spatially should continue without distorting the markets, through various market instruments, one cannot depend on them exclusively. The city authorities should also seriously consider eliminating the price distortions in the metropolitan regions and compensating for externalities through fiscal instruments. There are indeed a number of other related issues, such as whether aggregate employment in the economy as a whole would increase or decrease as a result of decentralised development, which also need to be considered, but unfortunately there is little empirical evidence on this.

In conclusion, it should be stressed that, if current trends in urbanisation in the Third World can be sustained, in accordance with the concept of sustainable development elaborated in Chapter 2, through the various measures discussed above, it would also contribute to a significant improvement in the rural environment by relieving the pressure of population on natural resources. A well-conceived urban development strategy is therefore a vital element in the formulation of a strategy of sustainable development.

References

Asian Development Bank 1991a. *Annual Report 1991*. Manila.

———. 1991b. *Asian Development Outlook 1991*. Manila.

Barnett, A. et al. 1978. *Biogas technology in the Third World: A multidisciplinary review*. Ottawa, International Development Research Centre.

Berry, R. 1977. *Inequality demand structure and employment: The case of India*. D.Phil. thesis (unpublished), Brighton (United Kingdom), University of Sussex.

Bifani, P. 1991. *Technology generation and transfer for sustainable development*. Paper prepared for the 1992 United Nations Conference on Environment and Development.

Castaneda, F. C. 1989. "The risks of environmental degradation in Bogotá, Colombia", in *Environment and Urbanization* (London, International Institute for Environment and Development), Vol. 1, No. 1.

Centre for Science and Environment. 1989. "The environmental problems associated with India's major cities", in *Environment and Urbanization* (London, International Institute for Environment and Development), Vol. 1, No. 1.

Cuenya, B. et al. 1989. "Land invasions and grassroots organisation: The Quilmes Settlements in Greater Buenos Aires, Argentina", in *Environment and Urbanization* (London, International Institute for Environment and Development), Vol. 1, No. 2.

Deshpande, S.; Deshpande, L. 1991. *Problems of urbanisation and growth of large cities in developing countries: A case study of Bombay.* Mimeographed WEP working paper (WEP 2-21/WP.177). Geneva, ILO.

HABITAT. 1989. *Urbanisation and sustainable development in the Third World: An unrecognised global issues.* Nairobi.

———. 1990. *People, settlements, environment and development: Improving the living environment for a sustainable future.* Nairobi.

Hardoy, J. E.; Satterthwaite, D. 1986. "Third World cities and the environment of poverty", in Repetto, R. (ed.): *The global possible: Resources, development and the new century.* New Haven, Connecticut, Yale University Press.

———; ———. 1988. "Small and intermediate urban centres in the Third World: What role for government?", in *Third World Planning Review* (Liverpool, Liverpool University Press), Vol. 10, No. 10.

ILO. 1970. *Towards full employment: A programme for Colombia.* Geneva.

———. 1991. *The urban informal sector in Africa in retrospect and prospect: An annotated bibliography.* International Labour Bibliography No. 10. Geneva.

———/JASPA. 1988. *Recent trends in employment, equity and poverty in African countries.* Paper prepared for the International Conference on the Human Dimension of Africa's Economic Recovery and Development, Khartoum (Sudan), 5-8 March 1988. Addis Ababa.

———/JASPA. 1989. *African Employment Report 1988.* Addis Ababa.

———/PREALC. 1978. *Sector informal: Funcionamiento y políticas.* Santiago (Chile).

Jagannathan, N. V. 1989. *Poverty, public policy and the environment.* World Bank Environment Department Divisional Working Paper No. 24. Washington, DC, World Bank.

James, J. 1980. "The employment effects of an income redistribution: A test for aggregation bias in the Indian sugar processing industry", in *Journal of Development Studies* (London, Frank Cass), Vol. 7, No. 2.

Jones, D. W. 1991. "How urbanisation affects energy use in developing countries" in *Energy Policy* (Guildford (United Kingdom), Butterworth), Vol. 19, No. 7.

Kaplinsky, R. 1987. *Micro-electronics and employment revisited: A review.* Geneva, ILO.

Khouri-Dagher, N. 1986. *Food and energy in Cairo: Provisioning the poor.* Tokyo, United Nations University, Food-Energy Nexus Programme.

Newland, K. 1980. *City limits: Emerging constraints on urban growth.* Worldwatch Paper 38. Washington, DC, Worldwatch Institute.

Pearson, P. (ed.). 1986. *Energy and the environment in the Third World.* Discussion Paper Series. Guildford (United Kingdom), Surrey Energy Economics Centre.

Reddy, A. K. N. 1986. "Energy issues and opportunities", in Repetto, R. (ed.): *The global possible: Resources, development and the new century.* New Haven, Connecticut, Yale University Press.

Renaud, B. 1989. "Urban employment policies in developing countries", in Tolley, G. S., and Thomas, V. (eds.); *The economics of urbanisation and urban policies in developing countries.* Washington, DC, World Bank.

Rodgers, G. 1989. "Introduction: Trends in urban poverty and labour market access", in Rodgers, G. (ed.): *Urban poverty and the labour market: Access to jobs and incomes in Asian and Latin American cities.* Geneva, ILO.

Rondinelli, D. A. 1983. *Secondary cities in developing countries: Policies for diffusing urbanisation.* London, Sage Publications.

———. 1986. "The urban transition and agricultural development: Implications for international assitance policy", in *Development and Change* (London, Sage Publications), Vol. 17, No. 2.

Sanyal, B. 1986. *Urban cultivation in East Africa.* Tokyo, United Nations University, Food-Energy Nexus Programme.

Schteingart, M. 1989. "The environmental problems associated with urban development in Mexico City", in *Environment and Urbanization* (London, International Institute for Environment and Development), Vol. 1, No. 1.

Sethuraman, S. V. (ed.). 1981. *The urban informal sector in developing countries: Employment, poverty and environment.* Geneva, ILO.

Sinclair, J. 1989. "Using today's technology to clean up the planet", in *Our Planet* (Nairobi, UNEP), Vol. 3, No. 3.

Singh, A. 1989. *Urbanisation, poverty and employment: The large metropolis in the Third World.* Mimeographed WEP working paper. Geneva, ILO.

Townroe, P. M. 1979. "Employment decentralisation: Policy instruments for large cities in less developed countries", in *Progress in Planning* (Oxford, Pergamon Press), Vol. 10, Part 2.

Tricaud, P.-M. 1987. *Urban agriculture in Ibadan and Freetown.* Tokyo, United Nations University, Food-Energy Nexus Programme.

United Nations. 1989a. *Technology, trade policy and the Uruguay round.* Papers and proceedings of a round table held in Delphi, Greece, 22-24 April 1989. New York.

———. 1989b. *Prospects for world urbanisation.* New York.

United Nations Development Programme (UNDP). 1990. "Special report: The urban challenge", in *Source* (New York), June.

United Nations Environment Programme (UNEP). 1981. *Biogas fertiliser system: Technical report on a training seminar in China.* Nairobi.

———. 1989. *Environmental data report.* Oxford, Basil Blackwell.

United States Congress, Office of Technology Assessment. 1991. *Energy in developing countries.* Washington, DC.

Vandemoortele, J. 1991. "Labour market informalisation in sub-Saharan Africa", in Standing, G., and Tokman, V. (eds.): *Towards social adjustment: Labour market issues in structural adjustment.* Geneva, ILO.

Wade, I. 1987. *Food self-reliance in Third World cities.* Tokyo, United Nations University, Food-Energy Nexus Programme.

World Bank. 1984. *World Development Report 1984.* Washington, DC.

————. 1990. *World Development Report 1990: Poverty*. Oxford and New York, Oxford University Press for the World Bank.

————. 1991a. *Urban policy and economic development: An agenda for the 1990s*. Washington, DC.

————. 1991b. *The Urban Edge* (Washington, DC), Vol. 15, No. 2.

————. 1991c. *Botswana: Urban household energy strategy study*. ESMAP Report No. 132/91. Washington, DC.

World Commission on Environment and Development (WCED). 1987. *Our common future*. Oxford, Oxford University Press (also known as the Brundtland Report).

SOME GLOBAL ISSUES [1]

A. S. Bhalla * and P. Bifani **

7

In Chapters 2 to 6 we covered environmental issues of mainly national concern. Global environmental issues going beyond national boundaries are the subject of this chapter. Global environmental and economic interdependence implies either that all countries have a stake in the natural environment or that the actions of any individual country affect the environment or welfare of other countries.

Several global environmental dimensions of development may be noted. The first case is where every country contributes directly to the environmental problem through impacts on the global commons, e.g. climate change and the atmosphere. Secondly, global environmental issues can also be associated with unidirectional types of externalities involving "upstream"-polluting countries and "downstream"-suffering countries. Examples of these are transborder pollution and acid rain. Third are the issues related to the environmental policies adopted by any country, which are likely to have implications for international flows of capital and goods and services through changes in terms of trade. Environmental policies and measures may cause trade distortions and thus affect the partners in international trade. Two cases illustrate this situation: trade barriers arising from environmental measures, and the relocation of industry, both of which are related to technological change and transfer. Therefore, the transfer of environmentally sound technology is also an important global issue.

The international concern with environmental problems has led to the adoption of standards and norms to protect the natural environment. Multilateral agreements, conventions, protocols or other types of international agreement relating to specific environmental issues are discussed and may be adopted, e.g. the Montreal Protocol on Substances

---

* ILO, Geneva.   ** Universidad Autónoma de Madrid.

[1] The authors are grateful to Lawrence Kohler for helpful suggestions on an earlier draft of this chapter.

that Deplete the Ozone Layer; the Basle Convention on the Control of Transboundary Movements of Hazardous Wastes and their Disposal; and, at the regional level, the Bamako Convention on the Ban of the Import into Africa and the Control of Transboundary Movement and Management of Hazardous Wastes within Africa. In addition, two important international agreements are at present being discussed, i.e. conventions on climate change and biodiversity.

These international environmental policy instruments are meant to be binding agreements which will have economic as well as social implications. The Basle Convention stipulates that industrial activities must reduce the amount of waste they generate, and the amendment to the Montreal Protocol adopted in 1990 sets the year 2000 as the target date to phase out five of the chloro-fluorocarbons (CFCs) and halons controlled by the Protocol, the year 2000 for phasing out carbon tetrachloride, and the year 2005 for methyl chloroform. Even these target dates are expected to be shortened as a result of recent scientific evidence concerning ozone depletion.

Our concern in this chapter is to examine the implications of global environmental issues, particularly for the developing countries. This is done in the first section. The second section discusses the implications of environmental policies for trade distortions, the decline of exports of developing country manufactures, and employment generation. The third section discusses the issues of technology transfer and the relocation of polluting industries to developing countries. The final section is concerned with possible international action to overcome the global consequences for the developing countries. In this context, the role of the ILO is also considered.

IMPLICATIONS OF GLOBAL ENVIRONMENTAL CONVENTIONS

The Montreal Protocol

The Montreal Protocol stipulates that, as of January 1993, no Party would be allowed to export substances controlled under the Protocol (e.g. CFCs and freon) to any State that has not ratified the Protocol. Many developing countries find this mandate unacceptable, since it is likely to affect adversely both their rate of growth and their rapidly growing industries producing refrigeration systems, air-conditioning equipment, solvents and so on, the manufacture of which involves the use of these substances. Its direct negative effect would occur through a reduction in the expansion of industrial activity related to CFCs. The adoption of the Montreal Protocol is also likely to have indirect negative implications for employment generation in developing countries by slowing down the rate of economic growth. It is worth mentioning here that at the time of writing

China and India, to name but two developing countries, have not signed the Protocol.

The economic growth of developing countries is likely to raise the demand for refrigeration and air-conditioning equipment; some countries (e.g. China, India and Brazil) are already developing major industrial activities to meet these demands and to export household refrigerators (India is actually exporting refrigerators to the former USSR and the Middle East.) India is producing nearly 100,000 room air-conditioners per year, each of which requires 1 kg of freon, and air conditioning is being increasingly used in new buildings. India's production capacity for CFCs is estimated at 18,000 tons per year, with demand estimated at around 5,000 tons in 1991 and 25,000 tons by the end of the century. (In 1988, a new CFC plant was built in the State of Gujarat, financed by the Industrial Development Board of India.)

In the light of the above, the phasing-out of CFCs seems very costly for India. It is not only their replacement that is costly but also the fact that the CFC/halon substitutes will most probably involve the redesigning of several parts and pieces of refrigerators and air-conditioning systems. The problem is complicated because of the following factors: the costs involved, the technological aspects, and competitiveness in external markets.

The magnitude of the additional cost can be appreciated through the following comparisons: in 1987 the price of 500 g of CFC-11, one of the most used CFCs, was about US$0.30. The expected price for its substitute, the HFC-134a to be marketed in 1994, is US$3. Moreover, some of the new equipment associated with the substitutes is at present less energy-efficient; hence, it implies increased costs resulting from a greater consumption of energy.

At present, India is not paying any royalty on CFC products, but a royalty may have to be paid in the event of redesign and the substitution of new technology. It is estimated that redesigning will raise the average cost of production per refrigerator. This higher cost will not only slow down domestic demand, but will also affect India's competitive position in foreign markets. Lack of competitiveness will clearly have adverse effects on the growth of employment in industry.

A similar situation seems to exist in China, which has undertaken an aggressive programme of industrialisation and manufacture of household appliances. Between 1980 and 1988 China's production of refrigerators increased substantially. Bearing in mind that at present only 10 per cent of Chinese households have a refrigerator, the potential demand is still very high.

In different international forums, developing countries have noted that they are not in a position to afford the high cost of preserving the ozone layer. Furthermore, they argue that "singling out developing countries as a main source of threat to the global environment obscures the fact that the ecological stress on the global commons has, in large, been caused by the North" (South Commission, 1990).

The Montreal Protocol provided for Parties to facilitate access to environmentally safe alternative substances and technology. It also provided for Parties to facilitate, bilaterally or multilaterally, the provision of subsidies, aid, credit, etc., for the use of alternative technologies and for substitute products.

Proposed Convention on Climate Change

A similar concern has been expressed in relation to the Convention on Climate Change that is currently being negotiated. This Convention is likely to have important implications for the motor vehicle industry, the production and use of fertilisers, the metal industry and, in general, all energy-intensive activities involving the burning of fossil fuels. If this Convention establishes stringent standards for global emissions of greenhouse gases (GHG) to be applied uniformly throughout the world, it is possible that developing countries could be at a disadvantage. Although the levels of emissions in these countries are far lower than those in the industrialised countries, their process of development will require an increase in GHG emissions.

The greenhouse effects are caused not by a single family of man-made products, but by at least half a dozen gases of different origin and not only carbon dioxide, as is frequently believed. It is estimated that carbon dioxide is responsible for about 50 per cent of the global warming effects of the 1980s, while methane accounts for 18 per cent, CFCs for 14 per cent, nitrous oxide for 6 per cent and other gases about 12 per cent. It seems impossible to compare the effects of their relative importance and of the possibility to limit emissions, which in fact is affected by the cumulative process not only of the past few years but of several decades since the Industrial Revolution.

The implications of global warming for tropical or subtropical developing countries are important in terms of the impact of changes in sea level and precipitation (Hulme, 1990). A rise in sea level will expose populations in low-lying countries such as Egypt, Bangladesh and the Maldives. Populations in densely inhabited delta regions of Bangladesh and India, which frequently suffer from cyclones, are likely to be particularly vulnerable. It is estimated that if the sea level rose by 1 m as a result of climate changes, much cultivable land in Egypt and Bangladesh would be inundated and about 8 and 10 million people, respectively, would be affected (Broadus et al., 1986; Hulme, 1990).

Global warming also induces precipitation changes, which tend to affect the availability of, and access to, the water resources of river basins shared by a number of countries, and this could lead to possible political tensions between them.

Therefore negotiations for a global agreement on the control of carbon emissions should be of interest to developing countries, notwithstanding the fact that, at present, these countries contribute much less to such emissions than the industrialised countries. One possible solution proposed is to lease carbon emission quotas to individual countries, which would give them the right to emit up to the global average of per capita carbon output (Grubb, 1989; Hulme, 1990, p. 14). The underlying principle of this proposal is a global market in which the developing countries with a low per capita carbon output could lease permits to the developed countries, thus earning revenue to finance their environmental programmes and projects.

TRADE, EMPLOYMENT AND ENVIRONMENTAL IMPLICATIONS

Environmental measures and policies are likely to have implications for economic relationships among countries to the extent that they affect trade between them. Depending on the subject and its scope, environmental regulations adopted by a country may have a positive or negative influence in the country itself, on other countries and on international trade in general. Stringent standards pertaining to the location and operation of domestic industries are likely to encourage imports and therefore stimulate exports in other countries. Regulations that require certain products to meet specific minimum environmental standards are liable to be detrimental to other countries. The economic and commercial impact of environmental measures is normally considered as one element of specific policies dealing with competitiveness, international trade, investments, protectionism, etc. (see UNCTAD 1991; GATT, 1992; and Anderson and Blackhurst, 1992; GATT, 1992). Whereas at the aggregate level the effects of environmental regulations may not be considered of critical importance, their prospective effect for industry and firms may indeed be significant. The same considerations are valid for individual countries: whereas the impact of international trade in general can be negligible, it may be extremely important for a single country specialising in the export of one or a few commodities which would be vulnerable to environmental controls imposed by importing countries.

The exports of food products from the developing countries are likely to be adversely affected when stringent standards are introduced. Products can be subject to "environmental" trade restrictions because of the characteristics of the product itself or by reason of its having been exposed to environmentally noxious agents (e.g. pesticides, herbicides, fungicide residues in food crops). In the early 1980s a UNEP/UNCTAD study noted that 53 per cent of OECD imports from developing countries were of environmentally sensitive products, e.g. meat, fish, fruit and vegetables.

The growth of these exports from developing countries has been slowing down since then, with obvious negative implications for employment generation.

Furthermore, negative effects on incomes and employment in developing countries can be felt through a decline in exports of products based on natural resources, e.g. textiles, leather and wood products which tend to be produced by pollution-intensive techniques. UNCTAD (1991) notes that "exports of these manufactures may be afected because of further restrictions on the chemical compounds and heavy metals contained in them."

However, as we shall see below, a decline in exports may also be partially compensated by an increase in exports from developing countries, thus resulting in either a positive or a negative *net* result. An increase in exports of manufactures can occur through a process of substitution of products, e.g. replacement of chemical-based products by organic fibres — packaging materials, furniture and construction components. Secondly, export opportunities for developing countries may improve in the wake of a reduction in the production of some agricultural products in the industrialised countries. Thirdly, there may be an increase in developing-country exports when the use of chemical inputs in agriculture is restricted. This measure can "provide export opportunities in terms of alternative inputs based on natural products such as pyrethrum" (UNCTAD, 1991).

Obstacles to trade (such as non-tariff barriers) introduced on environmental grounds can have three main origins: (a) environmental regulations which raise production costs in countries adopting increasingly stringent environmental policies, associated with the use of compensatory import charges sought as a shield against foreign suppliers; this kind of safeguard mechanism is clearly of a protectionist character; (b) environmental product standards imposed for both imported and domestically produced goods with no protectionist intention; and (c) environmental product standards applied for exclusively protectionist purposes.

Employment effects

The negative employment effects in developing countries of stringent environmental standards are likely to be similar to those resulting from protective barriers introduced by the industrialised countries. The growing export of labour-intensive manufactures from the developing countries has in the past led to a substantial increase in employment. A study of eight major exporters of manufactures from the Third World estimated that direct and indirect employment created about 5 million jobs for various years between 1960 and 1970 (Renshaw, 1981, p. 70; see also Tyler, 1976). The growth of employment opportunities in developing countries is likely to slow down if their exports are adversely affected. While it is difficult to quantify this impact, it may be appreciable, since most of the developing country exports (with a few exceptions, such as refrigerators) are likely to be labour intensive.

A study undertaken by the ILO World Employment Programme (WEP), with funding from the United Nations Environment Programme (UNEP), produced some quantitative estimates of the impact of pollution control measures in the United States on employment and incomes in selected developing countries, notably Thailand and the Republic of Korea (Koo, 1979; Kim, 1979). These two economies were selected since they have traditionally had close trade relations with the United States, and their development strategy was based on export expansion as a major means of stimulating growth.

The methodology used for quantifying the income and employment effects included case studies of the developing economies concerned, and the use of input-output tables for estimating the income and employment effects induced by changes in exports resulting from an increase in environmental control costs in the importing country. For example, the total possible impact of the trade deficit of Thailand (resulting from United States pollution control) on Thai national income and wage income was calculated on the basis of the input-output table for 1971. The loss of employee income was then converted into possible job loss (of about 5,400) by making specific assumptions about wage rates, which vary a great deal among different categories of worker. In the case of the Republic of Korea, the availability of labour input coefficients (which were not available for Thailand) made possible the direct estimation of the employment effects. These income and employment effects for the two countries are presented in table 13. The negative employment impact for the economy of the Republic of Korea is substantial. The estimate may have been exaggerated due to "the drastic assumption that the Korean pollution-intensive goods would lose their entire export market in the United States" (Koo, 1979; Kim, 1979, p. 103).

A heroic attempt was also made by the ILO/WEP study to estimate the direct income and employment effects of American environmental control measures on other developing countries or areas, i.e. Argentina, Brazil, Hong Kong, India, Israel, Pakistan and Singapore (Koo, 1979).

The above quantifications of the trade-environment-employment interactions are presented only for purposes of illustration. These estimates are based on a number of simplifying assumptions which may or may not be valid. First, the effects of changing terms of trade of developing countries, which would affect employment and incomes, do not seem to have been taken fully into account. Although with lower environmental standards the developing countries enjoy lower costs of production, the increased cost of imports of raw materials and machinery from the developed countries (owing to higher environmental costs in those

147

Table 13. Possible impact of United States pollution control measures on national income, employee income and employment in the Republic of Korea and Thailand

Country	National income	Employee income	Employment (thousands of jobs)
Republic of Korea (millions of wons)			
Increase resulting from increase in certain Korean exports	1 445		1 837
Decrease resulting from decrease in certain Korean exports	23 168		36 731
Net change	21 723		34 894
Thailand (millions of bahts)			
Increase resulting from increase in certain Thai exports	796	92	
Decrease resulting from decrease in certain Thai exports	1 068	178	
Net change	272	86	+5.4

Source: Kim (1979).

countries) would tend to raise the costs of production of the import-intensive goods.

Secondly, the impact of environmentally induced direct investment in developing countries cannot be easily estimated. The assessment of total employment effects would be possible through the use of income multipliers for each country. In the absence of data for marginal propensities to consume and import, it is difficult to estimate the indirect and total employment impact (Kim, 1979).

Thirdly, the estimates presented in table 13 assume that there is a net decline in exports resulting from a decline in the export of pollution-intensive goods to the United States. It is assumed that these goods could not be redirected to a third country — an assumption which is probably not valid. To the extent that all pollution-intensive exports do not suffer, the loss of employment estimated in table 13 may be exaggerated. However, there is some empirical support for the above assumption. Data for the United Kingdom and the United States for 1971 to 1976 show that "pollution-intensive imports have not grown as fast as imports in other categories; and share of pollution-intensive goods from developing countries has increased only slightly ..." (Duerksen and Leonard, 1980, p. 57). Similarly, an industry-by-industry breakdown of OECD country imports showed that "light, labour-intensive imports are greater than pollution-intensive imports" (Duerksen and Leonard, 1980, pp. 57-59).

So far, we have considered only the aggregate income and employment effects. If the data on commodity composition of trade were available,

Table 14. Possible impact of United States pollution control measures on both process and product pollution on the economy of the Republic of Korea in selected sectors

Sector	Income change	Employment change		
	Plus (millions of 1973 wons)	Minus (thousands of jobs)	Plus	Minus
Fishery	3.8	1 508	6	2 401
Fruit processing		3 201		11 160
Canning		1 925		3 869
Textiles	100	0	172	
Lumber and plywood	316	0	412	
Primary iron and steel	272	0	207	
Fabricated metals	152	0	238	
Electrical machinery	124	16 338	145	19 069

Source: Koo, 1979; Kim, 1979, p. 104.

similar effects could also be estimated for selected economic sectors and industries that would probably be affected by process and product pollution control in the advanced countries. The ILO/WEP study (Koo, 1979) described these sectoral employment and income effects for the Republic of Korea (see table 14).

Environmental standards

Environmental standards are likely to vary from country to country depending on the national and local conditions regarding environmental stress and degradation. Standards may also be more stringent at higher than at lower levels of development.

The international concern regarding standards and regulations poses a real dilemma. On the one hand, harmonisation of environmental standards and their uniformity across countries may be desirable if the objective is to discourage the introduction of non-tariff barriers for environmental reasons. On the other hand, imposition of uniform standards ignores country variations to which standards should be adjusted. For example, countries suffering from serious environmental degradation may need to introduce more stringent standards than those where such degradation is not so acute.

All food product standards applied to fruit, vegetables, fish and shellfish have, as measured by value of imports detained, a modest impact overall on global trade, but they can be quite significant for individual commodities (e.g. shrimps, mung beans) or countries. The problem of import detention for these two sectors appears to be greater for developing than developed countries, owing to the specific commodity composition of that trade and the less diversified structure of the exports of developing countries. It is difficult to assess accurately the impact of environmental product standards in the food sector, because very frequently they are closely associated with health and sanitary standards.

There is no doubt that environmental regulations can play a role in the context of protectionism. They can be used as a form of unilateral quantitative and qualitative restrictions. However, it is difficult to assess how important they have been or can be as trade barriers.

Environmental regulations may be justified on grounds of environmental protection; but they may also contribute to raising trade barriers, to which there is growing opposition. Care will be needed to devise environmental measures in order to minimise trade distortions and investment flows from the industrialised to the developing countries. The harmonisation of national environmental measures and standards may be a prerequisite if the negative effects of trade restrictions and trade sanctions, which may be introduced to enforce environmental objectives, are to be minimised. Such a harmonisation may not be attainable or feasible without international and multilateral action, procedures and supervision. This is particularly so in order to ensure that the relocation of industry and the transfer of technologies do not engender occupational and health hazards.

INDUSTRIAL RELOCATION AND TRANSFER OF ENVIRONMENTALLY SOUND TECHNOLOGIES

Relocation of industries

Issues relating to industrial plant relocation have both national and international implications. In this chapter we are concerned only with the latter. However, in both cases there are common considerations and motivations for relocation: changes in costs and market location, sources of supply of raw materials and other inputs, impact of environmental and other regulations, etc.

Environmental control measures and regulations which vary between countries can account for, inter alia, the relocation of industries and plants and industrial investments across national boundaries. Differences in environmental standards, particularly between the developed and the developing countries, lead to differences in costs of production and changes in the comparative advantage of countries in respect of trade, investment and capital flows. Since higher environmental standards in the developed countries are likely to be associated with higher production costs, it is argued that the firms in these countries would be induced to shift investments and relocate to developing countries so as to take advantage of lower costs.

It has frequently been claimed that one of the implications of the adoption of environmental regulations by the developed countries is the transfer of polluting industry to the developing countries, resulting in the degradation of their environment.

However, the issue of industrial relocation is not one of unmixed evil. From the point of view of developing countries (although not the developed ones), the relocation of industry and its associated investment and technology has beneficial income and employment effects which cannot be ignored. It is perhaps for this reason that the countries concerned may not object so strongly to relocation on environmental grounds as one might expect. High environmental standards may not be appropriate (at least in the short run), since they involve a financial burden for developing countries with low levels of economic development and development priorities that are different from those in the industrialised countries.

The argument in support of the relocation of industry to developing countries is also based on another premise, i.e. that the developing countries have a comparative advantage over the industrialised ones from an environmental point of view. This argument is intimately related to the concept of environmental assimilation capacity, which is assumed to be higher in the developing than in the industrialised countries. This argument is often supported by the fact that, in general, developing countries are characterised by a predominance of labour-intensive industries and technologies using natural materials such as wood, cotton, silk and wool which are less polluting than the artificial or man-made inputs that are being used more and more in the developed countries. This factor has clear implications for the choice and location of, particularly, processing industries. In addition to the replacement of natural materials, constant technical progress and technological obsolesence contribute to a change in the environmental assimilation capacity of countries. This latter factor also provides a "fillip" to the development of "clean" technologies and industries — which in turn raises the question of the supply and availability of polluting plants and technologies for the developing countries. And it is well known that a number of outward-looking developing economies have invited multinational enterprises to locate industries (including polluting industries) in order to accelerate their own industrialisation.

These arguments, particularly fashionable during the 1970s, are based on the premise that developing countries have environmental comparative advantage over the developed countries, and thus have a higher capacity to absorb polluting industries. However, this does seem to ignore the fact that the industrial areas of developing countries are extremely concentrated and polluted, like those in the developed countries. Thus, these areas within developing countries may have as low a capacity to absorb pollution as the industrialised countries.

According to studies carried out in the United States and Europe, environmental regulations did not seem to be a major factor in deciding where to locate new manufacturing plants. In fact, even for highly polluting industries such as steel, environmental considerations are ranked eighth or tenth in the list of location criteria. The traditional locational factors (markets, transport costs, availability of materials and labour and so on) continue to be much more important than the environmental costs, which form only a small proportion of the total costs (Davis et al., 1980; Leone, 1976; UNCTAD, 1991).

Whenever the relocation of dirty industries has occurred, the movement has been between industrialised countries rather than from developed to developing countries. Individual cases such as that of asbestos in the United States and Mexico cannot be generalised (Bifani, 1979). Besides, it has been demonstrated that American foreign investment in pollution-intensive industries such as chemicals, pulp and paper, metals and petroleum refining has gone mainly to other developed countries and not to developing countries (Duerksen and Leonard, 1980). The competitive advantage that can be gained by moving to "pollution havens" seems to be very marginal, since environmental costs represent only a small proportion of the total production cost.

Transfer of environmentally sound technologies

Related to the issue of industrial relocation is that of the transfer of technology that it entails, and the need for developing countries to have access to pollution-abatement and environmentally sound technologies. Although the concept of environmentally sound technology is not universally agreed upon, it is characterised by lower pollution, energy and resource intensity, a greater use of renewable resources and more recycling of waste products.

The control or abatement of the main global environmental problems discussed above will require the development of new technologies and the modification of existing ones. In relation to climate change, the report of the Energy and Industry Sub-Group (EIS) of the Intergovernmental Panel on Climate Change (IPCC) identifies three main approaches for reducing and limiting greenhouse gases (GHG) emissions. The first involves lowering the "carbon intensity" of energy, that is, reducing the ratio of GHG emissions per unit of energy consumption. This implies the replacement of fossil fuels by non-fossil fuels. The second approach is to raise the energy efficiency of the economy, or reduce the ratio of energy consumption per unit of GDP. This would call for technologies to improve conservation and to achieve higher fuel efficiency in vehicles, electricity generation and factories. The third approach involves greater reabsorption and reafforestation that can contribute to a net reduction in the quantity of GHG emitted into the atmosphere.

A reduction in GHG emissions can be achieved by replacing existing plants and equipment, installing improved plants, improving maintenance and management practices, changing products and designs, and modifying consumer demands. All these solutions involve technological decisions. It seems that there is a wide variety of technologies already developed, there are new high technologies and there are potential technologies at present at the development stage. These technologies should be complemented with know-how, training management and maintenance procedures.

The adoption and diffusion of environmentally sound technologies is at present limited even in the industrialised countries, not to speak of the developing ones. The United States Office of Technology Assessment estimates that "50 per cent of all environmentally harmful industrial wastes could be eliminated with the technology that was available in 1986 and another 25 per cent with additional research and development" (cited in UNIDO, 1991, p. 5).

While many environmentally sound technologies do exist, developing countries may not enjoy access to them, partly because they are of a proprietary nature and are thus not in the public domain (e.g. new biotechnologies). Some of these proprietary technologies may no longer be in use in the developed countries (e.g. coal for residential heating). Their access to these technologies may be further hindered by several other barriers: for instance, multinational enterprises expect to make low profits from sales of these technologies owing to limited markets; they may be discouraged from investing in developing countries also partly due to uncertainty about host-country policies with regard to nationalisation and/or privatisation; and the developing countries face difficulties in using the technologies for lack of infrastructure, slow rate of investment and consequent limited diffusion of new technologies, their high cost, etc. There may also be a disincentive to use "clean" technologies in place of "polluting" technologies which are cheaper.

Adequate evidence on comparative costs of "clean" and "polluting" technologies is not easily available. But the capital costs of newer and cleaner technologies are most likely to be higher. These costs are likely to be particularly high for small enterprises in developing countries (UNIDO, 1991, p. 16). For example, for the small family-based tanning units in developing countries the cost of obtaining a special drum for "hair" recovery (cleaner technology), including the necessary auxiliary equipment, may be twice as high as the conventional drum. The larger enterprises are more likely to enjoy access to environmentally sound technologies than the smaller ones. It is estimated that "in China, the budget for a pulp and paper chemical recovery system for a large-capacity mill . . . is US$4.5 million" (UNIDO, 1991, p. 17) which is simply beyond the investment capacity of small and even medium-sized enterprises.

Apart from the above barriers to the access by developing countries to available technologies that are environment friendly, there is the issue of their limited capacity to absorb these technologies, and to develop them wherever circumstances and resources warrant. Whether developing countries can develop new pollution-control and environmentally sound technologies will depend very much on their current stock of technological capabilities, R & D resources, scientific manpower and infrastructure, etc.

An efficient and effective use of environmentally sound technologies in developing countries presupposes that a demand for such technologies exists. However, the relatively lower environmental standards in these countries, as mentioned above, are likely to limit such a demand.

The use of environmentally sound technologies will have both direct and indirect employment implications. But it is not clear (in our present state of knowledge) whether the use of these technologies, in place of others, will lead to more or less aggregate employment (see Chapter 8).

INTERNATIONAL ACTION AND THE ROLE OF THE ILO

The foregoing discussion on global conventions, environmental standards, relocation of industry and transfer of environmentally sound technologies suggests that international action will be needed to tackle these global environmental problems, which are of concern to both industrialised and developing countries. For example, international mechanisms may be needed (perhaps through existing institutions like GATT) to settle any international disputes that may arise from the introduction and enforcement of national and global environmental protection measures. In addition, global resources will be required for the implementation of the provisions of global conventions and the development of environmentally sound technologies.

The international debate and negotiations on environment will culminate with the United Nations Conference on Environment and Development (UNCED) in Brazil (June 1992). The UNCED Action Programme — "Agenda 21" — discussed at the Fourth Session of the Preparatory Committee (New York, March-April 1992) embodies the views of developed and developing countries on the following major sets of issues: the social and economic dimensions of environment and sustainable development (fighting poverty, changing consumption patterns, promoting a sustainable pattern of human settlements); the conservation and management of resources for development (protection of the atmosphere and the oceans, and biodiversity, combating deforestation); strengthening the role of the major groups such as trade unions, youth, women, business and industry and the scientific and technological community; and mechanisms for ensuring the availability of adequate financial resources, the transfer of environmentally sound technology, the promotion of capacity building in developing countries and the promotion of education, training and public awareness.

One of the themes of "Agenda 21" is the "revitalisation of growth and development", which calls for the solution of such problems as trade, debt, development finance and related domestic policies. This volume has touched on the need for ensuring compatibility between environment and development to ensure sustainable levels of employment and standards of living, particularly in developing countries (Chapters 2, 5 and 6).

"Agenda 21" provides a good basis for linking global environmental issues with those related to development in the South and North-South dialogue. The developing countries are already preparing their negotiating position concerning "Agenda 21".[2] The emerging position of the South is that environmental issues cannot be divorced from those of development, the alleviation of poverty and global economic reform, namely, debt, development assistance, stabilisation of commodity prices and access of developing countries to markets in the North.

The developing countries' position on global environmental issues such as climate change and emission of greenhouse gases is that, as the countries of the North are largely responsible for these emissions, they should bear the major financial burden for controlling them. The developing countries are also interested in the creation of a global system for the transfer, on preferential and non-commercial terms, of environmentally sound technologies.

The various proposals for action discussed at recent international forums on environment can be broadly grouped into two main categories: funding mechanisms, and the transfer of environmentally sound technologies to developing countries which call for partnerships in research and development. We discuss these categories below.

Funding mechanisms

The overall costs involved in attaining the goals of international proposals on global environmental issues are enormous, particularly for the developing countries. Some global funding mechanisms will therefore be necessary to ensure the effective implementation of the proposals.

At the Ninth Non-Aligned Summit in Belgrade in September 1989, India proposed the creation of a Planet Protection Fund under the auspices of the United Nations. This Fund was to be created through annual contributions of 0.1 per cent of GDP by all countries except the

---

[2] In June 1991, ministers from 41 developing countries (from Africa, Asia and Latin America) met in Beijing to discuss the challenges posed by the norms of cooperation and better coordination between environmental and development issues. They issued a declaration on the subject. In September 1991, the South Centre set up a Working Group on "The South and UNCED" which met in Geneva and prepared a report entitled *Environment and development: Towards a common strategy of the South in the UNCED negotiations and beyond* (South Centre, 1991). In November 1991, the Second Meeting of the Summit Level Group for South-South Consultation and Co-operation (Group of 15) was held in Caracas and a Joint Communiqué was issued which, inter alia, stated the commitment of the developing countries to the protection of the environment (Group of 15, 1991).

least developed. The size of the Fund would thus be about *US$15.8 billion per year*. The Fund was to be used for the development and purchase of conservation-compatible technologies in critical areas. Such technologies would then be disseminated for the benefit of both developing and developed countries. In his address to the Summit, the then Prime Minister of India, the late Rajiv Gandhi, proposed that "all technologies over which the Fund acquires rights will be made available gratis, and without restriction, to all constituent members of the Fund".

The above proposal has not been implemented. However, in 1990, recognising the global environmental problems and the need to assist countries in the Third World to improve the global environment, the World Bank, UNDP and UNEP established a "Global Environment Facility" (GEF). GEF is a three-year experiment with financing of US$1.3 billion to provide resources for investment projects and technical assistance to protect the global environment, to transfer environmentally sound technologies and to support local institutions. Projects eligible for funding relate to four problem areas: global warming, the protection of the ozone layer, international waters and biodiversity (see UNEP, 1991). A Scientific and Technical Advisory Panel (STAP) of GEF has established for each of these four basic areas a set of criteria for identifying programmes and projects, and a list of priorities. By the end of November 1991, 29 projects had been reviewed, including proposals to promote non-conventional energy (and thus to reduce global warming) in India, and to preserve biodiversity in Malawi. Consideration is also being given to transforming the GEF experiment into a more permanent mechanism for funding future global environmental conventions.

It is clear that protocols and other international instruments should include mechanisms for making possible their adoption and implementation by developing countries. The original Montreal Protocol advocated technology transfer between rich and poor nations without providing any mechanism for this, and an Interim Multilateral Fund was later created (in 1990) for this purpose. This Interim Fund is established for a three-year period (from 1 January 1991 to 31 December 1993) to provide financial and technical assistance, including the transfer of technology to the Parties.

The only way to motivate developing countries to participate in the protection of the global commons is by facilitating their access to technology. A well-funded R & D programme involving scientists from developed and developing countries could tailor new technologies for use in the specific environmental conditions of developing countries. At the Ministerial Conference on Atmosphere Pollution and Climatic Change, held in Geneva in 1990, it was estimated that the international investment needed to stabilise the climate is of the order of US$30 billion to US$45 billion per year, which in fact represents less than 0.4 per cent of the total GDP of developed countries.

Technology transfer

The action proposals in this area are meant to address the issue of access to and affordability of environmentally sound technologies as well as their future development and management by the developing countries.

Proprietary technologies which do exist but are virtually no longer in use in the developed countries could be marketed to the developing countries, or adapted for application there, through partnerships between owners and potential users (see United Nations/General Assembly, 1991). Other proposals include a system of "carbon dioxide reduction credit" to stimulate investment by the developed countries in "cleaner" technologies for use in developing countries.

Access by the developing countries to "cleaner" technologies is limited only partly because of restrictions through patent protection. Other barriers to access relate to a lack of adequate information, and the absence of international mechanisms to enable public institutions to purchase licences from private owners in the industrialised countries and to make them available to developing countries. Therefore, barriers need to be overcome through such mechanisms as international information networks and regional clearing-houses, and proprietary information acquisition systems. The effective management and use of environmentally sound technologies by the developing countries also reinforces the need for international cooperation in systematic technology training and the building of endogenous capacities.

So far only the *utilisation* aspects of technology transfer have been considered. The building of endogenous capacities in developing countries also calls for the *development* of environmentally sound technologies within the Third World. This can occur only through long-term collaboration and international partnerships between developed and developing countries in the field of research and development. A network of international research centres along the lines of the Consultative Group on International Agricultural Research (CGIAR) is one example of such a partnership.

The ILO contribution

As was noted in the earlier chapters, greater compatibility between the environment, employment and sustainable development is an essential ingredient of sound environmental policies. But these issues have so far not received as much attention as they deserve. The ILO, with its rich experience and long-standing work on poverty alleviation, employment generation, technology, adaptation and transfer, strengthening of technological capabilities, the role of tripartism and the improvement of the working environment, can play an important catalytic role in this direction. The UNCED Preparatory Committee's examination of issues relating to poverty and environmental degradation, and its objective of "sustainable livelihoods", are in line with the ILO's own objectives.

The ILO can contribute, through advising governments on policy, to ensuring both that their *environmental* policies more effectively reflect employment opportunities, and that their *employment* policies more effectively reflect environmental considerations as well as those relating to sustainable development for the satisfaction of the basic needs of the population.

The ILO was founded, one can argue, to avoid the trade wars which could arise if particular trading patterns violated labour standards and lowered the price of labour. One of the driving forces behind the international environment debate today is similar, namely an attempt to avoid trade practices which would lower environmental standards and the price of natural capital.[3]

The international labour standards promoted by the ILO are not only directly related to the working environment, but often, and to an increasing extent, are closely interrelated with the general environment too. Seven of the ILO's environment-related Conventions were identified for examination by the UNCED. These are the Radiation Protection Convention, 1960 (No. 115); the Benzene Convention, 1971 (No. 136); the Occupational Cancer Convention, 1974 (No. 139); the Working Environment (Air Pollution, Noise and Vibration) Convention, 1977 (No. 148); the Occupational Safety and Health Convention, 1981 (No. 155); the Asbestos Convention, 1986 (No. 162); and the Chemicals Convention, 1990 (No. 170). In addition, the Indigenous and Tribal Peoples Convention, 1989 (No. 169), explicitly deals with the interrelationship between these peoples and their land, natural resources and development opportunities.

The objective of setting environmental standards is, inter alia, to improve the quality of human life by making natural resources, such as air and water, cleaner. Apart from making possible a better quality of life, these standards are also likely to improve the health and productivity of workers — objectives which underlie many of the international labour Conventions cited above. Improving the working environment, which is at the core of the ILO's mandate, is essential for achieving both environmental and development objectives. As a major follow-up to the Meeting of Experts on the Prevention of Major Hazards (October 1990), which adopted a Code of Practice on the subject (ILO, 1991), preparatory work began on the possible adoption of a Convention and/or Recommendation on the prevention of industrial disasters (major hazard control system). In this area, the close linkage between the working and the general environment became particularly evident after the major accidents

---

[3] This point is due to Rolph van der Hoeven, ILO, Geneva.

of Chernobyl and Bhopal; but the significance of sound working conditions for the general environment is also apparent in areas such as the dismantling of nuclear power stations, offshore oil drilling, or the transport and storage of oil and chemicals.

References

Anderson, K.; Blackhurst, R. (eds.) 1992. *The greening of world trade issues.* Hemel Hempstead (United Kingdom), Harvester-Wheatsheaf.

Bifani, P. 1979. *Environment and industrial location.* Unpublished paper. Nairobi, UNEP.

Broadus, J. et al. 1986. "Rising sea level and damming of rivers: Possible effects in Egypt and Bangladesh", in Titus, J. G. (ed.): *Effects of changes in stratospheric ozone and global climate,* Vol. 4: *Sea level rise* (Washington, DC, United States Environmental Protection Agency/UNEP).

Davis, B. A., et al. 1980. *The effects of environmental amenities on patterns of economic development.* Washington, DC, The Urban Institute.

Duerksen, C.; Leonard, H. J. 1980. "Environmental regulations and the location of industries: An international perspective", in *Columbia Journal of World Business* (New York, Columbia University Press), Vol. XV, No. 2.

General Agreement on Tariffs and Trade (GATT). 1992. *International trade 1990-91,* Part III, Vol. I, Geneva.

Group of 15. 1991. *Joint communiqué.* Second Meeting of the Summit Level Group for South-South Consultation and Co-operation, Caracas, 27-29 Nov.

Grubb, M. 1989. *Climate change and international politics: Problems facing developing countries.* London, Royal Institute of International Affairs.

Hulme, M. 1990. "Global warming in the twenty-first century: An issue for less developed countries", in *Science, Technology and Development* (London, Frank Cass), Vol. 8, No. 1.

ILO. 1990. *ILO contribution to environmentally-sound and sustainable development.* Report of the Governing Body of the International Labour Office to the 44th Session of the General Assembly in response to General Assembly resolutions 42/186 and 42/187. Reproduced as Annex I in ILO: *Environment and the world of work,* Report of the Director-General (Part I), International Labour Conference, 77th Session, Geneva, 1990.

——. 1991. *Prevention of major industrial accidents: An ILO code of practice.* Geneva (also available in French and Spanish).

Kim, S.-Y. 1979. "The effect on selected developing countries", in Koo, A. Y. C., et al., 1979.

Koo, A. Y. C., et al. 1979. *Environmental repercussions on trade and investment.* East Lansing, Michigan, Michigan State University, on behalf of the ILO.

Leone, R. A. (ed.). 1976. *Environmental controls and their impact on industry.* Lexington, Massachusetts, Lexington Books.

Renshaw, G. (ed.). 1981. *Employment, trade and North-South co-operation.* Geneva, ILO.

South Centre. 1991. *Environment and development: Towards a common strategy of the South in the UNCED negotiations and beyond.* Geneva.

South Commission. 1990. *The challenge to the South: The report of the South Commission.* Oxford, Oxford University Press.

Tyler, W. G. 1976. "Manufactured exports and employment creation in developing countries: Some empirical evidence", in *Economic Development and Cultural Change* (Chicago, University of Chicago Press), Jan.

United Nations/General Assembly. 1991. *Ways and means of ensuring the participation of developing countries in international co-operation for research on and development of environmentally sound technologies, and the rapid and effective transfer of such technologies to the developing countries.* Report of the Secretary-General to the Intergovernmental Committee on Science and Technology for Development at its Eleventh Session. New York, doc. A/CN.II/1991/2, 20 Mar.

———/———. 1992. *Report of the Secretary-General of UNCED on transfer of environmentally sound technology.* Preparatory Committee for UNCED, Fourth Session, New York, 2 Mar.-3 Apr., doc. A/CONF.151/PC/100/Add.9.

United Nations Conference on Trade and Development (UNCTAD). 1991. *Environment and international trade.* Report of the Secretary-General of UNCTAD submitted to the Secretary-General of the Conference (UNCED) pursuant to General Assembly resolution 45/210 (doc. A/CONF.151/PC/48).

United Nations Environment Programme (UNEP). 1991. "The Global Environment Facility", in *Our Planet* (Nairobi), Vol. 3, No. 3.

United Nations Industrial Development Organization (UNIDO). 1991. *Barriers facing the achievement of ecologically sound industrial development.* Working Paper No. II for the Conference on Ecologically Sustainable Industrial Development, Copenhagen, 14-18 October 1991 (doc. ID/WG.516/1). Vienna.

CONCLUSIONS AND FUTURE PERSPECTIVES

8

A. S. Bhalla *

On a broad subject such as environment, development and employment, it is dangerous to make generalisations. This is all the more true since, as we noted in Chapter 1, the concept of environment itself has very broad interpretations.

At the beginning of this volume, we posed a number of questions concerning the relationships between environment and development, between environment and poverty and between environment and employment, and about environmentally sustainable development. If there is one general conclusion that we can make, it is that there are, at our present state of knowledge, no clear-cut answers to these questions. Knowledge about environmental degradation varies from country to country and from region to region, and particularly between the developed and the developing countries.

In this volume the two main concepts, namely "environmental degradation" and "sustainable development", have been defined, particularly in Chapter 2, which also deals with broader conceptual issues. In this chapter we attempt some general conclusions concerning the concepts used and interpreted, the evidence on the employment implications of environmental degradation, and the research and policy gaps that need to be filled.

CONCEPTS

This volume has devoted a good deal of attention to the concepts of environmental degradation and sustainable development, which we believe are not properly defined, especially in the context of developing countries. Not all examples of environmental resource depletion

---

* ILO, Geneva.

necessarily mean degradation. In developing countries, which have population growth, industrialisation and economic development as features common to most of them, some environmental repercussions are inevitable and may be considered as a necessary price to be paid. In the early stages of development, a strategy of industrialisation may call for some depletion of the environmental resource base.

Secondly, we believe that a systematic analysis of the unsustainability of developing economies, measured in the light of such criteria as economic performance, development strategies and technological and employment policies adopted, are rarely undertaken. Yet such analyses are essential to determine the sustainability of the development path for the developing countries.

As noted in Chapter 2, non-sustainability, particularly in the least developed countries, is the result of economic stagnation and technological backwardness, rather than poor natural resource endowment. Therefore, for these countries, issues of environmental policy may be linked much more closely with underdevelopment than in other, more advanced developing countries characterised by growth and technological dynamism. Consequently, building the stock of capital through employment generation may be more important for their long-term sustainability than maintaining the stock of natural resources for ecological reasons alone.

Several definitions of the concept of sustainable development have been proposed in the current literature. Most of them are based on the assumption/condition of the constancy of the natural capital stock; and thus it does not allow for any resource depletion. This volume provides an empirical analysis of sub-Saharan African countries which illustrates a broader definition of sustainable development in terms of feasible growth paths. For developing countries in general, an appropriate definition of sustainable development may be in terms of the *minimum* rate of feasible growth that is necessary for meeting the basic needs of the population (see Chapter 2).

Thus defined, the concept of sustainable development is closely related to that of poverty. It is generally believed that extreme poverty in developing countries is the main cause of environmental degradation, reflected in deforestation, soil erosion and waterlogging, etc. We have tried to show that, while poverty is generally associated with the overexploitation of natural resources, it is not the only factor explaining environmental degradation (see Chapters 2 and 5). Poverty by itself cannot explain serious environmental degradation, which is also associated with high incomes and consumption styles in the rich countries, for example. Furthermore, deterioration of agricultural resources cannot be attributed to the rural poor, especially in Latin America with its highly concentrated landownership involving 5 per cent of the farmers owning 80 per cent of farmland (Chapter 5).

Thirdly, the analysis of environmental issues is complicated by the fact that scarce environmental resources are like public goods. Externalities associated with these imply that the costs cannot be reflected in actual or potential market exchanges. Chapter 2 discusses the environmental problems associated with incomplete or missing markets. Those environmental resources often called "global commons" are cases in point. The problem of missing markets is identified with a lack of property rights in the case of degradation of such environmental assets as atmosphere, oceans, forests and grazing lands.

The missing markets further complicate the analysis of environmental problems and the implementation of various pre-emptive and corrective policies and measures. This is particularly so in developing countries with a predominance of subsistence agriculture (see the section "Policy issues" below).

The economic instruments of policy (Chapter 4), applied at present mostly (though not exclusively) in the developed countries, are intended to provide correct price signals to resource users. Such signals are unlikely to be effective in non-market subsistence economies. The "polluter-pays-principle" (PPP), which underlies the economic instruments used in the developed countries, assumes the existence of well-developed markets and exchange relationships (see Chapter 2), an assumption which does not always hold good in many developing countries.

EMPLOYMENT IMPLICATIONS

Two types of income and employment implications of environmental protection are considered in the volume. The first relates to the income and employment implications of *national* environmental protection on employment and incomes within a country concerned. The second aspect of employment and income effects is more *global* — environmental standards and measures introduced in developed countries have repercussions on the developing countries through trade (changes in relative costs and prices of tradable goods), capital flows and technology transfer.

At the national level, as a result of environmental policies and measures, employment may be affected in several ways. First, additional jobs may be created in the new industries which manufacture pollution control equipment and devices (e.g. filters, recycling equipment, precipitators, cooling towers, water treatment components). Jobs may also be created through software associated with licensing and consulting services and the dissemination of pollution control technology. However, these positive employment effects are likely to occur mainly in the developed countries, where most of the pollution control industry is at present located. But such gains in employment are likely to represent only a small fraction of total employment. In the absence of any international cooperation in R & D on the development of pollution control technology, it is unlikely that most of the developing countries can expect to reap these potential employment benefits.

Secondly, positive employment effects are also likely to accrue from the growth of economic activities which are environment-compatible, i.e. renewable energy and recycling, which tend to be labour intensive. Labour-intensive measures to arrest soil erosion can generate substantial employment in the least developed countries. But this gain has to be set against the loss in industries being phased out.

Thirdly, there are negative employment implications through the closure of polluting plants and industries, through the ban on polluting products such as certain packaging materials, and through a rise in product prices leading to a decline in demand, output and employment. However, these negative employment effects in the short term may be more than offset by positive growth in the long term.

At the supranational and global levels, there are two sets of employment implications, one for the developing countries and another for the developed ones, as we noted in Chapter 7. Developing countries may suffer from employment losses if their exports of pollution-intensive goods decline in the wake of the environmental control measures in the developed countries. However, relocating polluting industry from the industrialised to the developing countries might imply a loss of output and employment in the former. Thus, employment losses of the former countries might mean employment gains for the latter. This would imply a trade-off in the sense that developing countries are prepared to accept a lower environmental quality in return for more employment. Such possible employment gains and losses are illustrated in table 15.

As noted in Chapters 3 and 7, the empirical evidence on the employment impact of environmental measures is at present very scarce even in the developed countries, not to speak of the developing countries. Whatever macro-economic, sectoral and micro studies exist are based on weak methodology and questionable assumptions. It would therefore be unwise to make any hasty generalisation. In many cases the positive and negative employment effects may cancel each other out and may lead to no appreciable change one way or another. In the long run the outcome may be less indeterminate and more positive.

The review of various studies in Chapter 3 suggests that, on balance, the employment impact of environmental measures introduced in the developed countries is generally likely to be positive; but more rigorous data collection and analysis is needed before any definite conclusions can be made.

At the global level, empirical evidence of employment gains and losses is particularly hard to find. But illustrative examples presented in Chapter

Table 15. Employment gains and losses

	Employment change	
	Gain	Loss
National		
New industries on pollution control (related hardware and software)	+	
Expansion of existing environment-compatible activities (e.g. recycling)	+	
Closure of polluting plants and industries		–
Ban on polluting products		–
Net change	+ or –	
Global		
Expansion of exports	+	
Decline in exports		–
Increase in investment	+	
Decline in investment		–
Net change	+ or –	

7 seem to suggest that, at least for developing countries, the employment losses resulting from shrinkage of exports may outweigh any gains through inflow of capital and polluting industry. Besides data shortcomings there is a lack of an analytical framework that could combine the micro- and macro-level effects on employment to draw conclusions on aggregate employment. Further, there are questions of equity — would positive employment effects accrue to the poor and unskilled?

POLICY ISSUES

Having clarified the concepts and provided empirical evidence on the employment impact, we move on to the national policy concerns, in both developed and developing countries, for overcoming their growing environmental problems.

Policies directed towards environment

National policy measures were examined in Chapters 4 to 6. There are first the economic instruments, both direct and indirect, whose effective implementation calls for functioning markets and price responses to incentives. Taxes and subsidies are cases in point. Secondly, there are controls and regulations (e.g. quotas and emission regulations) which are not market-based. Finally, government production or expenditures (e.g. purification, waste disposal and clean-up) can also be cited as measures for achieving environmental protection.

From the point of view of developing countries, two issues are particularly relevant: (a) does environmental protection lead to less growth and less employment? and (b) if environmental protection is desirable, what policy instruments would be the most effective? Our present state of knowledge does not permit any definitive answers to these questions.

There are pros and cons of using the economic as well as non-economic instruments. The experience of the industrialised countries suggests that the administrative cost of enforcement may be high. Very few developing countries have yet had long enough experience of these instruments. Also, as noted in Chapter 2, the PPP has limitations of application in developing countries. Extreme cases of poverty in the latter mean that the capacity of many polluters to pay for the environmental costs is extremely limited, even though the high-income population in these countries can afford to pay. Governments may have to give subsidised loans now (to reconstitute the stock of natural resources) in order to raise productivity in the long run.

In view of the above constraints and the case of missing markets discussed earlier, economic policy instruments may not always be effectively applied in the developing countries. Therefore, enforcement of standards through direct control may be more important. More research is needed to make an assessment of different types of instruments in the light of the criteria of employment, technology and feasibility of implementation under conditions prevailing in developing countries.

Policies directed towards other issues

Three types of policy issues of particular relevance to developing countries relate to population, energy and technology.

Chapter 5 noted that growing population pressures in developing countries can directly lead to environmental degradation and the marginalisation of labour. It also noted that national policies should link population and environmental degradation to technological change and employment creation. This link further brings into focus the excessive consumption styles and patterns through which degradation of the environment may occur, as has happened in the developed countries (see Chapter 5).

Population growth and a rise in living standards in developing countries are bound to raise the demand for energy. An appropriate energy policy will need to ensure that the additional demand for energy is met through environment-friendly sources, and that unnecessary waste of energy is minimised. It should be the objective of population policy to ensure that environmental protection and economic development are compatible. Depending on the employment and technological considerations, the economies that are similar in respect of population growth rates and population-natural resource ratios may move along divergent development paths.

The issues relating to technology policy have both national and international dimensions. A national technology policy can raise the level of sustainability or "carrying capacity" to sustain larger populations through technological developments and increased food production, for example (see Chapter 5). It can also prevent the misuse, or excessive use, of technology which may cause environmental degradation. For example, land degradation in many developing countries resulted from specific policies associated with agrarian strategies and the overuse or misuse of fertilisers.

The international dimension of technology, noted in Chapter 7, has more to do with international transfers of environmentally sound technologies to developing countries at reasonable cost and terms and conditions. Policy recommendations for such technology transfers presuppose the existence of these technologies, which is not always the case. Even when such technologies do exist, they may be more costly than those which are less environment-friendly. Thus greater cost may limit access to environment-friendly technologies. If these technologies do not exist, they may have to be developed through the allocation of R & D resources. There may be scope here for global partnership between developing and developed countries. In the absence as yet of any global implementation machinery, the international policy issues essentially come down to the formulation of global mechanisms and the feasibility of their implementation through global partnership between developed and developing countries, their political commitment and mutual goodwill.

Another policy dimension relates to the role of the State versus that of the market. A proper balance needs to be struck between the two. As noted in several chapters, the State can play both direct and indirect roles, through controls and standards and through market-based policy instruments.

Alternative development strategies

Apart from the policies considered above, the broad development strategies adopted by the developing countries may have to be modified to take account of environmental goals. Different levels of development, infrastructure and national capacities of administration and implementation, and technological capabilities also suggest that these countries may have to follow different development paths from that chosen by the industrialised countries. This may imply that these countries may have to avoid mimicking the consumption styles of the North. For example, Chapter 5 noted the wasteful consumption styles and patterns in the industrialised countries. Those patterns which raise the demand for energy may have to be altered. Furthermore, Chapters 5 and 6 discussed how rapid economic growth and urbanisation raises energy intensity and pollutes the urban environment. Yet to achieve environmental goals, a development strategy will need to aim at planning for the production and consumption of products which save on energy and natural resources. This is likely to call for changes in technology as well as product mix. In the industrialised countries an increasing number of regulations, e.g. registration and certification of chemical products, restrictions and bans, product quality standards, labelling and so on are already being introduced in the product markets with a view to cutting down on the consumption of polluting products and encouraging the use of environmentally sound ones (UNCTAD, 1991a, 1991b).

Product standards may need to be adjusted to the specific environmental conditions prevailing in individual countries. Countries will need to explore ways and means by which a change in consumption patterns towards less energy-intensive products can be combined with substitution of natural products (which are more environment-friendly) for man-made and synthetic products. Technical possibilities for such substitution need to be explored. Suitable economic instruments would also need to be introduced to ensure that substitution in consumption and production actually takes place (see Chapter 5).

Thus the redistribution of income and consumption and a change in product mix may need to become major components of development strategies to make them compatible with environmental objectives. The economic rationale of these strategies and their political expediency are important factors to consider.

FUTURE PERSPECTIVES

The subject of environment-employment relationships is relatively new. While it has attracted much attention in the industrialised countries, the environmental issues have not yet received as much attention in the developing countries. Much of the literature is of a general nature and fails to come to grips with the sort of questions that were posed in Chapter 1.

Our gaps in knowledge remain quite large. The first type of gap pertains to conceptual and methodological analyses about the interrelationships — complementarities and trade-offs — between environment, development and employment. Chapters 1 and 2 made some attempts in this direction, but much remains to be done. All one can say in our present state of knowledge is that there are cases where trade-offs may exist between environment and growth and between environment and employment. There are other cases where complementarities may be found. This is not very illuminating either for building a knowledge base or for the policymakers who need to minimise the trade-offs and maximise complementarities through appropriate policy design and implementation.

The second type of gap relates to the estimation of income and employment effects. One may argue that methodologies to estimate direct, indirect and total employment effects do exist. While this may be true, they are not easily applicable for lack of adequate "environmental" information. Environmental accounting, which is currently being developed, may help to fill this gap. Special surveys and inquiries will be needed to generate new data. At present, whatever quantitative employment evidence exists in developing countries cannot be easily attributed to environmental degradation. This brings us to the third type of gap, namely, lack of adequate and robust data.

Chapters 3 and 7 described the inadequacies of available data and studies on the employment and income effects of environmental protection measures. These lacunae can be filled in future through systematic national studies on primary data generation. The ILO has already made a beginning in this direction. Apart from conceptual and analytical studies (Markandya, 1991; Pereira, 1991; Perrings, 1991a), country case studies have been carried out in Bangladesh (Alauddin, Mujeri and Tisdell, 1992), Malaysia (Jonish, 1992a) and the Philippines (Norris and Sathiendrakumar, 1991) in Asia; Botswana (Perrings, 1992b), Senegal (Golan-Hardy, 1991) and Zambia (Thampapillai, 1991) in Africa; and Mexico (Jonish, 1992b) in Latin America. In rural Bangladesh, case studies of three separate villages were undertaken to examine the effects of income, employment and environmental effects of major technological changes in agriculture.

Additional investigations need to be undertaken on the output and employment effects of environmental regulations in the agricultural sectors of developing countries. Despite a few studies that are available, the distributional and employment implications of different incentive structures remain uncertain. Changes in relative prices of resources may be a necessary but not sufficient condition for achieving sustainable development. In addition, land use patterns, land tenure systems and migration patterns may also need to change. Systemic and macro-economic investigations of a more rigorous nature than have been done to date will be necessary for a better understanding of the potential output and employment impact and the environmental costs of a system of regulations and incentives.

It is also "not obvious that labour-intensive technology is necessarily more environmentally sound than capital-intensive technology" (Perrings, 1991a, p. 31). Studies need to be undertaken on the industrial sectors of developing countries to analyse "the impacts of alternative regulations, both in terms of their economic costs as well as their employment and environmental effects . . . the relative impacts on the formal and informal sectors, the financial implications of government-financed controls and the problems of enforcement" (Markandya, 1991, p. 41).

At a global level, apart from the methodological requirements necessary to estimate employment effects for developing and developed countries, an issue that has not been settled is that of the implications of environmental standards for changes in costs and prices, patterns of trade, capital movements and employment. For example, it is not clear whether differential standards between developed and developing countries are sufficiently large to induce major plant and industrial relocations to the developing countries. It is equally uncertain whether the developing countries with lower per capita incomes are necessarily reluctant to introduce environmental standards. In theory, one can argue that the demand for a cleaner environment is higher at higher levels of income. Although people in poor countries may value clean air and water as much as those in the rich ones, they may be much less able to afford them. What is not clear, however, is whether the real world situations confirm the above hypothesis or not. We noted in Chapter 4 that some developing countries at lower levels of income have also introduced environmental standards.

Chapter 7 presented some evidence from the 1970s which suggested that environmental standards and associated costs were not an important factor in explaining plant relocations across countries which occurred even before these standards were introduced. Since environmental standards have repercussions on output, employment and the quality of life (health and safety of workers, their productivity and standard of living), more empirical studies analysing their implications at a disaggregated level (for countries and specific industries) are badly needed.

References

Alauddin, M. et al. 1991. *The environment, employment and environmental protection in rural Bangladesh: An overview*. Draft manuscript. Geneva, ILO.

——. 1991. *Employment, economic and environmental impact of natural resource utilisation in agriculture and forestry: Case studies from rural Bangladesh*. Draft manuscript. Geneva, ILO.

Golan-Hardy, E. 1991. *Policy options for soil conservation: A study from Senegal*. Draft manuscript. Geneva, ILO.

Jonish, J. 1992a. *Forestry in Malaysia: Policies, practices and options for sustainability*. Draft manuscript. Geneva, ILO.

——. 1992b. *The river as an international environmental resource: The case of the Colorado-US-Mexico Salinity Agreement*. Mimeographed WEP working paper (WEP 2-22/WP.221). Geneva, ILO.

Markandya, A.. 1991. *Technology, environment and employment: A survey*. Mimeographed WEP working paper (WEP 2-22/WP.216). Geneva, ILO.

Norris, W. K.; Sathiendrakumar, R. 1991. *The Green Revolution, biotechnology and environmental concerns: A case study of the Philippines.* Draft manuscript. Geneva, ILO.

Pereira, A. F. 1991. *Technology policy for environmental sustainability and for employment and income generation: Conceptual and methodological issues.* Mimeographed WEP working paper (WEP 2-22/WP.215). Geneva, ILO.

Perrings, C. 1991a. *Incentives for the ecologically sustainable use of human and natural resources in the drylands of sub-Saharan Africa: A review.* Mimeographed WEP working paper (WEP 2-22/WP.219). Geneva, ILO.

———. 1991b. *Incentives for the ecologically sustainable use of human and natural resources: A case study of Botswana.* Draft manuscript. Geneva, ILO.

Thampapillai, D. J. 1991. *Environmental policies and their impacts on employment and income growth in Zambia.* Draft manuscript. Geneva, ILO.

United Nations Conference on Trade and Development (UNCTAD). 1991a. *Informal encounter on international trade and environment.* Oslo, 28 February-1 March 1991. Doc. UNCTAD/VIII/2, GE.91-50739. Geneva.

———. 1991b. *Environment and international trade.* Report of the Secretary-General of UNCTAD submitted to the Secretary-General of the Conference (UNCED) pursuant to General Assembly resolution 45/210 (doc. A/CONF.151/PC/48). Geneva.

SELECT BIBLIOGRAPHY

Alfthan, T. et al. 1990. *Employment and training implications of environmental policies in Europe.* Training Discussion Paper No. 52. Geneva, ILO.

Anderson, D. 1990. *Economic growth and the environment.* Selected Papers. London, Royal Dutch/Shell Group.

Anderson, K.; Blackhurst, R. (eds.). 1992. *The greening of world trade issues.* Hemel Hempstead (United Kingdom), Harvester-Wheatsheaf.

Barbier, E. B. 1989. "Cash crops, food crops and sustainability: The case of Indonesia", in *World Development* (Oxford, Pergamon Press), Vol. 17, No. 6.

———. 1989. "The contribution of environmental and resource economics to an economics of sustainable development", in *Development and Change* (London, Sage Publications), Vol. 20, No. 3.

———. 1990. "Alternative approaches to economic-environmental interactions", in *Ecological Economics* (Amsterdam, Elsevier Science Publishers), Vol. 2.

Bezdek, R. et al. 1989. "The economic and employment effects of investments in pollution abatement and control technologies", in *Ambio* (Stockholm, Royal Swedish Academy of Science), Vol. 18, No. 5.

Blaikie, P. 1990. *The political economy of soil erosion in developing countries.* London, Longman.

Browder, J. O. 1988. "The social cost of rain forest destruction: A critique and economic analysis of the Hamburger debate", in *Interciencia* (Washington, DC), Vol. 13, No. 3.

Castaneda, F. C. 1989. "The risks of environmental degradation in Bogotá, Colombia", in *Environment and Urbanization* (London, International Institute for Environment and Development), Vol. 1, No. 1.

Centre for Science and Environment. 1989. "The environmental problems associated with India's major cities", in *Environment and Urbanization* (London, International Institute for Environment and Development), Vol. 1, No. 1.

Conway, G. R.; Barbier, E. B. 1990. *Sustainable agriculture for development.* London, Earthscan.

Dasgupta, P. 1990. *The environment as a commodity.* WIDER Working Paper No. 84. Helsinki.

———; Maler, K. 1990. *The environment and emerging development issues.* Paper presented at the World Bank Annual Conference on Development Economics, 26-27 April 1990.

Desai, A. V. (ed.). 1990. *Energy economics.* New Delhi, Wiley Eastern.

———. 1990. *Patterns of energy use in developing countries.* New Delhi, Wiley Eastern.

Duchin, F. et al. 1991. *Strategies for environmentally sound economic development.* Mimeographed. New York, Institute for Economic Analysis.

Eckholm, E. P. 1976. *Losing ground: Environmental stress and world food prospects.* New York, Norton.

Environmental Resources Ltd. 1989. *Employment and training implications of actions to improve the environment: A case study.* Mimeographed. London.

Fearnside, M. 1986. "Agricultural plans for Brazil's Grande Carajas: Lost opportunity for sustainable local development", in *World Development* (Oxford, Pergamon Press), Vol. 14, No. 3.

General Agreement on Tariffs and Trade (GATT). 1992. *International Trade 1990-91.* Part III, Vol. I. Geneva.

Goldemberg, J. et al. 1988. *Energy for a sustainable world.* New Delhi, Wiley Eastern.

Gopalakrishna, K. 1987. *Ethiopian famines 1973-1986: A case study.* WIDER Working Paper No. 26. Helsinki.

Grainger, A. 1990. *The threatening desert: Controlling desertification.* London, Earthscan.

HABITAT. 1989. *Urbanisation and sustainable development in the Third World: An unrecognised global issue.* Nairobi.

———. 1990. *People, settlements, environment and development: Improving the living environment for a sustainable future.* Nairobi.

Herath, H. M. G. 1985. "Economics of salinity control in Sri Lanka: Some "exploratory results", in *Agricultural Administration* (Barking (United Kingdom), Elsevier Applied Science Publishers), No. 18.

ILO. 1990. *Environment and the world of work.* Report of the Director-General (Part I), International Labour Conference, 77th Session, Geneva, June 1990.

International Union for Conservation of Nature and Natural Resources/United Nations Environment Programme/World Wide Fund for Nature (IUCN/UNEP/WWF). 1991. *Caring for the earth: A strategy for sustainable living.* Gland (Switzerland).

Jagannathan, N. V. 1990. *Poverty-environment linkages: Case study of West Java.* World Bank Environment Department Divisional Working Paper No. 1990-8. Washington, DC, World Bank.

———; Agunbiade, A. O. 1990. *Poverty-environment linkages in Nigeria: Issues for research.* World Bank Environment Department Divisional Working Paper No. 1990-7. Washington, DC, World Bank.

James, J. 1978. "Growth technology and the environment in LDCs: A survey", in *World Development* (Oxford, Pergamon Press), Vol. 6, Nos. 7 and 8.

Jansen, K. 1991. "Structural adjustment and sustainable development", in *International Spectator* (The Hague), Vol. 45, No. 11.

Jayawardena, L. 1991. *A global environmental compact for sustainable development: Resource requirements and mechanisms.* WIDER Research for Action Series, Aug.

Kreisky, B. 1989. *A programme for full employment in the 1990s: Report of the Kreisky Commission on Employment Issues in Europe.* Oxford, Pergamon Press.

Kumar, S. K.; Hotchkiss, D. 1988. *Consequences of deforestation for women's time allocation: Agricultural production and nutrition in the hill areas of Nepal.* Research Report No. 69. Washington, DC, International Food Policy Research Institute.

Leonard, H. J., et al. 1989. *Environment and the poor: Development strategies for a common agenda.* Washington, DC, Overseas Development Council.

Lewis, K. 1991. *Employment and training implications of the waste management industry.* Mimeographed. Geneva, ILO.

Livingstone, I.; Assunçao, M. 1989. "Government policies towards drought and development in the Brazilian Sertao", in *Development and Change* (London, Sage Publications), Vol. 20, No. 3.

Lopez, M. E. 1987. "The politics of lands at risk in a Philippine frontier", in Little, P. D. et al. *Lands at risk in the Third World: Local level perspectives.* Boulder, Colorado, Westview Press.

Lutz, E.; Daly, H. 1990. *Incentives regulations and sustainable land use in Costa Rica.* World Bank Environment Department Working Paper, No. 34. Washington, DC, World Bank.

Markandya, A. 1991. *Technology, environment and employment: A survey.* Mimeographed WEP working paper (WEP 2-22/WP.216). Geneva, ILO.

Matthews, W. H. (ed.). 1976. *Outer limits and human needs: Resources and environmental issues of development strategies.* Uppsala (Sweden), Dag Hammarskjöld Foundation.

Metz, J. J. 1991. "A reassessment of the causes and severity of Nepal's environmental crisis", in *World Development* (Oxford, Pergamon Press), Vol. 19, No. 7.

Organization for Economic Co-operation and Development (OECD). 1978. *Employment and environment.* Paris.

———. 1978. *The macroeconomic evaluation of environmental programmes.* Paris.

———. 1984. *The impact of environmental policy on employment.* Background paper. International Conference on Environment and Economics. Paris.

———. 1985. *Environment and economics: Results of the International Conference on Environment and Economics.* Paris.

———. 1985. *The macroeconomic impact of environmental expenditure.* Paris.

———. 1989. *The application of economic instruments for environmental protection: Summary and conclusions.* Paris.

———. 1991. *Environmental management in developing countries.* Paris.

Pearce, D. W. 1991. "Growth, employment and environmental policy", in *Economic Report* (London, Employment Institute), Vol. 6, No. 1.

Pearce, D. W. et al. 1988. *Sustainable development and cost-benefit analysis.* Paper presented at the Canadian Environment Assessment Workshop on Integrating Economic and Environmental Assessment. Vancouver, Canadian Environmental Assessment Research Council.

———. 1990. *Sustainable development: Economics and environment in the Third World.* London, Earthscan.

————; Turner, R. K. 1990. *The economics of natural resources and the environment.* Hemel Hempstead (United Kingdom), Harvester-Wheatsheaf.

Pereira, A. F. 1991. *Technology policy for environmental sustainability and for employment and income generation: Conceptual and methodological issues.* Mimeographed WEP working paper (WEP 2-22/WP.215). Geneva, ILO.

Perrings, C. 1991. *Incentives for the ecologically sustainable use of human and natural resources in the drylands of sub-Saharan Africa: A review.* Mimeographed WEP working paper (WEP 2-22/WP.219). Geneva, ILO.

Pezzy, J. 1989. *Economic analysis of sustainable growth and sustainable development.* World Bank Environment Department Working Paper No. 15. Washington, DC, World Bank.

Plateau, J.-P. 1988. *The food crisis in Africa: A comparative structural analysis.* WIDER Working Paper No. 44. Helsinki.

Renner, M. 1991. *Jobs in a sustainable economy,* Worldwatch Paper No. 104. Washington, DC, Worldwatch Institute.

Repetto, R. 1985. *Paying the price: Pesticide subsidies in developing countries.* Washington, DC, World Resources Institute.

Schramme, G.; Warford, J. J. (eds.). 1989. *Environmental management and economic development.* Baltimore, Maryland, Johns Hopkins University Press.

Schteingart, M. 1989. "The environmental problems associated with urban development in Mexico City", in *Environment and Urbanization* (London, International Institute for Environment and Development), Vol. 1, No. 1.

Single, J. S. (ed.). 1985. *Environmental regeneration in the Himalayas: Concepts and strategies.* New Delhi, Kay-Kay Printers.

Teitenberg, T. H. 1984. *Environmental and natural resource economics.* Glenview, Illinois, Scott, Foresman and Co.

————. 1990. "Economic instruments for environmental regulation", in *Oxford Review of Economic Policy* (Oxford, Oxford University Press), Vol. 6, No. 1.

Timmer, P. C. 1988. "Indonesia: Transition from food importer to food exporter", in Sinclair, T. (ed.). *Food price policy in Asia: A contemporary study of origins and outcomes.* Ithaca, New York, Cornell University Press.

United Nations Conference on Trade and Development (UNCTAD). 1991. *Environment and international trade.* Report of the Secretary-General of UNCTAD submitted to the Secretary-General of the Conference (UNCED) pursuant to General Assembly Resolution 45/210 (doc. A/CONF.151/PC/48). Geneva.

————. 1991. *Informal encounter on international trade and the environment,* Oslo, 28 February-1 March 1991. Doc. UNCTAD VIII/2, GE.91-50739. Geneva.

United Nations Environment Programme (UNEP). 1992. *Status of desertification and implementation of the United Nations Plan of Action to Combat Desertification.* Report of the Executive Director. Nairobi.

United Nations Industrial Development Organization (UNIDO). 1991. *Barriers facing the achievement of ecologically sound industrial development.* Working Paper No. II for the Conference on Ecologically Sustainable Industrial Development, Copenhagen, 14-18 October 1991 (doc. ID/WG.516/1). Vienna.

Warford, J. 1987. *Environment and development*. Washington, DC, World Bank/IMF Development Committee.

Wood, C. et al. 1989. *Environmental impact assessment, employment and training*. Mimeographed. Manchester, University of Manchester.

World Bank. 1985. *Desertification in the Sahelian and Sudanian zones of West Africa*. Washington, DC.

———. 1991. *The World Bank and the environment: A progress report*. Washington, DC.

World Commission on Environment and Development (WCED). 1987. *Our common future*. Oxford, Oxford University Press. (Also known as the Brundtland Report.)

Younis, A. S. 1987. *Soil conservation in developing countries*. Washington, DC, World Bank.